To Commander Liam Hulin,
Patriot and Warrior

Stories of my war!

VALOR IN VIETNAM

by

Allen B. Clark

June 19, 2017

Go Navy and Army

Beat Everyone!

Southeast Asia 1963–1977

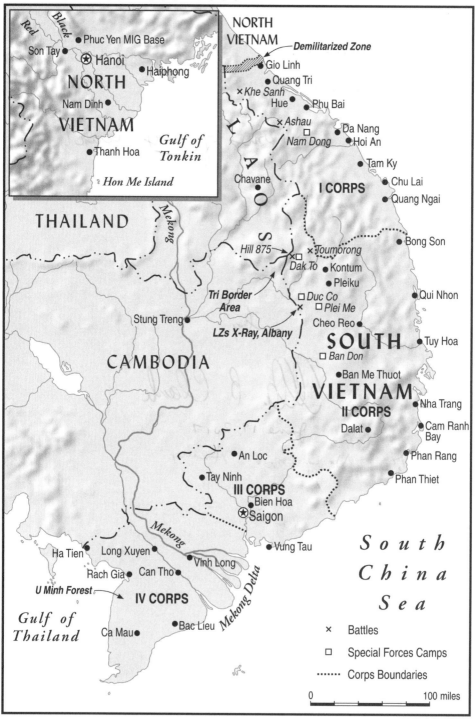

NORTH VIETNAM

Red

Black

Son Tay ●

● Phuc Yen MIG Base

⊛ Hanoi

● Haiphong

NORTH

Nam Dinh ●

VIETNAM

Gulf of Tonkin

● Thanh Hoa

Hon Me Island

NORTH VIETNAM

Demilitarized Zone

● Gio Linh

● Quang Tri

× *Khe Sanh*

Hue ● ● Phu Bai

× *Ashau*

□ *Nam Dong* ● Da Nang
● Hoi An

● Tam Ky

Chavane ● ● Chu Lai
● Quang Ngai

I CORPS

● Bong Son

Hill 875 → □× × *Toumorong*
Dak To ● Kontum

● Pleiku

□ *Duc Co* ● Qui Nhon

Tri Border Area

× □ *Plei Me*

Stung Treng ● Cheo Reo ●

LZs X-Ray, Albany

SOUTH ● Tuy Hoa

□ *Ban Don*

CAMBODIA

●Ban Me Thuot

VIETNAM

● Nha Trang

II CORPS

Dalat ● ● Cam Ranh Bay

● An Loc ● Phan Rang

● Tay Ninh ● Phan Thiet

III CORPS

● Bien Hoa

⊛ Saigon

Mekong

● Vung Tau

Ha Tien ● Long Xuyen ●

Vinh Long ●

Rach Gia ● Can Tho ●

U Minh Forest →

IV CORPS

Gulf of Thailand

Ca Mau ● ● Bac Lieu

THAILAND

Mekong

LAOS

South China Sea

Mekong Delta

× Battles

□ Special Forces Camps

······· Corps Boundaries

0   100 miles

VALOR IN VIETNAM

Chronicles of Honor, Courage, and Sacrifice
1963–1977

ALLEN B. CLARK

CASEMATE

Philadelphia & Oxford

Published in the United States of America and Great Britain in 2012 by
CASEMATE PUBLISHERS
908 Darby Road, Havertown, PA 19083
and
10 Hythe Bridge Street, Oxford, OX1 2EW

ISBN 978-1-61200-095-4
Digital Edition: ISBN 978-1-61200-108-1

Cataloging-in-publication data is available from the Library of Congress and
the British Library.

10 9 8 7 6 5 4 3 2 1

Printed and bound in the United States of America.

For a complete list of Casemate titles please contact:

CASEMATE PUBLISHERS (US)
Telephone (610) 853-9131, Fax (610) 853-9146
E-mail: casemate@casematepublishing.com

CASEMATE PUBLISHERS (UK)
Telephone (01865) 241249, Fax (01865) 794449
E-mail: casemate-uk@casematepublishing.co.uk

———————

All photographs are from author's collection unless otherwise noted.

Contents

Dedication

To our comrades-in-arms, who did not return with us from Vietnam, and to those who did, but carry scars in body, soul and spirit.

Heroes are forged on anvils hot with pain,
And splendid courage comes but with the test.
Some natures ripen and some natures bloom.
Only on blood-wet soil, some souls prove great.
Only in moments dark with death or doom
God finds His best soldiers on the mountain of affliction.

Streams in the Desert, *pg. 437-438*

Foreword

Library shelves groan under the weight of books on the Vietnam War. They run the usual gamut of battle and campaign history, personal memoir, apologia, strategy, and so on.

This one is different. It is, literally, unique.

It verges on being allegorical—portraying and explaining the abstract by means of concrete forms. In this case, the forms are drawn from among those who served in Vietnam.

That war was surely abstract in the understanding of many. In its own time—and since—it was quite difficult to grasp, a conflict seeming perversely to elude full comprehension, even for those who fought in it. Reasons abound: the exotic setting; its very length in years; its changing nature over those years; its location half way around the world; the eerie sense of "business as usual" at home; the shameful obfuscations by politicians and activists of all stripes. No wonder Americans still don't know quite what to make of it. For all too many it remains a frustratingly abstract episode in our nation's history.

Allen Clark grapples with that abstraction through real stories of actual participants, stories portraying the honor, courage, and, especially, sacrifice of those who went when their country said go and did what their country said do.

Clark selects twenty-one exemplars and describes in splendid prose the exploits of each. Those accounts, tied neatly together by brief inserts provided by Lewis Sorley, the most authoritative voice on the scene today, merge to paint a grand panorama of the legions of young men and women who answered the call to arms. Those selected are representative of the host whose service in a woeful war was magnificent and who certainly deserved better than the national cold shoulder they received upon returning home. They are representative, as well, of the caliber of those who did not return, the fallen whose names appear in somber row upon row on the Vietnam Memorial on our National Mall.

As the Vietnam War slips inexorably further and further into the past (it is now nearly four decades since Americans watched the final horrific scenes of helicopters lifting frantic survivors from Saigon roof-tops), increasing numbers of researchers are striving to draw clearer water from a well seriously poisoned by the politics of the time. Their aim is to provide a fuller and more objective rendering of the war than has existed for far too long. This book about authentic heroes fits squarely into that genre.

Actually, the book features twenty-two individuals, not twenty-one. The presence of the author is evident throughout. Allen Clark was physically in Vietnam only once—an experience that cost him both his legs. But emotionally and spiritually the war has never left him. His own story is an inspiring backdrop for the others he modestly pushes to the front.

Veterans of that long ago and far away war—and, of course, their descendents—will want to have this volume in their libraries. It is their story.

May 2012   Dave R. Palmer, Lt. Gen., U.S. Army (ret.)
           Author of *Summons of the Trumpet: U.S.-Vietnam in Perspective*

Introduction

E very war continues to dwell in the lives it touches or in the lives of those living through that time. The Vietnam War lives on famously and infamously, dependent on political points of view, but those who have "been there, done that" have a highly personalized window on their own time of that history.

Herein are first-hand narratives by Vietnam War participants: highly intense, emotional, and personal stories. Connecting the stories is commentary contributed by Lewis Sorley that covers the historical setting of that period of the war, the geography, setting, and strategy, which are denoted in italics.

This is the Vietnam War as seen through the eyes of people who experienced it. It is my hope and prayer that these stories reflect the commitment, honor, and dedication with which we performed our duty in the Vietnam War.

The Vietnam War lasted for a long number of years and American troops in regular units were deployed to South Vietnam over an eight-year period in four geographical or corps areas. As a Vietnam veteran my information was limited to my year in my location. We ask each other where were you and in what unit did you serve? Unless that was our corps area or unit, we have little to no knowledge of their experiences.

Terms such as SOG, special forces, Phoenix program, Gulf of Tonkin, China Beach, *Chieu Hoi*, Pleiku, and Kit Carson Scouts are unknown to many people, even some Vietnam veterans. If we were not in combat units, we cannot understand the details of the horror and complexities of heavy action.

Some of us participated in the war, but definitely wish we had not. Most of us lost many friends during and after the war.

This book becomes the product of my life exposed to the military and veteran world for seventy years. Through army-brat childhood, West Point cadetship, five years on active duty, fifteen months in an army hospital recuperating from double-leg amputation and post-traumatic stress disorder, and thirteen years in the Department of Veterans Affairs (four of which were as a presidential appointee requiring Senate confirmation) it has been my privilege and pleasure to have known many citizens of our country who have served the cause of peace and freedom in active military service. Most of us have our own stories and they are our personal legacies. My collection of other veterans' stories runs the gamut of battlefield courage on land, air, and sea. These stories also relate the legacy of pain, sorrow, and suffering due to our commitment and dedication to our country. Unfortunately, it was my misfortune to suffer immensely from my dedication to serve my country in Vietnam. A general officer wanted me to serve in Korea as his aide-de-camp, but my personal dedication to the ideals of West Point, my loyalty to my country, and my personal honor dictated that I volunteer for service in the Vietnam War.

When I arrived in Vietnam in August 1966 as a military intelligence officer I volunteered for the army's 5th Special Forces Group and was assigned to Detachment B-57, a secret unit with the mission of obtaining intelligence on the North Vietnamese army's use of Cambodia as a privileged sanctuary.

While assigned at Dak To special forces A-team camp near the tri-border area on 17 June 1967, I was wounded in an intense enemy mortar barrage on our camp. Following this action I was awarded the Silver Star, Purple Heart, and Combat Infantryman's Badge. For the next fifteen months I was a patient at Brooke General Hospital at Ft. Sam Houston, Texas. My stay there included fourteen weeks in a closed psychiatric ward to heal from extreme emotional trauma related to my amputations. In the medical center and since I have endured a total of twenty surgeries.

Six years of psychotherapy until 1973 found me ready for the real healing I finally achieved through a strengthening of my spiritual dimension by taking my Christian faith very seriously. Since then, I have needed no psychiatric counseling or antidepressants. What I have learned about healing from war trauma, especially PTSD, is available on my web site www.combatfaith.com. Published in 2007, *Wounded Soldier, Healing Warrior: A Personal Story of a*

Vietnam Veteran Who Lost his Legs but Found His Soul, covers my personal story: service in Vietnam and my recovery from the resulting physical, psychological and spiritual injuries.

Veterans of Vietnam, readers of war stories and histories, and those proud people who appreciate the service of friends and family members who have served in the military, will all find a compelling story in this book. It encompasses history from the special forces teams who began serving in the early 1960s through the evacuation of Saigon in 1975 through to the conditions in South Vietnam after the war. Some books tell only war stories, some relate only the history, but it has been my goal to meld both history and highly-personalized stories, not only of what happened and why in the war, but how we felt, what we saw, and what we learned

Unfortunately many of the stories of those who served in Vietnam do not have happy endings. Families of MIAs will never know the fates of their

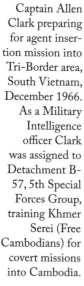

Captain Allen Clark preparing for agent insertion mission into Tri-Border area, South Vietnam, December 1966. As a Military Intelligence officer Clark was assigned to Detachment B-57, 5th Special Forces Group, training Khmer Serei (Free Cambodians) for covert missions into Cambodia.

family members. Others grieve forever for our casualties killed in action. Those wounded in body and soul rub their scars, pray their prayers, "pop" their pills, and go about their lives: staying busy and in some cases healed, in others remaining in constant fogs from the war. Many were men and women of valor, very few would "love" Vietnam, and all would have preferred not to have gone to Vietnam. However, most of us are proud for what we attempted and know that we were a part of history, as convoluted, complicated, and contrasting as it is.

❖ ❖ ❖

May God rest our souls and heal our spirits and bodies.

Historical Overview: The War in Brief

*T*he Vietnamese had been at war for a long, long time by the point at which Americans began to be involved. Fighting against Japanese invaders during World War II, they were then divided in their reaction to French efforts to reestablish their colonial rule in Indochina after the allied victory in that global conflict. The Geneva Accords of 1954 divided Vietnam into North and South, supposedly temporarily, by a demilitarized zone stretching across the 17th parallel. As matters evolved, however, that boundary held until the final Communist victory on 30 April 1975.

Individual views of the nature of the war and its conduct vary widely, being shaped primarily by when and where a person served. South Vietnam (the Republic of Vietnam) was itself a very diverse nation in terms of terrain, weather, and spheres of economic activity, not to mention the enemy encountered. Then the nature of the war evolved over time, introducing further variables into the service of each person "in country." And, of course, over time a good many Americans returned for second or even more tours of duty in the combat zone, often encountering significantly different conditions than those experienced earlier.

American participation in the war may conveniently be divided into several phases. The initial period, primarily that of advisory and logistical assistance, lasted until the spring of 1965. Opinions vary as to when this period should be viewed as beginning, but as early as 1955 American advisors and military assistance had come to South Vietnam's aid. Over the years the level of this presence grew significantly, providing, in addition to advisory input, a number of other important kinds of support, including military equipment, training, intelligence, communications, logistics, and of course funding.

When, during late 1964 and the early part of 1965, it appeared that South Vietnam would be overwhelmed if the United States did not introduce ground forces into the conflict the decision was made to take that fateful step. Thus, beginning in March 1965, and on a much larger scale in the summer of that year, U.S. Army and Marine Corps forces were deployed to South Vietnam along with supporting air and naval forces and logistics and other sustaining elements of every type. Over the next four years this commitment continued to grow. By the end of April 1969 a total of 543,400 men were in country in addition to many thousands more in supporting air and naval elements elsewhere in Southeast Asia and contiguous waters.

In the years of the buildup American forces conducted a war of attrition with the focus on killing large numbers of enemy troops in large scale battles often conducted in the deep jungles adjacent to South Vietnam's western borders with Laos and Cambodia. Meanwhile South Vietnam's armed forces were relegated to what was then considered the secondary role of pacification, a situation in which they were also given low priority when it came to modern weapons and communications equipment.

Dramatic changes ensued in the wake of the enemy's Tet Offensive of 1968. The overall U.S. commander in Vietnam was replaced by his deputy, an officer with a much different outlook on the nature of the war and how it should be conducted. He abandoned the war of attrition, with its emphasis on body count, in favor of what might be termed a war of population security in which progress in protecting the people of South Vietnam became the measure of success. Increased emphasis on the importance of intelligence, and combat operations to clear-and-hold the populated regions, replaced earlier search-and-destroy operations as the predominant mode. In what was termed "one war," improvement of South Vietnam's armed forces and pacification of the rural areas were given equal importance to combat operations, with combat operations being dramatically reconfigured in favor of a multitude of small-unit patrols and ambushes as opposed to the "war of the big battalions" favored earlier.

A new phase began in 1969 when, with a new administration in office back home, it was decided to "Vietnamize" the war and, regardless of what the enemy did, progressively withdraw American forces. Thus, the buildup of the earlier period was systematically reversed with the first of what turned out to be fourteen withdrawal increments, euphemistically called "redeployments," pulling out in July and August of 1969. The initial 25,000 were followed by another 40,500 by the end of that year in what became a steady, continuous and irreversible process.

While the unilateral withdrawal of American forces was underway, expansion of South Vietnamese armed forces was supported, particularly the territorial forces who were to provide the "hold" in clear and hold, along with the provision of greatly improved weaponry and other equipment. During this period pacification was also accorded priority equal to that given conventional military operations. As a result of these initiatives security of the populace was greatly improved, as was the ability of the South Vietnamese to replace the departing U.S. and other allied forces in providing for their own defense.

In 1973 yet one further phase began with conclusion of the Paris Accords, an agreement that in theory ended the conflict, while at the same time providing that allied troops would be withdrawn from South Vietnam and prisoners of war would be exchanged. Ominously, however, no mention was made of the large number of enemy forces deployed inside South Vietnam. With practically no surcease the fighting began again and, so long as the United States continued to provide the necessary military and financial wherewithal, South Vietnam held her own. When, however, the United States Congress drastically cut this support, while North Vietnam's Communist patrons dramatically increased support for their client state, South Vietnam was doomed. At the end of April 1975, with the fall of Saigon, the long struggle ended.

CHAPTER 1

Early Special Forces "A" Teams in Vietnam

CAPTAIN RAMON A. "TONY" NADAL, II, USA

(NAM DONG SPECIAL FORCES CAMP, 1963–1964)

The bravest are surely those who have the clearest vision of what is before them, glory and danger alike, and yet notwithstanding go out to meet it.
—Thucydides

SPECIAL FORCES

U.S. Army special forces came into their own during the Vietnam War. In the typical employment small teams of Americans trained and led indigenous forces, composed most notably in the Central Highlands of the native Montagnard peoples, establishing a string of camps along South Vietnam's borders with Laos and Cambodia. There the mission was to observe and report on enemy infiltration of troops and supplies and, where possible, to interdict or at least impede such movement into South Vietnam from the enemy's Ho Chi Minh Trail network. Of course the static camps were tempting targets for enemy raids and attacks by fire, and over the long years of the war many fierce battles took place in and around these camps.

The Ultimate Volunteer

At a young age in his native Puerto Rico, Tony Nadal knew he was meant to be a soldier. His father graduated from West Point in 1928 and no other choice but West Point made any sense to him. Upon graduating in 1958 he desired to prepare himself the best possible way for soldiering and joined many of his classmates at the Infantry Officer Basic Course followed by Airborne and Ranger schools. He volunteered for the infantry, without argument the most dangerous branch of the U.S. Army. His first Vietnam tour would be an illuminating and illustrious example of the early Vietnam War history.

Special Forces

It was only natural for him to volunteer for special forces who were engaged in combat action, however limited it was at the time, in Laos and Vietnam. He had barely heard of Laos and Vietnam, but learned that SF soldiers had served on mobile training teams in Laos since 1959 and in Vietnam since early 1961. He quickly realized the "romanticism" of this type of soldering and knew that was where he wanted to serve. (Stanton: 26) After applying a second time for an SF assignment it was his good fortune to be assigned to the 7th Special Forces Group at Ft. Bragg, North Carolina, and soon after he became qualified as a special forces officer. Then he volunteered a second time to lead a special forces A detachment to Vietnam.

Prior to his assignment to Detachment A-727, Nadal was sent to Ft. Knox, Kentucky, for two months where he trained a battalion of Cuban volunteers that was to take part in the planned invasion of Cuba as the vanguard of the liberation of Havana in order to create the impression that the invasion of Cuba during the Cuban Missile Crisis was a Cuban affair. Also included in the invasion plan were the 82nd and 101st Airborne, 1st Armored, and 2nd Marine divisions This massive invasion force had been organized to prevent Soviet nuclear missiles from being stationed in Cuba.

After returning from Ft. Knox, he received his assignment as team leader for the newly-formed SF Detachment A-727, a twelve man A team, bound eventually for South Vietnam and the special forces camp at Nam Dong in the northern section of the country. Several of the other eleven members of his team had already been to Laos and their experience was welcomed by Captain Nadal. He would now be serving with soldiers at a level of quality that he had not previously experienced. Their training, motivation, physical hardiness, mental discipline and expertise were outstanding and their ability to accomplish their tasks with limited guidance or supervision was a lesson that he quickly learned. Special forces missions, "demanded rugged individuals who were able to master critical military skills needed to train and lead guerrilla warriors [and] to take care of themselves and others under harsh combat conditions." (Stanton: 21) These were Nadal's kind of warriors. He would fit seamlessly into this culture. After two months of training at Ft. Bragg they were ready for deployment to Vietnam.

His team sergeant, MSgt. Theodore Finch, remains to this day the best enlisted soldier Nadal ever met. A long-serving SF soldier, Sergeant Finch was as qualified in the various skills of an A team as the incumbent sergeants holding the positions of communications, weapons, intelligence, or engineering. However, Finch himself would probably have admitted that the team medic may have been somewhat better qualified in that skill position. In addition to their military occupation specialties the senior sergeants in each position were also qualified as combat leaders, with several being veterans of the Korean War. "Doc" Wilson, their senior medic, had served in the 101st Airborne Division in World War II as well as in the Korean War. First Lieutenant Walter Nelms, his team executive officer, who had been in Laos previously, would become a valuable asset in camp administration and patrol leadership once they reached Vietnam.

Special Forces in Vietnam

The major reasons the United States became involved in Vietnam were to counter a possible move by China to absorb Indochina and to thwart Ho Chi Minh from extending his "war of national liberation" into South Vietnam. The special forces camp effort in South Vietnam began in 1961 with the establishment of a Central Intelligence Agency (CIA) program to build border surveillance camps to monitor North Vietnamese army (NVA) troop movements into South Vietnam. By late 1961 the Communists already had been very successful in recruiting the inhabitants as Viet Cong (VC) loyalists opposed to the central government of President Ngo Dinh Diem in the western highlands of Vietnam and the border areas adjoining Laos and Cambodia. In cooperation with the American army, special forces A teams, initially funded by the CIA, established a series of camps in the central part of South Vietnam around Pleiku and Dak To. Montagnards, the aborigine inhabitants scattered around numerous South Vietnamese hill tribes, were originally recruited to serve as Strike Forces (camp fighters). Each camp was overseen by an American SF "A" team, ostensibly serving only in an advisory capacity to the Army of Vietnam special forces (VNSF) team and the Strike Force members. The success of the initial program led to its expansion and in early 1963 A teams from the 7th Special Forces Group were sent to northern South Vietnam to establish four new camps, one of which was Nam Dong. In mid-1963 the U.S. Army assumed full responsibility for this program, much to the regret of the A teams, which had become accustomed to the much more lenient structure, freedom of action, and generous resources provided by the CIA. By September 1963 there were thirty-seven special forces camps such as Nam Dong scattered all over South Vietnam, primarily along the Laotian and Cambodian borders. The CIA had originally planned and strategized for these camps to stop Viet Cong troop movements and resupply from Laos and Cambodia. (Stanton: 82)

Assignment: Nam Dong

After a long, leisurely trip by air across the Pacific Ocean, Nadal's team in-processed at Nha Trang and Da Nang. On 30 July 30 1963 a trio of Marine Corps CH-34 helicopters transported detachment A-727 from Da Nang on the coast approximately thirty kilometers over heavy jungles and mountains to their new home, the isolated outpost of Nam Dong, located approximately fifteen kilometers from the Laotian border and forty kilometers south of the A Shau Valley. As the special forces Detachment A-727 commander, Captain Nadal faced the daunting task of running a camp of four hundred Vietnamese in the mountainous northern jungles of South Vietnam. The camp was located in Thua Thien Province, South Vietnam's second province south of its border with North Vietnam

A stream flows through the village of Nam Dong, also shown as Ta Rau on the map, and the only access to the valley is a very rough dirt road, which could easily be ambushed in the narrow mountain passes between the mountains and the coastal plains. Surrounding the valley are three thousand foot-high steep-sided mountains covered with dense primary jungle that was very difficult to traverse. The stream through the village originates in another valley to the east which is separated from Nam Dong by a narrow gorge through which the river flows.

The task was very challenging, but Nadal was up to it. "No military duty was more difficult or potentially more challenging than border duty . . . the northwestern outposts, in close proximity to North Vietnam and the dreaded A Shau Valley (just northwest of Nam Dong), were the most feared assignments." (Stanton: 84) He felt confident in the ability of his team members and himself to accomplish their mission. His training and desire gave him assurance that he would succeed because he reflected the positive attitude that all military personnel should possess. Extraordinary confidence was especially critical for these original American special forces soldiers, the vanguard of the U.S. military effort in Vietnam, when they were in such isolated locations with little logistical support or backup.

On arrival they were met by the outgoing Nam Dong A team members who were very helpful and took several of the A-727 detachment members on a one-day patrol to familiarize them with their jungle environment. Nadal immediately realized that it would be necessary in their six month tour to focus on building up the camp and training the Strike Force, which was not only understrength, but also not well-trained.

Nam Dong Camp

One of the pleasant surprises in the camp was when they learned that the team they were replacing was the first team in Vietnam to have hired Chinese Nungs for an A team camp to act as body guards and, most importantly, as competent fighters. The Nungs were a fascinating Chinese tribal group from southern China that had been fighting the Communists since the early days of Mao Tse-tung. They were chased out of China, fought for the French, moved to South Vietnam after the French were defeated, and were now fighting with American special forces or being used to guard special forces headquarters units. There were approximately thirty Nungs in Nam Dong with their own team house and kitchen. Their leader was an old soldier named Le-Tse-tung who had been an NCO with a French unit. They were protective of the Americans and good allies in a fight. Whenever Americans went on patrol, three or four Nungs always joined them. Nadal was always curious as to what happened to the Nungs following the fall of South Vietnam.

Nam Dong village was established in 1962 as part of the South Vietnamese government's strategic hamlet program which was designed to provide land to move farmers from the populated areas to the seemingly unpopulated highlands. The location had originally been built as a small French outpost. Many of these hamlets were located near the Laotian and Cambodian border. Unfortunately, native hill-tribe Montagnards, living as they did three hundred years ago, surviving through hunting and slash-and-burn agriculture, had inhabited the mountain areas first. Historic antagonism between the two groups, Vietnamese and Montagnard, created continuous difficulties where the cultures collided. The outpost protected five thousand Vietnamese in the surrounding valley which served as a direct enemy infiltration route to the cities of Da Nang and Phu Bai on the coast. (Stanton: 93) Later in the Vietnam War a senior SF officer, Charles M. Simpson, III, reported that, "the greatest portion of the peasant population was not committed ideologically to either side, wishing only to be left alone to survive." (Simpson: 98)

When Nam Dong Camp was established in the spring of 1963, there had been little previous contact with the Montagnards in the area. The Katu tribe, which inhabited this area, had a history of hostility to the Vietnamese and most chose to stay deep in their jungle valleys. Because of this, the Strike

Force at Nam Dong was Vietnamese, recruited from the lowlands and cities along the coast. Colonel Simpson commented that some of the Strike Force members for the SF camps in northern South Vietnam were a unique group obtained when "The mayors of Da Nang and Hue [obtained recruits] from the . . . teenage hoodlums, who had been scraped off the water front." (Simpson: 109) This was unfortunate because they lacked the jungle lore and wisdom that the Montagnards possessed, did not bond with the Americans as did the Montagnards, and were often infiltrated by the Viet Cong. As an example, on July 6, 1964, after Captain Nadal's team had returned from their tour, Nam Dong was attacked by a Viet Cong battalion; the attack so fierce that the camp almost was overrun. Only the heroic defense by the A team, the Nungs, and the Vietnamese special forces allowed the team to survive. The first Medal of Honor of the Vietnam War was received after that battle by Captain Roger Donlon, the team commander. In 1995 Donlon returned to the camp site and a former Viet Cong (VC) informed him that 20 to 30 percent of his Vietnamese Strike Force had been Viet Cong. Donlon related he now understood why so many of my Vietnamese were found in their beds with their throats slit or their necks broken. Some even had their hearts and livers cut out." (Donlon: 218)

The Nam Dong camp was built as two concentric ovals, defined by trenches and barbed wire. Between the outer and inner ring lived the Vietnamese Strike Force near their fighting positions in small thatch and palm tree frond huts. Inside the inner oval were the main camp buildings, which included a communication shack for the radios, a headquarters building for the team, a dining house for the Americans, an aid station, and a dormitory for the rest of the team members. This was generally replicated for the VNSF team. Also inside the second fence were the mortar, machine gun, and various fighting positions for the Nungs and Vietnamese special forces.

Strike Force Training

While Nadal or other team members were leading patrols, back at camp the training and recruiting of Strike Force members went on continuously. Recruiting was primarily the responsibility of the Vietnamese, but the Americans equipped and trained the civilian irregular defense group (CIDG) force. The CIDG members were fulltime members of the camp complement and were quartered inside the outer circle of defenses. By the time the tour ended the Strike Force had been built to nearly four hundred members organized into three companies. There were constant training cycles focusing primarily on weapons competency, immediate action drills, and ambush tactics. Training was the primary responsibility of Sfc. Charles Dodds, a large, very competent soldier, who earned everyone's respect by his undying patience and gentle manner when dealing with the Vietnamese. Unfortunately, not much was able to be done about discipline and morale. Nadal wondered if they should have spent more time on close order drill and other rudimentary military training. Since the Americans had no power to enforce discipline and minimal language skills, it was difficult to improve motivation, unit cohesion, or morale, and the VNSF detachment commander did not choose to exert himself to remedy these problems. From the original foundation of the organization of Luc Luong Dac Biet (LLDB), Vietnam's airborne special forces, although there were exceptions, many of the officers were incompetent. Captain Nadal was unfortunate that his counterpart was one of the weaker officers.

Medical and Civic Action

Establishing good relations with his Vietnamese counterparts was important and always depended on establishing rapport with divergent personalities. Inasmuch as the U.S. Army was paying the CIDG troops, Nadal evolved to be in command of the camp. Fortunately, the initial VNSF detachment commander did not much care to be in charge and deferred to Captain Nadal.

The focus was on three activities: combat patrolling towards the Laotian border to determine enemy infiltration and ambushing or capturing the enemy, protection of the village of Nam Dong, and gaining the trust of the villagers through civic action projects. Nadal personally led many of the patrols, participated in civic action projects, and left protection of the local area to the VNSF Strike Force. One of the SF team's accomplishments came to fruition just prior to their departure: they obtained the services of a team from a naval construction battalion (Seabees), which came to the camp with heavy equipment and built a bridge across the river, improved the camp's defensive fighting positions, and built an airstrip nearby.

The most successful civic action project, however, was clearly the use of the camp medics to treat the villagers. The SF medics were highly qualified and competent in treating many types of medical problems, to include some minor surgery. It always pleasantly surprised Nadal to see how quickly a child, whose head was covered with pus-filled sores, would heal after a shot of penicillin to the child and a bar of soap to the mother. Within days the sores would dry up and the mother would become a loyal friend. In the camp there were also female Vietnamese nurses who assisted in conducting sick call in the village. Most conversations with villagers were conducted through the camp interpreters who were invaluable and generally competent.

Combat Operations

It was amazing that Nadal and his team members were able to conduct combat operations by communicating all instructions through an interpreter. This communications challenge dictated for all the patrols that the action always took place within a small core group of American SF, Nungs, and a few Vietnamese SF. The majority of the Strike Force soldiers seldom played a role because they were generally unmotivated and difficult to control in combat.

Shortly after Detachment A-727's arrival Nadal decided to lead his first patrol. After completing a terrain analysis and choosing an objective area in the valley to the east he planned what he thought would be a short, one-day orientation patrol. Several of his SF team members participated as well as a few Nungs and twenty Strike Force members. They left in the early morning and around 1600 hours reached the objective area, which the original plan called for reaching three hours earlier by 1300. Nadal had significantly underestimated the difficulty of traveling in the mountainous terrain.

After they crossed a river, they found a trail that could have been a demonstration lane at Ft. Bragg for improvised man traps. There were large rocks hung on vines and covered with punji stakes (sharpened bamboo sticks), that would swing from a tree when someone tripped a vine stretched across the trail. Pits were filled with punji stakes on the far side of fallen trees so that a person would fall in to the pit as they stepped over the log. More stakes were placed among the vegetation by the side of the trail so a passersby would impale themselves if they jumped to the side of the trail. Fortunately, the Nungs were astute enough to locate these traps and no one was hurt. These booby traps had all been established to discourage anyone from following the trail, which led to an enemy training area that was discovered on a later patrol. Nadal learned not to follow trails, but instead to move along the sides of the mountains. Unfortunately, Captain Nadal would receive a Purple Heart for a puncture wound caused by an encounter with a punji stake during a later patrol.

After examining the trail for a couple of hundred meters, it became dark and they had to spend the night in the jungle, something Nadal had not planned for on this patrol. As everyone else strung out their hammocks, he huddled next to a tree as he had not brought sleeping gear. Seeing his predicament, Le-Tse-tung, the chief Nung, directed his soldiers to weave

Nadal a hammock made from tree vines and gave him a canteen cup full of hot rice and dried shrimp, which was delicious and highly appreciated. A major lesson learned on this patrol was that the Vietnamese cooked their rice every night on 10-20 cooking fires that created a beacon to the enemy signaling their exact location.

The Young Man in the Blue Shorts

Two of Nadal's personal needs were satisfied by excitement and action. Both needs were fulfilled on his next patrol. Leading his second patrol since arriving at the camp he had established an ambush on a trail where it crossed a twenty or thirty foot wide stream. Three of his SF A team members, two VNSF soldiers, four Nungs, several Strike Force members, and their interpreters joined Nadal for this patrol. After a one day march from the camp, they organized an L-shaped ambush with a machine gun positioned to fire up a trail, and positioned themselves parallel to the long side of the L. It was hot; the jungle, thick with large-leafed plants and vines with sharp thorns, was populated with two-inch long leeches that stuck to you and sucked out your blood. A Nung was beside Nadal, who held in his left hand the trigger mechanism for a Claymore mine and laid a World War II carbine across his lap. Since they had been lying in the same place since the previous afternoon, fatigue was affecting Nadal and his head started bobbing as he fought to stay awake.

Suddenly, the Nung tapped him on the arm and with his eyes directed Nadal to look down the trail. There were two men walking toward the ambush. The shirtless lead man, wearing blue shorts, carried a bolt action rifle in his right hand. He was no more than ten feet away when Nadal blew the Claymore. It was an automatic reaction by him, without thinking of consequences or moral issues. Unfortunately, the two men had gotten so close that they went past the kill zone of the Claymore mine. However, when the Claymore mine exploded, several other ambush members opened fire, killing the lead man. In an amazing demonstration of survival instincts the second man made an impossible leap across the stream and escaped.

Adrenaline was pumping through each one of them as they examined the body. Nadal felt a sense of success. Seven years of infantry, ranger and special forces training had been brought to fruition in this, his first combat action. The entire consequences of this incident were not felt by him until many years later when he would be reminded over and over of this event.

It made no sense to try to chase the second man because the patrol was in his territory and it would be an opportunity in turn for their small force to be ambushed. Now Nadal faced a quandary. They had an enemy body, and they did not know what to do with it, but eventually he decided to carry the body back to camp. No one seemed to argue with the idea and the Vietnamese camp commander, who was on this patrol, agreed. After the body was trussed up on a pole with the Vietnamese Strike Force members carrying the body, they began their return. Carrying the dead man along the stream bed and through the jungle was not an easy task. Subsequently, Nadal learned to leave the dead where they fell. The enemy would bury their own dead. During their return, while crossing rapids at a stream, the Vietnamese dropped or lost the body in the stream and it floated down among some rocks and sunk out of sight. Having made the decision to bring the body back, Nadal was determined to recover the body, so he took off his web gear and dove into the stream to a depth of eight to ten feet where he retrieved the body and brought it to the surface. They made it back to their camp and the camp commander, who was the commander in name only, exhibited the corpse in the village as a warning not to collaborate with the enemy. Captain Nadal would never shake the memory of this ambush or the young man who was killed that day.

Counterpart Cooperation
Detachment A-727 also became known for good relations with its Vietnamese counterparts as reported by the Vietnamese chain of command to Nadal's superiors. All his team members made an effort to cooperate and help the Vietnamese special forces. Initially, the VNSF team leader was somewhat reluctant to conduct frequent and aggressive patrols, but eventually he was either convinced or ignored, and after the first month, in addition to local security patrols, there were almost constant patrols of several days duration into what was slowly discovered to be a major crossing area on the route from Laos to the lowlands and cities of northern South Vietnam.

Isolation of the Special Forces Camps
The camp was located over thirty miles away from their support base at the Da Nang air field. Nam Dong camp was accessible from the east only by a tortuous trail that needed to be secured by placing Strike Force troops on the passes whenever it became necessary to take the camp's old World War II-vintage trucks to Da Nang to procure supplies. Usually resupply was made by air, either by marine CH-34 helicopters or by parachute with bundles dropped by army Caribou aircraft or Air Force C-123s. Even live animals

were parachuted into the camp. Chickens were delivered in cages and they would begin flapping their wings attempting to fly as soon as they exited the aircraft. Pigs, tied together two to a bundle, were also air dropped. Once, even cows were dropped, but the cows had not been properly trained in parachute landings and several broke their legs so they had to be killed and eaten immediately as there was no refrigeration available.

The major problem with the isolation of Nam Dong and most of these early special forces camps was the fact that in case of a major night attack there was no way to reinforce the camp rapidly. This was demonstrated by the July 6, 1964, VC attack on Nam Dong when relief troops arrived the following morning, well after the attackers had fled. The second major problem was communicating with the outside world. The only radio with the range to reach Da Nang or to enable communication with the camp when on patrol was the AN/GRC-9, originally designed for use in World War II by Office of Strategic Services (OSS) agents. It could receive and transmit only in Morse Code. The radio did not use batteries and power was provided by a heavy, hand-cranked generator. A long, wire antenna had to be hung between trees and properly oriented in order to send a message. This whole process took twenty to thirty minutes so there was no way of calling for immediate assistance if a patrol became engaged in a firefight. If ambushed, the special forces patrols knew they were on their own because the likelihood of additional support was nonexistent.

Despite all the risks and dangers faced by the brave special forces soldiers, they accepted their missions and remained in harm's way. On one patrol Staff Sergeant Zamarripa, the junior weapons sergeant, knelt on a punji stake that penetrated under his knee cap. The patrol was two days march from the camp and he could not walk. This was the only time on Nadal's tour that they unlimbered the GRC-9 radio in an emergency to call for assistance. (A patrol would normally communicate twice a day: when it stopped for the evening and before it began moving the following day.) It took over twenty minutes to set up the radio antenna, another ten minutes to make contact with the Da Nang-based SFB team and transmit a message, and over an hour before a marine CH-34 arrived to hoist Sergeant Zamarripa from a stream bed. Not only was communication limited, but there were no reinforcements available in Da Nang to come to their assistance in the event of an attack by a superior force.

The Stay-Behind Patrol

The most significant patrol led by Captain Nadal occurred midway through the tour at Camp Nam Dong. Early in November 1963 Nadal conducted a reconnaissance flight in an L-19 flying from Da Nang over his area of operations. In the far end of the valley to their east he noticed smoke rising from the jungle in an area located in a draw at the base of a mountain. He could follow the route of a stream that led towards the smoke so he knew if there was some type of habitation there, that they also had a source of available water.

By now they had learned that all the trails in that valley were guarded by outposts that would fire warning shots as soon as they approached. He returned to camp and organized a rather large patrol, consisting of about forty men including the Nungs, interpreter, VNSF, Strike Force members, and four of American SF. Relying on his instincts and training, he decided to follow a route that took them halfway up the mountain ridge where they moved at that elevation to the far end of the valley. As in all mountainous country, he knew there would be a trail along the top of the ridge as well as along stream beds on the valley floor, but they would be guarded. No one, however, placed outposts half way down a steep mountain side.

Traveling for three days half way up the mountain through primary jungle was very difficult physically. Ankles were twisted, water was in short supply, the Vietnamese complained, but Nadal learned how to get behind the early warning outpost line. The trees and vines provided hand holds and kept the patrol members from sliding down the mountain.

This valley was in a part of Vietnam that was so remote that it had not yet been mapped and their map sheet's upper right hand corner was blank. Navigating by land reckoning, they descended into the valley floor about five hundred meters short of the draw he had seen from the air. As they reached the valley floor, he had two Strike Force members climb the large trees to describe what they saw. They then set off towards the draw. Upon their approach, a shot rang out, after which they moved forward quickly and discovered a camp consisting of three recently vacated Montagnard long houses. They found cooking fires still burning, rice in pots, documents, hand grenades, rifle cartridges, marksmanship targets and other items. After examining the camp, Nadal ordered the buildings burned. Then he decided to establish an ambush at the camp and sent the bulk of the patrol downstream about a mile with orders to be prepared to defend themselves. Two of his team members, one VNSF, and three Nungs remained with him on the outskirts of the camp where he planted some Claymores. While they waited, it began to rain with monsoon intensity. He reasoned that, at some point, someone had to come back to this camp to see what had been done. All night in the rain they observed the burnt camp site. They had no knowledge of what size force originally might have been based there. They were leech bait during the night. The following morning a group of four or five enemy entered the camp. The Claymores were triggered, killing several of the enemy and the small ambush group ran to escape before a larger force could react to confront them.

The postscript of this patrol occurred about a month later, while Nadal was on yet another patrol, when several Vietnamese helicopters came to the camp, brought a band and several dignitaries, and conducted an awards ceremony in which they decorated the Vietnamese camp commander and some of his teammates. The camp commander had been on the patrol, but had been sent back with the main body while Nadal remained in the enemy camp for the ambush. The Americans all laughed upon their return to camp from the latest patrol with the irony of his decoration because he had missed the real action when Nadal and his group had ambushed the enemy upon their return to the destroyed camp.

From left to right: Sfc. Commerford, Capt. Tony Nadal, SSgt. McPherson, members of U.S. Army Special Forces Team A-727, November 1963, at Nam Dong Special Forces camp upon return from a combat patrol.

Meanwhile Back at the White House

During Nadal's six month tour in Vietnam, back in the Oval Office at the White House momentous decisions were being made. Michael Forrestal, a Vietnam specialist, served on the staff of the National Security Council under McGeorge Bundy. "In the waning days of summer in 1963, Forrestal was one of the Kennedy administration insiders who helped to draft and clear a weekend cable that would change the course of the war." (Goldstein: 77)

The cable was written and sent to Ambassador Henry Cabot Lodge in Saigon on August 24, 1963, without adherence to the normal approval process. (Goldstein: 78) The bottom line of the instructions dictated that South Vietnamese President Diem must replace many of his government and military leaders and if he refused, to plan for an overthrowing of Diem. (Goldstein: 78) Many senior U.S. officials had been left out of the loop on this decision. Basically, this directive left Diem's future up to the Vietnamese military.

On October 2, 1963, at a meeting in the White House General Maxwell D. Taylor, who at the time was chairman of the Joint Chiefs of Staff, reported to President Kennedy that the mission to prop up South Vietnam could be almost complete by the end of 1964 and therefore withdrawal of our advisors could be completed by the end of 1965. (Goldstein: 82, 83)

Attention then turned to discussion of the plan to replace Diem by effecting contact with other potential Vietnamese leaders. (Goldstein: 84) By the end of the month of October there apparently was significant discussion about the ramifications of an overthrow of Diem. (Goldstein: 86)

On November 1, 1963, "President Diem and his brother were bound and shot to death in the rear hold of a South Vietnamese army personnel carrier." (Goldstein: 88) It is reported that President Kennedy was deeply disturbed that the coup ended with the murder of President Diem.

President Kennedy was assassinated three weeks later on November 22, 1963. Author Goldstein summarizes, "The events of November 1963 punctuate what is arguably the end of the first act of America's entanglement in Vietnam. An autocratic leader in Saigon had been overthrown by generals in his armed forces. A determined but strategically dispassionate U.S. President who had rejected Americanizing the war was abruptly murdered." (Goldstein: 93) Eight days before his death President Kennedy had been opposed to the insertion of combat troops into Vietnam.

When Lyndon Johnson became President on November 22, 1963, his course was set for 1964. McGeorge Bundy recalled that Johnson really put Vietnam on the back burner and focused on his election after which he would be able to focus on major policy issues. (Goldstein: 98) In December 1963 it was reported to Johnson that the situation in Vietnam was really much more negative than previous reports reaching the White House. (Goldstein: 107)

Conclusion of Tour

In late 1963, the U.S. government was still denying that the enemy action in South Vietnam was being largely supported and led by the North Vietnamese government. After one particular patrol, when Nadal reported finding a major trail entering from Laos, where steps had been built into the sides of the mountains, hand rails had been erected, and many signs of traffic had been detected, a colonel from special forces headquarters flew to Nam Dong to try to dissuade Nadal from reporting all he had discovered. Nadal offered to lead another patrol to the location if the colonel would come along to investigate personally. He declined and nothing was ever heard again about Nadal's report.

Captain Nadal and his team learned to operate very proficiently in this forbidding environment. The competency and success attained by the time the team was replaced, was mentioned in a report by the B detachment commander who stated, "Captain Nadal's team had more patrols, enemy engagements, and enemy killed than the other four A teams in our I Corps combined."

Aftermath

Special forces Detachment A-727 rotated back to the United States from Nam Dong on January 11, 1964. Captain Nadal's experiences at Nam Dong served him in very good stead as what he experienced was utilized in his later tour as a company commander in the 7th Cavalry. He had learned to operate independently, navigate in the jungle, locate enemy sites and lead by personal example, all of which benefited him in his next tour in Vietnam.

In his life he will always cherish his extraordinary and undying pride in the performance and accomplishments of Detachment A-727. Captain Nadal and his special forces soldiers had entered an isolated and dangerous environment to be a part of America's effort to save South Vietnam from Communist domination. Even by the time special forces teams like Captain Nadal's had infiltrated enemy country, the enemy had been slowly building their infrastructure and influence for several years. Under Nadal's leadership his team accomplished their mission and brought great credit to the army's Green Berets. Nadal found his action and excitement. However, there is a recurring and troubling memory he cannot seem to shake of a young man in

blue shorts, walking down a trail, unaware he was going to die. Killing someone in an ambush eventually struck Nadal as profoundly different to killing
someone in his later battle at LZ X-Ray where everyone was shooting at
everyone else. In the hindsight of life and with the passing of time he is troubled that the killing of the young man might really be akin to murder. If
actions such as these are really murder, then the gates of heaven will be closed
to many warriors of ages past. Truly it was killing in the fulfillment of a military mission, not murder, but nevertheless, actions in the years of our youth
torment many warriors in the years of our old age.

Retired army Colonel Roger Donlon, who later commanded Nam Dong
when he was a captain, described some personalized details of the July 6,
1964, attack at Nam Dong. As many as a hundred of the three hundred Vietnamese Strike Force members ended up being Viet Cong sympathizers and
when the VC battalion attacked the camp, these Strike Forcers turned their
guns on the Americans, Nungs, and VNSF in the inner perimeter, and joined
the attacking force. Donlon's Vietnamese army (ARVN) counterpart and several of his staff members were discovered to have been Viet Cong. The Nungs
fought valiantly alongside the Americans. Two of Donlon's team members,
MSgt. Gabriel R. Alamo and Sgt. John L. Houston, were killed along with
Kevin Conway, an Australian warrant officer. Nine of Donlon's twelve team
members were wounded, with several being wounded multiple times. The
attackers eventually left without overrunning the camp. The four Vietnamese
female nurses survived, remained loyal, and tended to the wounded after the
attack. The camp remained open until September 4, 1964, so the enemy
would not be able to claim an immediate victory. The Nung security force
commander, Le Tse-tung, survived the attack, but died later in the war. Donlon heard that a large enclave of Nungs relocated after the war to the high
deserts of California. His executive officer was Lt. Jay Olejniczak, who had
been in the author's cadet company at West Point.

When Captain Nadal served in the 7th Special Forces Group, his group
commander during the Cuban Missile Crisis had been Colonel Clyde Russell, whom Captain Nadal never met. In 1963 Colonel Russell was assigned
to Military Assistance Command Vietnam (MACV) to form a new classified
operation that would become quite unique. Many of the participants in
Colonel Russell's operation would be veterans of the early special forces
camps in South Vietnam.

CHAPTER 2

"How's it Feel to be the Man that Started World War III?"

COLONEL CLYDE R. RUSSELL, USA
(MACVSOG, 1964–1965)

A special breed of man will sacrifice everything for the security and freedom of so many unthankful others.—Author Unknown

MACVSOG

The acronym SOG, standing for Studies and Observation Group, was a euphemism for a semiautonomous element of the U.S. Military Assistance Command, Vietnam, which in fact answered directly to the Joint Chiefs of Staff in Washington (in the person of the Special Assistant for Counterinsurgency and Special Activities). The SOG mission was conduct of clandestine operations throughout Southeast Asia by U.S. members of the various services and by indigenous personnel. Agent insertions, ambushes and raids, rescue missions, deep reconnaissance, and interdiction were among the typical SOG cross-border missions.

A Man of Firsts

Colonel Clyde Russell was a man of firsts. A parachutist with the famed 82nd Airborne Division during World War II, Russell was the first to jump in his battalion during the D-Day landings at Ste. Mere-Eglise, in Normandy, France. (Langdon: 49) His battalion commander, Lieutenant Colonel Benjamin Vandervoort, later portrayed by John Wayne in the movie *The Longest Day*, was right behind him in the stick. He made all four combat jumps with his division in World War II. He was one of the first ashore with the 7th Infantry Division in Inchon, during the Korean War. In 1963, as one of the first U.S. Army advisors with the Military Assistance Command Vietnam (MACV), Russell set in motion the scenario leading to the 1964 Gulf of Tonkin incident. This swiftly led to full American involvement in the war in Vietnam.

The "fruit salad" on Russell's uniform included the Distinguished Service Medal, Silver Star, the Purple Heart with oak leaf cluster, two awards of the Combat Infantryman's Badge, and ten campaign ribbons for three wars.

Clyde Russell's family was as colorful as he was. An insurance salesman in Iowa prior to World War II, Russell married a woman named Jini. When Clyde went off to war, Jini divorced him, but joined the war effort herself, as a Red Cross worker assigned to the 101st Airborne Division with the famed 506th "Band of Brothers" Parachute Infantry Regiment (PIR). When Clyde was wounded during Operation Market Garden, Jini tracked him down at a field hospital in England and remarried him. A mannequin of Jini in her wartime uniform is displayed today at the 101st Airborne Division Museum in Ft. Campbell, Kentucky.

Special Forces

In the late 1950s upon completion of the Army War College, at Carlisle Barracks, Pennsylvania, the Russells were transferred to Germany. There were four of them now: Clyde, Jini, daughter Polly, and son Chris. After a year in Stuttgart at the 7th Army headquarters, Russell became the executive officer of the 10th Special Forces Group (SFG), located in the picturesque Bavarian Alps town of Bad Tolz, which was situated but a few miles south of Munich. It was there, in January 1960 that Jini Russell died one night while then Lieutenant Colonel Russell was away on duty in Berlin. Shortly afterward, recently-promoted full Colonel Clyde Russell and his children, Polly and Chris, returned sadly to Ft. Bragg, North Carolina.

Back at Ft. Bragg, it wasn't long before Clyde Russell had been introduced to a young college professor from Syracuse University named Helen Persons, and they were soon married. It was at this point in his career that Russell was given command of the 7th Special Forces Group at Ft. Bragg. The Cuban Missile Crises was in full bloom and the world stood on the brink of the nuclear war. The 7th SFG was tasked with the Area of Operations (AO) of Central and South America. This included Cuba, and the 7th SFG stood ready to go into harm's way as the vanguard of America's finest in the armed forces of the United States. No sooner had the Cuban Missile Crisis cooled down than the drums of war could be heard in distant corners of

Southeast Asia in a country called the Republic of South Vietnam. Clyde Russell couldn't resist the call and in 1963 he volunteered for duty in Vietnam where he reported in late September 1963. He was tagged by the Pentagon to write the plans for special operations and so for his first few months in country he devised and then wrote the top secret plans for the Military Assistance Command Vietnam Special Operations Group (MACVSOG). When asked what the name SOG meant, not wanting to reveal the real meaning behind SOG, he simply replied that it was a "Studies and Observation Group." Under this innocent sounding name SOG became the U.S. deep-cover clandestine operation of the Vietnam War conducting secret missions and collecting intelligence against North Vietnam.

November 1, 1963, had been the original planned date for the CIA covert operations to be converted to U.S. Army control (Operation Switch-back) under Colonel Russell. The November 1963 assassinations of President Diem of South Vietnam and President John Kennedy delayed the official transfer until January 24, 1964 when Colonel Russell assumed command of SOG. (Plaster *Photo History:* 17)

General William C. Westmoreland arrived in South Vietnam in January 1964 as the deputy to General Paul D. Harkins, who commanded U.S. Military Assistance Command, Vietnam. General Westmoreland would replace General Harkins in June 1964. Captain Dave R. Palmer was his first aide-de-camp in Vietnam. (Westmoreland: 41) Palmer later would become a three-star general and Superintendent of West Point.

SOG was established with a chain of command outside Harkin's and Westmoreland's MACV channels. "SOG would answer directly to the Joint Chiefs of Staff in the Pentagon via a special liaison, the special assistant for counter-insurgency and special activities (SACSA). In Saigon only General Westmoreland and four non-SOG officers were even briefed on SOG." (Plaster *Photo History:* 18)

During the time that Colonel Russell was organizing SOG, his family, consisting of second wife Helen, Chris (then a high school senior), and daughters, Polly and newly-born Janet, moved to Saigon in June 1964. His family was able to join him because with the SOG assignment his original thirteen-month tour had been extended. Older daughter, Polly returned to college in the United States in September. Because MACVSOG was so highly classified, Colonel Russell did not "talk shop" with his family. Still, they recognized the hush-hush secrecy involved in his job even if they weren't told any of the specifics. Helen said he frequently left the villa at eleven at night, not returning until early the next morning. She asked him once what was the best route to his office and he said, "There is no best route. My driver takes me a different way every day."

Agent training was conducted by SOG at Camp Long Thanh about thirty miles east of Saigon. This was a secret camp where Chris visited once and test fired multiple weapons affixed with silencers, participated in a native wild chicken hunt, and watched his father parachute from a helicopter during the visit. Chris later learned that this was the training camp for agents who subsequently were to be parachuted (infiltrated) into North Vietnam on top secret SOG missions.

Colonel Clyde Russell giving cans of milk to a Montagnard village chief, whose wife had died in child birth.

In February 1965, when the Vietnam War began to heat up, all the military and embassy families, including the Russells, were evacuated back to the United States with a scant one week's notice.

SOG

Colonel Russell knew that he needed some of the best and the brightest special operations minds to help him create his Studies and Observations Group, so he requisitioned several of his old special forces comrades from their days together in the 10th SFG and the 7th SFG. Men like Lt. Col. Bob Bartelt, Lt. Col. Ed Partain, Lt. Col. Hans Manz, Marine Corps Col. Jimmy Johnson (his SOG executive officer) and others. The logistics for SOG were run out of an office in Okinawa by another old friend of Russell's: Col. Robert (Bob) Scherer. As the SOG plans were being devised, Russell formatted and sent a budget request to the Pentagon and as Chris was told later, Congress awarded SOG with a $5 million budget. With this money Russell sent Lt. Col. Hans Manz to Norway to purchase the "Nasty" class PT speedboats which were later implicated in the Gulf of Tonkin Incident. These Nasty class speedboats were manned by South Vietnamese and were designed to run raids against the North Vietnamese north of the DMZ. No Americans accompanied these missions.

Russell realized early on that SOG needed operational intelligence to be able to conduct its business. The problem was that the needed intelligence was only known by the CIA. The military, that is MACV, simply had not been in country (in Vietnam) long enough to acquire such intelligence on their own. It took a major effort for Colonel Russell to obtain the cooperation SOG needed from the CIA.

With the advent of SOG, Russell immediately began raiding the coastline of North Vietnam with the newly acquired Nasty PT boats. After Russell's family returned to the United States, he shared living quarters with Lt. Gen. John Throckmorton (deputy commander of MACV in 1964 and 1965), which became known as the "White House East." This BOQ (bachelor officer quarters) was so named because all SOG operations were being run out of the White House through the Joint chiefs rather than through MACV in Saigon. As it was later explained to Chris, there was a somewhat leery attitude toward SOG operations because they were questionable in so far as to their international legality. After all, the 1956 Geneva Conventions that divided Vietnam proscribed the United States from conducting military operations in the neighboring countries of Cambodia, Laos, and North Vietnam.

Colonel Ed Sayre, who was personally interviewed by the author, was on the MACV staff from 1964–1965 as an assistant G-3(operations section). Ed Sayre knew Clyde Russell very well as they were old 82nd friends from World War II when Sayre had been the Able Company commander while Russell had been commander of Easy Company, 505th Parachute Infantry Regiment. As a captain in Sicily, following the combat jump by the 82nd Airborne Division, Sayre was awarded the Distinguished Service Cross for his valorous actions in battle.

In 1961 Colonel Sayre had been on the staff of the U.S. Army, Pacific (USARPAC) and had an interesting perspective on the decision-making process for our involvement in Vietnam. One evening he had dinner in Honolulu with Lt. Gen. Thomas H. Trapnell who was transiting through Honolulu en route back to Washington, D.C., from a fact-finding mission to South Vietnam for President Kennedy. Previously Sayre had been a battalion commander in Trapnell's regiment. General Trapnell had also been a recipient of the Distinguished Service Cross from 1942 combat action on the Bataan Peninsula. Sayre said Trapnell told him he would recommend to the president that the United States proceed no deeper with our support for South Vietnam. Trapnell believed deeper American involvement in Vietnam would end up being a big mistake. Sayre said Trapnell's advice to President Kennedy was not what the president wanted to hear. Sayre became the message carrier for official correspondence between General Westmoreland and Maxwell D. Taylor, who became the Ambassador to South Vietnam in July 1964.

North Vietnam Raids

In 1977 Colonel Russell was diagnosed with cancer. This was before science had developed the life-saving therapies that many cancer patients can avail themselves of today, and the diagnosis of cancer was a death sentence. Russell succumbed to his cancer in November 1979. His funeral service was overflowing as more than three hundred of his friends attended. At the funeral home, Lt. Gen. John Throckmorton, Clyde R. Russell's former roommate at the White House East in Vietnam, appointed himself to greet everyone who came to the wake. It was during this time that General Throckmorton told Chris Russell the story of how Chris's father had "started the Vietnam War." General Throckmorton related to Chris the history and background of his father's time as chief of SOG. Throckmorton related that the senior commanders were very insistent about plausible deniability in the event that some international incident was to come to light as a result of SOG activities. After all, America was not supposed to be in Laos, Cambodia, or North Vietnam, which were the area of operations (AO) for SOG. It was against international law and the 1956 Geneva Conventions to be doing what the SOG teams were doing. It was these very actions that would later be revealed when the infamous "Pentagon Papers" were brought to light by the antiwar activist Daniel Ellsberg. In any event—and again according to General Throckmorton at Russell's funeral—on the Sunday morning preceding the events that led up to the Gulf of Tonkin Incident, Colonel Russell had gone down to his office in the embassy in Saigon.

The following highly-personalized historical information was related to Chris at his father's funeral by General Throckmorton and has been indelibly imprinted in his memory. Here it is as recollected by Chris:

General Throckmorton received a telephone call from his boss, General Westmoreland, early on a Sunday. (Most probably Asia date August 2, 1964, Washington date Saturday August 1, 1964.) Westmoreland told Throckmorton that he had just received a call from the White House in Washington, D.C., asking what was going on. He said that there was a radio report coming out of Hanoi, transmitted by China and Japan and then heard at Hickam Air Force Base in Hawaii, saying that there had been a firefight in North Vietnam waters!

Washington wanted to know what was going on. Throckmorton said that he didn't know, that he hadn't given any orders authorizing an offensive firefight in North Vietnam. As an aside, it should be noted that up until this point in the war, the standing order was that Americans were to shoot only if shot at, that is in self defense. Apparently, someone had authorized an offensive engagement with the North Vietnamese. However, if Westmoreland and Throckmorton, the top two U.S. generals in Vietnam didn't know anything about it, then this begs the question of, who did? It was at this point in the conversation that both Generals Westmoreland and Throckmorton said at the same time, "Where's Russell?" General Throckmorton said he wasn't sure but said that he'd check his room. He told Chris that he checked Colonel Russell's room but that he wasn't there. He reported back to Westmoreland that "He's not here," and General Westmoreland said, "Find him." With that, General Throckmorton walked into Russell's covert SOG office.

He said that when he entered the room, he could see that Russell was the only person in the room. He said that the colonel stood up at attention and when Throckmorton then said to him, "Clyde, how's it feel to be the man that started World War III?", Russell looked around the room and said with a grin, "Well, where is that SOB, sir, I'd like to shake his hand."

Chris Russell said that his father obviously said this with tongue in cheek. Now, who knows whether this was an accurate description of what happened that morning? Chris remembers this as it was told by Lt. Gen. Throckmorton at the funeral.

Admittedly, Colonel Sayre is an old soldier, but he has an incredible recollection of facts from those days forty-eight years ago. In his opinion SOG was established "to get us into the war."

A study of the historical record related to the Gulf of Tonkin incident, much of which has just come to light as late as 2007 involves, "an official National Security Agency (NSA) history of signals intelligence (SIGINT) in Vietnam, written in 2002, [which]was released in response to a Freedom of Information Act Request." (Schuster: 29)

The above referenced article also stated, "one element of American assistance to South Vietnam included commando raids against North Vietnam's coastal transportation facilities and networks." (Schuster: 30) These raids were conducted by "Nasty" class PT boats in the SOG OPLAN-34A program. OPLAN 34A had been approved on September 9, 1963, by Chairman of the Joint Chiefs of Staff Maxwell D. Taylor even before Colonel Russell arrived in Vietnam and started SOG. The plan comprised, "an array of covert operations to be directed against Hanoi. . . . These actions were aimed at causing the leadership of North Vietnam to divert resources from, and in time stop supporting, its insurgency in the south." (Schultz: 35) When Lyndon Johnson became president after Kennedy's assassination, he inherited the OPLAN 34A program and as research shows knew about the SOG raids at least as early as the summer of 1964. "What the Pentagon Papers call 'an elaborate program of covert military operations against the state of North Vietnam' began on Feb. 1, 1964, under the code name Operation Plan 34A. President Johnson on the recommendation of Secretary McNamara, ordered the program with the hope, admittedly held very faint by the intelligence community, that 'progressively escalating pressure' from the clandestine attacks might eventually force Hanoi to order the Vietcong guerrillas in Vietnam and the Pathet Lao in Laos to halt their insurrections."(*Pentagon Papers:* 235) Colonel Russell oversaw OPLAN 34A. In late July 1964, under SOG control, the

South Vietnamese had been conducting cross-beach attacks on North Vietnam targets.

Meanwhile Back at the White House

As 1964 began McGeorge Bundy related to author Goldstein that Johnson was in a mode of not rocking the boat in Vietnam. (Goldstein: 98) President Johnson began spending a great amount of time at his Texas ranch. Immediately after President Kennedy's funeral, Johnson met with Ambassador Henry Cabot Lodge and read him the riot act. Johnson, according to Bundy, had not supported the idea of the coup that culminated in the murder of President Diem.

After Johnson had heard the bad news about how the war was really proceeding, he sent Secretary of Defense Robert McNamara on a fact-finding visit to Vietnam and his report on December 21, 1963 declared that the country could fall to the Communists within a short period of time.

In January 1964 the Joint Chiefs of Staff began to propose "the initial steps to Americanize the war." (Goldstein: 108)

Johnson began to stall, but the argument began to be made for the "domino theory", that it was important to take a stand in Vietnam or the rest of Southeast Asia would follow in Communist takeovers. The alternative of a neutralized South Vietnam came from French President de Gaulle. President Johnson began to be concerned about China entering the war as they had in 1950 in Korea.

In the summer of 1964 as the election loomed, more and more discussions were held in the White House relative to a higher degree of direct U.S. military actions and the need for congressional approval to increase the military pressure against the north. (Goldstein: 116) SOG's raids provided the perfect setting for the justification with congressional approval to escalate military actions.

Gulf of Tonkin

Secretary of Defense Robert McNamara had his finger right on SOG operations. Secretary McNamara sometime in the summer of 1964 ordered a new level of attacks. "McNamara asked his military advisers if it might make more sense to switch from cross-beach raids to standing offshore and bombarding coastal targets with ship-based heavy weapons." (Conboy and Andrade: 116) Colonel Russell had new orders and offshore bombardment restrictions were lifted. Apparently this did not yet include U.S. Navy ship bombardments at shore targets. The unit Russell used to conduct this new mission was Naval Advisory Detachment (NAD) at Da Nang.

There has intermittently surfaced some speculation and discussion that the intensified SOG missions and offshore U.S. Navy DESOTO operations, such as the intelligence-gathering patrol by the destroyer USS *Maddox*, were a set-up to provoke an enemy attack and assist Lyndon Johnson in his upcoming election. In the book *Tonkin Gulf and the Escalation of the Vietnam War*, author Edwin Moise states, "If the United States had wanted to avoid a violent incident, then, during a week when the United States was sponsoring repeated raids against the North Vietnamese coast, it would not have sent a U.S. destroyer so close to that coast, under conditions where the captain would feel he had no choice but to fire first when approached." (Moise: 89) However, information reported by Admiral U.S.G. Sharp, who at this time was Commander in Chief Pacific (CINCPAC), would tend to refute any deliberately planned provocation when he concluded: "*Maddox* had been told to keep clear of the South Vietnamese patrol boat actions, and her schedule was arranged so that the two operations would not be in the same area at the same time. It was my view at the time and remains so, that while the North Vietnamese may have been agitated by the South Vietnamese harassment operation, they had absolutely no reason to attack a U.S. ship, even close to their coast, much less far out in international waters." (Sharp: 42) (It is noteworthy that MACV was a subordinate command of Pacific Command, that is, Westmoreland was a subordinate of Sharp.)An examination of the telephone conversations between Secretary McNamara and President Johnson during August 2–4, 1964 sheds different light on the issue of provocation.

Colonel Sayre recollects from his personal experience at the time that our U.S. Navy ships in 1964 would position themselves just outside the twelve-mile offshore limit, but would cross the line to obtain a reaction from the North Vietnamese. The SOG raids and U.S. Navy ships off the North Vietnam coast eventually provoked the reaction apparently desired by the political establishment in Washington.

As a navy lieutenant, Dallas, Texas, resident Jack Jennings was assigned to the SOG covert maritime operation from 1965 to 1966. He has studied and written on the history of the Nasty boat operations. The Nastys were launched from the Da Nang facility whose American staff consisted of "SEALS, Marine Corps intelligence officers and other specialists experienced in guerrilla operations." (Jennings and Do Cam: 1) These Americans did not accompany the South Vietnamese on the raids.

Jennings wrote, "On 30 July 1964 impressed with the operational success, the JCS ordered to triple the August schedule [of attacks] over that of July. ... On the night of July 30th, the more aggressive schedule involved a night-time raid on Hon Me and Hon Nieu islands off Thanh Hoa coast." (Jennings and Do Cam: 1) This raid into North Vietnam was the farthest north of any raid thus far by SOG Nasty boats, closer to Hanoi than it was to Da Nang. Jennings believes the North Vietnamese complained to the International Control Commission about this previously unprecedented attack and personally theorizes that this attack precipitated the around-the-world radio announcement by the North Vietnamese that was what General Westmoreland heard about and about which Throckmorton confronted Russell.

Jennings said when he was with the SOG maritime detachment in 1965, each Friday he was required to submit through his chain of command a report of the operational and maintenance status of the unit's boats. One Friday he submitted an erroneous report and the following week a censure of his inaccurate report was made and he read it. The message was signed "McNamara." He thought at the time the war would be lost if such a mundane detail as his unit boat status was coming to the attention of the secretary of defense. This knowledge of SOG operations surely indicates strongly that McNamara did in fact know about SOG and could not claim denial of its operations, much less the unit's existence. But isn't that the game played during wartime by the politicians?

On August 2, 1964, the infamous Gulf of Tonkin incident occurred in which North Vietnamese PT boats attacked the U.S. destroyer *Maddox*. Plaster wrote, "Although he made no reference to the SOG raids, of which he was well-apprized, President Johnson warned Hanoi that another high seas attack would have dire consequences, and ordered the destroyer *Turner Joy* to reinforce the *Maddox*." (Plaster *SOG*: 27)

SOG went back into action the night of August 3 when SOG Nasty boats hit the radar station at Vinhsan. "The next night [August 4, 1964] the *Maddox* and *Turner Joy* reported themselves under attack, leading to the first U.S. retaliatory bombing and the Congressional Gulf of Tonkin Resolution." (Plaster *Photo History*: 21). There has been repeated controversy whether in fact the NVA attacks actually occurred on the 4th. "Since the attacks were now front-page news, SOG assumed the worst: that an investigation would expose its operations against the north."(Conboy and Andrade: 121). News of the entire set of incidents circled the globe. "Hanoi denied the second attack [by its boats against the U.S. Navy ships] took place while at the same time publicly blasting Washington for the multiple commando raids being conducted along its coast." (Conboy and Andrade: 121).

Obviously the North Vietnamese would never accept that the *Maddox*, performing intercepts of messages off the North Vietnamese coast, was not cognizant of and in fact was not a part and party to the SOG shore bombardments. The North Vietnamese could have been said (and believed themselves) to have been performing offensive actions as a defensive reaction to the new style and intensity of SOG raids. In an official U.S. congressional briefing it was reported that South Vietnamese junk boats had performed the coastal bombardment. If the truth had been evident, SOG's cover would have been blown because in fact they were conducted by the armed Nasty boats.

The North Vietnamese attacks on our navy precipitated the Tonkin Gulf Resolution of August 7, 1964. The resolution apparently had been drafted several months before for such a contingency as this, awaiting a suitable provocation. "The Pentagon papers disclose that for six months before the Tonkin Gulf incident in August, 1964, the United States had been mounting clandestine military attacks against North Vietnam while planning to obtain a Congressional resolution that the Administration regarded as the equivalent of a declaration of war." (*Pentagon Papers*: 234). Plaster's research found, "After the second incident, the Johnson administration further tightened controls on SOG, with each raid painstakingly reviewed by Deputy Defense Secretary Cyrus Vance." (Plaster *Photo History:* 21)

Summary of these events: "SOG, conceived as a means of showing American resolve short of war, had helped precipitate one." (Conboy and Andrade: 123) Colonel Sayre believes that the SOG raids irritated the North Vietnam enough to precipitate their attacks on the *Maddox*. As will be recalled he was a close friend of Colonel Russell and he believes there was no question in Colonel Russell's mind that his mission was to get the United States into a war with North Vietnam.

It would appear that a conclusion could be drawn that Russell, following orders and direct oversight from the Pentagon, had upped the ante on offensive actions on North Vietnam by covert SOG operations and the Vietnam War had its official *casus belli*. Of course by this time the North was developing its own provocation by secretly moving its regiments down the Ho Chi Minh Trail through Laos and Cambodia, preparing for its invasion of the South with full-scale direct military intervention. They were on the verge of substantially widening the war before our actions, limited as they were against coastal installations, were committed. It was complicated in mid-1964 from a socio-political standpoint.

The Smoking Gun Part One

During the Iran-Contra hearings in the late 1980s the questions were asked about President Ronald Reagan, "What did he know and when did he know it?" When research is conducted on SOG OPLAN 34A missions, U.S. Navy ship positioning, and President Lyndon Johnson's political decisions relative to his approach to widening the war in Vietnam beyond our already large advisory effort, and his actions during August 2–7, 1964, it becomes fair to ask of President Johnson, "What did he know, when did he know it, and what was the political landscape for his election campaign in the summer of 1964?"

Robert Dallek, a biographer of President Lyndon Johnson, wrote that, on November 24, 1963, two days after President Kennedy's death, President Johnson desired to "follow in concert with Kennedy's plans" in regard to Vietnam. Actually there were mixed signals sent by President Kennedy prior to his assassination. Although Kennedy desired "to preserve Saigon's autonomy" and had presided over an increase from 685 to 16,700 advisers, he supposedly had planned to bring 1,000 advisers home by the end of 1963 and was opposed to the introduction of American ground troops. President Johnson did not have a definitive sense of Kennedy's true direction so he chose a strategy "not to allow a Communist conquest." (Dallek: 1)

The political implications for Johnson of his Vietnam policy were all-encompassing: (1) If Vietnam went Communist, he would be blamed; (2) A Communist victory would encourage more aggressive actions by Russia and China; (3) He did not want his domestic agenda for America imperiled. (Dallek: 2)

President Johnson's Republican opponent for president in 1964 was Senator Barry Goldwater who proclaimed his insistence to take the war into North Vietnam. President Johnson did not want to lose South Vietnam to the Communists, but he also needed to counter Goldwater's bellicosity and wanted to be perceived as the peace candidate.

An examination of audio tapes from seven telephone conversations between 1030 hours August 3 and 1100 August 4, 1964, between President Johnson and Secretary of Defense Robert McNamara shed a bright light on many of the questions of the Gulf of Tonkin incident. They are available on a National Public Radio site from programs broadcast by Walter Cronkite on August 2 and August 6, 2004, the fortieth anniversary of the incident. (Cronkite: 1)

Listening to the actual conversations and broadcast introduces the following information:

1. President Johnson had in fact been aware of OPLAN 34A operations. Of course, he had approved the program earlier in the year. No Congressmen or Senators knew of 34A.

2. McNamara informed President Johnson of the SOG coastal raids of July 30, 1964 and the presence of U.S. Navy ships off the shore of North Vietnam. Cronkite's opinion was that they were "laying bait for the fox." McNamara said the July 30 raid [by SOG Nastys] had no doubt provoked the August 2, 1964, attack on the *Maddox*. McNamara even specified that "one-thousand rounds" had been expended in the raids.

3. There was extensive discussion [with CINCPAC Admiral Sharp's input] on the exact positioning of the destroyers inside the twelve-mile limit, as if deliberately to be attempting to draw a second attack, which Johnson warned against after the first attack.

4. Before the second attack had occurred, and in the course of intense discussions anticipating that a second attack would reflect sufficient provocation [thereby justifying an air attack on the north by U.S. carrier-based planes], the president suggested that McNamara, "Pull one of those things that you have been doing on one of their bridges." This probably referred to consideration of further SOG raids. McNamara was heard to say, "In the event the second attack occurs. . . ." and then the two discussed Admiral Sharp's suggestion of moving the navy ships up to the three-mile limit.

5. Eventually, in the 1100 hours, August 4th call, the conversation discussed the report from Admiral Sharp that a second attack had occurred: a torpedo attack on two destroyers. By the end of the day this second attack had been reported by the media and this was enough provocation for President Johnson to order air attacks for that night on North Vietnam's targets, preplanned weeks before.

6. On the August 6, 2004, Cronkite program, prominent American

historian and author Robert Dallek said, "LBJ was worried that Goldwater would make this a campaign issue." Another conversation between Johnson confidant Robert Anderson and the president mentioned that the NVA wanted to put a stop to the "covert operations."

The Smoking Gun Part Two

In 1984 Vice Admiral James Stockdale coauthored with his wife Sybil *In Love and War.* He was a first-hand witness to what did and did not transpire on August 4, 1964, with regard to the alleged second attack on our destroyers *Maddox* and *Turner Joy.* On August 2, 1964, he was flying a Crusader and in fact fired on and hit a North Vietnamese PT boat that had attacked our ships. (Stockdale: 5) He confirmed the first attack by the PT boats. He was in the air again on August 4, 1964, and thus in a position to support or deny reports of a second attack on our ships and wrote of that night, "No boats, no boat wakes, no ricochets off boats, no boat gunfire, no torpedo wakes—nothing but black sea and American firepower." (Stockdale: 21) He returned to the USS *Ticonderoga,* and began to read the communications log from the *Maddox* that indicated, "denial of the correctness of immediately preceding messages, doubt about the validity of whole blocks of messages, ever more skeptical appraisal of detection equipment's performance, the mention of overeager sonar operators, the lack of any visual sightings of boats by the destroyers, and finally there were lines expressing doubt that there had been *any boats out there that night at all.* (Stockdale: 22) Stockdale was livid! On August 5, 1964, the navy pilots were ordered on reprisal bombing raids. There would be no turning back now. On February 20, 1968, Secretary of Defense Robert McNamara was called to testify before the Senate Committee on Foreign Relations regarding the events and decisions of early August 1964. Admiral Stockdale studied the testimony and concluded, "I cannot avoid the conclusion that McNamara wound up using August 2nd material when analyzing events of the 4th. I know this sounds like a simple and tragic way to commit a nation to war, but that's the way I read it." (Stockdale: 459)

I will accept Admiral Stockdale's opinion as my own.

❖ ❖ ❖

According to Colonel Sayre, at some point in early 1965 General Westmoreland, who had been of the opinion that we should not become involved in Vietnam to the extent of introducing ground force American combat units, received a message from Honolulu-based Admiral U.S.G. Sharp, Commander in Chief, Pacific (CINCPAC). Sharp's message indicated Westmoreland had stalled long enough on the plan to introduce U.S. ground troops into the war and Sharp wanted to see the plan in one week. Colonel Sayre carried Westmoreland's plan to Honolulu for Westmoreland and presented it to Admiral Sharp. It was obvious the decision had already been made to proceed. During the meeting a Marine Corps general recommended a combat landing by marines to initiate the new strategy. Westmoreland did not agree with this plan upon Sayre's return, but being the professional soldier he was, he began to carry out the directive though opposed to the decision. Since Sharp and not Westmoreland commanded the Pacific area marines, on March 8, 1965 a combat landing of marines was made at Da Nang and that fateful turn of course was made for the Vietnam War.

Concurrently at this time, Colonel Russell, as one of his final SOG responsibilities before his reassignment back home, was able to plan and begin conducting SOG surveillance missions into southern Laos along the Ho Chi Minh Trail to begin to develop intelligence on those NVA troops being introduced into the south. This was a significant broadening of the SOG mission because these missions would now for the first time be led by U.S. Army special forces personnel.

> **COMBAT LEADERSHIP LESSON:** Colonel Russell told his son Chris that you were not to be too concerned about whether people liked you or whether you were popular but what was important was that others respect you as a leader. The way to earn respect was through one's honesty and integrity. He would expound on these two character traits: honesty *and integrity*. He told Chris that the only way to be successful in life was via hard work. Great and important advice for military leaders.

Aftermath

It should be mentioned that, out of respect for Colonel Russell, the late Lt. Gen. Edward A. Partain, Russell's protégé within special forces, named the XVIII Airborne Corps headquarters building at Ft. Bragg in Russell's honor on August 11, 1981. The Russell Building stands today in honor and tribute to this courageous soldier.

Russell's son, Chris, became a U.S. Army lieutenant and several years later served with MACV's Joint U.S. Public Affairs Office (JUSPAO) in the

Mekong Delta. Chris finished our conversations by stating that his father was not only a soldier of the highest caliber, but also a father of unparalleled love and devotion.

Author's Opinion

President Johnson knew everything about the SOG operations plan. He and McNamara believed the SOG raids of July 30 provoked the first attack on the *Maddox*. President Johnson was searching for a means to counter Goldwater on the war issue. And, the provocation of the second attack on August 4th or a specious analysis of the "facts" of the second attack all contributed to President Johnson deciding to pursue his strategy to save South Vietnam from Communist domination by utilizing the Gulf of Tonkin incident to move the course of a war in a new direction that would then last for nine more years.

❖   ❖   ❖

Thirty five months later after the Gulf of Tonkin, your author suffered wounds in Vietnam that would require amputation of both legs below the knee. Notwithstanding why we entered the war, how we fought the war, or how faulted was our political leader, nothing can ever detract from the dedicated and valorous service of almost three million patriotic Americans who served in the next nine years in Vietnam and other areas of Southeast Asia including adjacent waters, several of whose stories are captured in the following pages. An unknown author's comment of an earlier American war was made, "Even though the war be wrong, we are in it."

As Colonel Russell was finishing his tour in Vietnam in mid-1965, Lieutenant Gary Coe was beginning his tour and his experiences related to the movement into the Central Highlands of those NVA combat troops being infiltrated into the south from the Ho Chi Minh Trail, now being monitored by SOG Reconnaissance patrols. The frequency and success of these patrols was enhanced in the ensuing years under the leadership of the subsequent SOG chiefs, Colonel Donald D. Blackburn and Colonel John K. Singlaub.

CHAPTER 3

Vietnamization to Americanization
LIEUTENANT GARY COE, USA
(PLEIKU CENTRAL HIGHLANDS 1965–1966)

We should not attempt to take over the war from the Vietnamese . . . no lasting solution can be imposed by foreign armies.— Hubert H. Humphrey, Senator from Minnesota, Washington, D.C., September 12, 1964

U.S. ADVISORS TO THE SOUTH VIETNAMESE

As the war progressed, American advisors were assigned further and further down the South Vietnamese chain of command, placing a heavy demand on junior commissioned officers and experienced non-commissioned officers. At one point, for example, it was calculated that several divisions' worth of these key leaders were serving as advisors, stripping them from the U.S. units where they would normally have been assigned. This in turn reduced the experience and maturity levels of U.S. leadership. Advisory duty was extremely challenging and often difficult, especially for those advisors with South Vietnamese units and with province and district advisory teams. Living with their advisees, advisors had to adapt to the local culture while striving to build harmonious and productive relationships with their counterparts. As the war continued for year after year, long-serving South Vietnamese went through one advisor after another, as most advisors were on tours of limited duration, making it increasingly difficult for each new advisor to establish rapport and gain influence. Often this challenge was compounded by the fact that the South Vietnamese being advised had far more combat experience than his American counterpart. Beyond simply providing advice to the commanders and units they advised, however, advisors often functioned as the link to much-desired American support, both logistical and combat, such as, air strikes, medical evacu-

ation, and artillery. In addition to cultural differences, the disparate outlooks deriving from short-term time horizons—advisors on limited duration tours—and longer-term ones—Vietnamese who had been at war for years and had no other prospect but continuing to fight—made the advisory role uniquely challenging.

Career Army

Gary Coe spent several years in Venezuela where his father worked for an oil company. Since high school options were limited there, he returned to the United States to attend a military high school near Nashville that was designated as an honor military academy enabling its students to compete for nominations to West Point. He was appointed to West Point and graduated in 1963. He admits he was poorly motivated as a cadet, but intended to give the army his best and if it did not work out, then he would attempt to find success in the civilian world. As it turned out, he grew to love the army, became ranger-qualified, and remained an officer for twenty six years.

Vietnam Heats Up

On April 5, 1965, Secretary of Defense Robert McNamara and the Joint Chiefs of Staff held a critical meeting at the Pentagon that resulted in authorization by President Lyndon Johnson for the use of regular army and marine combat units in offensive operations in Vietnam. In the previous week the American embassy in Saigon had been bombed and the first air battle between North Vietnamese MiG fighter planes and U.S. Air Force jets resulted in the loss of two of our planes. Lieutenant Gary Coe was getting geared up to get into the fight in Vietnam. So urgent was the need for American advisors that Coe was sent without the normal Vietnamese language training. His story represents the period when the historical shift began occurring in 1965 from our advisory effort to the South Vietnamese military to an effort driven by introduction of the U.S. regular units authorized on April 6, 1965, by President Johnson.

Assignment: Pleiku, South Vietnam

In June 1965 Coe received a command briefing by Military Assistance Command, Vietnam (MACV) staff. During the intelligence briefing he learned about the buildup of Peoples Army of Vietnam (PAVN) in the Central Highlands wherein it was theorized that they were planning an offensive aimed at cutting the country in half at Pleiku which might be placed under siege not unlike the siege of Dien Bien Phu that culminated Ho Chi

Minh's successful campaign against the French a decade earlier. The theory was given further credence by the fact that North Vietnamese forces (PAVN) were commanded by General Giap, the commander of the forces against the French at Dien Bien Phu. The briefing left the attendees with the feeling that an assignment to Pleiku was the kiss of death. It wasn't long before he had orders in his hands assigning him to II Corps as a Regional Force/Popular Force advisor, headquartered in Pleiku.

Near the conclusion of the command briefing General Westmoreland personally addressed the group. He welcomed everyone for "volunteering" for the assignment to Vietnam and said that in their hearts they all knew that they belonged in Vietnam because "this is where the action is." For Coe he was right; the young officer believed that his tour in Vietnam could become one of the most significant events in his life. As our fathers had participated in World War II, it would be our role to affect history by our participation in the Vietnam War.

Finally Coe's in-processing was complete and he was at Tan Son Nhut Air Base on Sunday, June 27, 1965, ready to head up country to Pleiku. On his same plane was Maj. Ralph Walden, who had just completed his after-action report on what had been a triple ambush in a harrowing battle west of Pleiku at Le Thanh village earlier in that month.

Obviously this engagement had been of sufficient importance to have called the major to Saigon for a briefing. Coe's initial understanding was a little vague about Le Thanh but as he learned more, it all fit in with the intelligence briefings he had received about the enemy buildup in the Central Highlands. He was heading into the current hot spot in the war. As it evolved, the Le Thanh action had been quite an operation. This is what transpired.

On the 1st of June 1965 the monsoon season was in full swing, so, as expected, it was raining. It was early in the morning-about 0315 hours at Le Thanh District Headquarters, which were located at Le Thanh Village, off Highway 19 near the Cambodian border and not far from the special forces outpost of Duc Co.

The silence of the night was interrupted by the tremendous sound of loudspeakers. Threats rang out in Vietnamese, the, "Put down your arms and walk out of the village. We will not harm you or your families. We only want the Americans who we know are with you. It is useless to resist. We have a reinforced battalion and have the capacity to level your villages. We will do just that if you do not comply. Put down your arms . . ."

Except for a squad of loyal patriots, who were eventually killed, all of the Regional Force and Popular Force who formed the local garrison, about thirty-six in all, followed the intimidating instructions that were coming out of the dark, leaving the district headquarters to be summarily overrun. Fortuitously, no Americans were present because early the day before the Le Thanh Sub-Sector American Advisory Team, consisting of Maj. Ralph Walden, SSgt. Jimmy Hall, and Staff Sergeant Centershad been called back to Pleiku City. Intelligence had indicated a build-up of forces in the western part of the province. The newly-assigned senior sector advisor, Lt. Col. Bernard Dibbert, who had only been on the job for twelve days, was seriously concerned about the situation. Dibbert, Walden, and several American NCOs proceeded from Pleiku towards Le Thanh along highway 19 in a convoy commanded by Lieutenant Colonel Ba, Pleiku province chief, to determine what happened. About ten miles from Le Thanh one of the Popular Force soldiers who had escaped from the attack was encountered. He confirmed that Le Thanh had indeed been attacked and overrun.

Major Walden recommended against continuing onward with the relief force until air support could be made available. Initially, the relief force waited, but air cover was not forthcoming and Lieutenant Colonel Ba decided to proceed with the forces he had. Lt. Col. Dibbert decided that the American advisors would accompany their counterparts. In spite of Major Walden's recommendation Dibbert felt that he had a responsibility to support his counterpart, Lieutenant Colonel Ba, regardless of the risks associated with the Vietnamese officer's decision. So, Ba's convoy proceeded towards Le Thanh without air cover. The security force proceeded until it was ambushed. For an effort that won him the Silver Star, but cost him his life, Lt. Col. Dibbert attempted to rally a counterattack, moving towards the ambushing force and firing at the enemy. Dibbert took a bullet through the neck.

COMBAT LEADERSHIP LESSON #1: Emotions can sometimes override wise decisions and the decision to proceed without air cover proved to be disastrous.

Major Walden assumed command of the surviving American advisors and the firefight continued for about forty-five minutes to a point where Regional Force soldiers were beginning to desert. Major Walden was beginning to see the hopelessness of the situation so he began efforts to escape and evade the enemy. Carrying a wounded Sergeant Hall, he ran through the enemy lines followed by Sergeant Centers, the other surviving American. A medevac helicopter would soon find them ending their ordeal. A relief column was ambushed twice more.

By the end of the day, the Viet Cong had achieved a significant victory. The attacks confirmed that a large PAVN force was accumulating in the Vietnamese Central Highlands. The triple ambush on June 1 became the latest in a series of North Vietnamese actions of increased intensity.

Coe's C-130 flight from Tan Son Nhut to Holloway Army Airfield in Pleiku was less than two hours. Little could be seen of the countryside since there was cloud covering most of the way. June was in monsoon season. Ham Rung Mountain, located just south of Pleiku City, was the first landmark seen as the flight began its descent. The Montagnards believed that in times past that there was a great deluge that flooded the earth. When the floods subsided, a man and woman survived on top of Ham Rung Mountain. This man and woman began the Montagnard race. Perhaps stories of Noah's flood even reached Indochina.

Coe reported into the Pleiku Sector Advisory Team with great trepidation and anticipation. In Walden's absence, Vietnamese mourners silently, but ominously, sat around the senior American advisor's compound in Pleiku City. The events of this day marked a change in the nature of the war both for the locals and the countries of Vietnam and the United States. A new senior advisor, Lt. Col. Edward Smith, replaced Dibbert. The events that followed over the next few months were dramatic not only with respect to the operation of the advisory team, but with respect to the overall effort of the war.

The massive buildup of North Vietnamese regulars in the province created an urgent need to revive provincial security forces and the Pleiku Sector Advisory Team. The 173rd Airborne Brigade arrived in country about the same time as Coe. They were the only American combat unit available early in Coe's tour. Firepower and mobility provided by the Americans was a major advantage for the Republic of Vietnam forces against the Viet Cong and the People's Army of Vietnam.

The strategy adopted by Military Assistance Command, Vietnam (MACV) and the Vietnamese was based on the British model of strategic hamlets used in the guerrilla wars in Malaya. The environments were different in many ways, but that model seemed useful and appropriate. The approach was called by different names at different times for changing political concerns, but was generally known as development, redevelopment, pacification, or reconstruction. The theory of redevelopment was first to provide security to a strategic village that would enable the village to perform routine tasks such as farming, managing livestock, and commerce. Security was achieved by various methods including search and destroy operations that required military units to police a sufficiently large area with a regularity that would discourage Viet Cong guerrilla activity in that area. Other methods included psychological warfare and civil affair activities designed to achieve the trust of the targeted population by providing them with government services that they needed or by convincing them that the South Vietnamese government was a better option to the approach of the Viet Cong. Unless the government provides the people security in an insurgent environment, the enemy will prevail.

There were problems for Pleiku province villagers opting for either the South Vietnamese government or the Viet Cong. The government could be unreliable or ineffective. The Viet Cong could be brutal.

The Viet Cong had their own strategy for the hearts and minds of the Vietnamese people, contrasted to the approach of MACV and the South Vietnamese government. The Viet Cong claimed that they were the true government and supported this claim by collecting taxes in a variety of ways. For instance, the French-owned Cateka Tea Plantation located to the north of Highway 19 near Thanh Binh reportedly paid annual taxes totaling about a million dollars. They also paid taxes to the South Vietnamese government and apparently their bottom line still remained in sufficiently good shape to maintain a profitable business. To undercut South Vietnamese authority the Viet Cong would visit villages and murder the local leaders that included teachers, doctors, administrators, and American advisors. The Viet Cong took special effort to discredit Americans. One method was to disembowel Americans killed in combat. After they were killed, their testicles or entrails would be cut off and stuffed into their mouths. Viet Cong leaders were incorporated into the village infrastructure where possible. Self-criticism sessions would then be implemented according to Communist doctrine. The Viet Cong implemented their own form of psychological operations that tried to sell communism as the legitimate approach to government. They also spent a lot of their time cutting trenches across roads to limit the economic access of the South Vietnamese government to villages and even set up checkpoints to collect fees for road usage. While these methods were used throughout South Vietnam, they were of limited success in Montagnard territories. While it is known that some Montagnards were persuaded to support the

Viet Cong, in general Montagnards really didn't seem to care for Vietnamese irrespective of their political beliefs.

The triple ambush and the related massive increase of PAVN troops into the Central Highlands was changing MACV's strategy. In order to deal with the increasing enemy forces, American units would need to take on a greater role in destroying the PAVN units.

There was conflict between the Americans and Vietnamese in their respective approaches to war. These differing views seemed to exist at all levels in the chain of command. Coe agreed that the Vietnamese and Americans were measuring the situation with different scales. The following are Coe's thoughts on the difference in viewpoints between Americans and South Vietnamese:

> I believe that the Vietnamese had significantly different expectations about the war than that of the United States. It's hard to pin down what expectations South Vietnamese really had, but the instability in the central government was a factor. During my tour, the government changed several times so it was difficult to realize any cohesiveness in purpose by the Vietnamese senior leadership.
>
> Also, it seems that there was a contrast in the definition of "victory" in our minds versus theirs. Recall that we saw the war as an effort to stop the "dominos" from succumbing to communism. However, Ho Chi Minh expected the country to be unified after the Viet Minh defeated the French at Dien Bien Phu. When the Geneva Accords of 1954 partitioned Vietnam at the 17th parallel, this had to be a hard pill for "Uncle Ho" to swallow. South Vietnamese emerged from a population, dominated by Catholics and other religious and ethnic groups, who feared for their lives because of the antireligious posture of the Viet Minh. So, for the Vietnamese, this was a civil war; while for America, we were trying to make the world safe for democracy. I know our counterparts saw Americans as naive because in their minds we had a simplistic view of the world, and they tried to use that naiveté to whatever advantage they could.
>
> More to tactics, the French had a defensive philosophy in combating the Viet Minh, which historians believe saw as leading to the downfall of the French in Southeast Asia. The South Vietnamese seemed to mimic the defensive philosophy of their French mentors. Consider the system of special forces camps in the country.

These camps were useful in that they provided bases for patrols that could learn about the movement of Viet Cong units in the area. Also they did help provide protection of nearby villages. However, these defensive outposts made great targets for the VC by creating ambushes of the inevitable relief force. The main problem with this defensive mentality of the South Vietnamese is that it forfeited the initiative to the enemy. The VC always chose the time, place, and condition for attack and the Vietnamese reacted.

I believe the culture of super-caution in Vietnamese decision-making for combat operations was a result of defeatist mentality. By the time U.S. Forces were introduced into the war, the war was evolving badly for the South Vietnamese. So it was very hard to get them to think about combat in a positive way. Moreover, when engagements occurred, as discussed above, they always occurred on the enemy's terms.

Another factor is that we initially bought into the strategic hamlet concept that was successful for the British in Malaya. This model failed in Vietnam because we couldn't control the countryside. Therefore the need evolved for U.S. combat forces and a change in emphasis to "Search and Destroy." After having sold many Vietnamese on the Strategic Hamlet, I believe that many were unable to accept that concept failing in Vietnam. To be engaged in a war zone for years makes the war routine. In fact, our normal work day ran from about 0800 until 1700 with two hour siesta. Sundays were off. When Vietnamese took a few days off to Dalat, it was likely that some of the other guests there were VC. This was assumed, but there was no concern. It was like a timeout for both sides. It was difficult to create urgency in the South Vietnamese minds.

Coe's primary duty on paper at least was to advise the Popular Force Training Center five miles west of Pleiku. It was in an unsafe area and Coe always went there with air cover and security forces. During one visit, Coe received a complete tour of the facilities and then retired to the office of Captain Beo, the head officer, who had a company guidon leaning up in one corner.

While they were talking through an interpreter, one of the non-commissioned officers brought a trainee to Beo's office for his immediate attention. The interpreter explained that the trainee had been caught stealing from a buddy. He was a barracks thief and even in the American Army this carries the seriousness of a horse thief in the old west.

Beo increasingly became incensed with the trainee's responses until he finally reached for one of the guidon staffs. He used the staff to beat the trainee first on one side of the trainee's body, then on the other. "Dai Uy" (Captain) Beo then turned to Coe and commented something that was translated that we simply couldn't tolerate barracks' thieves. Coe didn't offer his opinion about Beo's disciplinary techniques. They were clearly unacceptable in the context of the American military, but he didn't have any leverage to impose his moral views to Beo, so he kept quiet.

Cultural conflicts between the Americans and the Vietnamese were frequent and problematic to the relationship with counterparts. One day a VC soldier walked into Pleiku and surrendered. He was visibly happy to leave the discomfort of living in the jungle and all were happy with his decision to leave a VC unit. Coe would have thought that the province should have made him a positive example for rewarding him for his decision to surrender. Contrary to this belief, a few days later Coe witnessed Vietnamese intelligence officers torturing this same prisoner. He was placed in a room on the other side of the wall of Coe's office. Coe heard his screams, which caused him to peer through cracks in the walls where he could see the VC tied to a chair. They had battery cable wires attached to an ear and testicles. On the other end they were attached to terminals of a field phone which operated with a hand-cranked generator normally used to send a ring signal to a receiver on the other end of the telephone wires. They were asking the prisoner questions and when he failed to provide the desired response, they would turn the crank and send a jolt of electric current through the prisoner's body. Coe complained to Colonel Smith about what he had seen, but was told that they didn't have any control over this situation. They could register their complaint with the province chief, but this wasn't their country since they were only advisors.

Duc Co

In late July 1965, culminating a month long buildup of enemy forces, the special forces camp at Duc Co near the Cambodian border was attacked by a VC regiment which completely surrounded the camp with its patrols driven back within the perimeter defensive wire. In spite of numerous air strikes, the VC had dug in mortars and recoilless rifles that were shooting directly into the camp. Their positions were next moved so close, and their fires became so heavy, that helicopters could not land. With the camp isolated from resupply and helicopter medical evacuation, the corps commander, Brigadier General Vinh Loc, decided to commit the corps' airborne task force to break the siege and destroy the VC surrounding the camp.

Colonel Smith invited American advisors of the ARVN airborne task force to stop by the villa for a discussion about Duc Co before their unit was thrust into battle. They were Maj. Norman Schwartzkopf and Lt. Pat Canary. Schwartzkopf later commanded forces for the first war in Iraq.

Preceded by a heavy air strike to suppress VC fire, the airborne task force landed by choppers at the airstrip on the edge of the camp. After landing, it launched the operation designed to drive back the VC and give elbow room to the camp. During this operation the task force uncovered a strong VC fortified position, the fighting became intense, and the VC drove the airborne task force back to the airfield. The enemy soon reestablished its positions so that it again became difficult to resupply and evacuate the wounded.

A successful enemy move on Duc Co would have been a serious threat to the entire Pleiku province, so another South Vietnamese task force was formed to attempt to break the siege and it moved west on August 5th. They ran into a well dug-in and camouflaged position which was attacked and seized.

At this time, the airborne task force at Duc Co was ordered to attack down Highway 19 to the east to link up with the relief force. Threatened with entrapment between these two attacking forces, the enemy broke contact and withdrew leaving only small deploying forces, snipers, and mines along the road. The battle of Duc Co ended with the VC defeated with heavy losses and the government troops in control of the battlefield. The battle of Duc Co raised the morale of ARVN troops. They had overcome the worst the VC could throw at them, held on, then made the enemy break contact and flee, leaving weapons and dead on the battlefield. The battle was the first major contact with North Vietnamese forces operating in South Vietnam and more importantly was the first victory for these forces.

This significant victory was celebrated by visits to the Duc Co camp by General Westmoreland and principal Vietnamese government officials headed by General Thieu, the Vietnamese head of state.

The engagement at Duc Co satisfied the anticipation for a major operation that summer in the Central Highlands, but there was more to come.

Meanwhile Back at the White House
Author Goldstein had detailed conversations and interviews with McGeorge

Bundy before his 1996 death. Goldstein wrote, "'Johnson's machinations to connect events in the Gulf of Tonkin to win advantage with the Congress as well as the electorate was an unassisted triple play', Bundy said, concluding, 'It was the right response politically, and the time was right.'" (Goldstein: 134)

The Gulf of Tonkin incident laid the groundwork for President Johnson to begin enlarging the war which actually began in 1965. Soon after the election Bundy recommended to President Johnson that "a strategic bombing campaign against North Vietnam" be initiated. (Goldstein: 143)

After the 1964 Christmas Eve bombing of the Brinks Hotel, a major American BOQ in Saigon, President Johnson moved decisively to support introduction of U.S. ground forces into South Vietnam and begin the expansion of the war. (Goldstein: 151)

On February 7, 1965, while McGeorge Bundy was visiting South Vietnam the Communists attacked two locations in Pleiku. It is possible this personal experience for Johnson's national security advisor prompted him to be more intent on military retaliation measures. (Goldstein: 156) These attacks probably signaled a major tipping point for the war. Senator Michael Mansfield and Undersecretary of State George Ball were vehemently opposed to the introduction of U.S. ground forces. (Goldstein: 160)

In early 1965 President Johnson presided over a group of senior officials who all had differing opinions about whether ground troops or bombing or neither were the proper course. (Goldstein: 161)

President Johnson enjoyed the support of former President Dwight Eisenhower, who believed, that once begun the war must be fought to be won. (Goldstein: 161)

Eisenhower supported General William Westmoreland's recommendation to insert American ground troops and further believed South Vietnam was important not to fall to the Communists. (Goldstein: 162)

A policy of deception began in that escalation began, but it was downplayed, if not totally conducted without public announcement.

Maxwell D. Taylor, now U.S. Ambassador to South Vietnam and celebrated World War II army commander, was vehemently opposed to introduction of U.S. combat units, but Westmoreland's recommendations prevailed and on March 8, 1965, marines landed at Da Nang.

Strategy began to be implemented to put increased pressure on the north to eventually bring about a settlement. (Goldstein: 165)

In 1965 it became obvious that Bundy saw the escalation and Americanizing of the war as a means "of protecting its (America's) global credibility, the imperative not to be rendered a so-called paper tiger." (Goldstein: 167) So it began. International and domestic credibility became the driving force to introduce U.S. ground troops. (Goldstein: 168) On April 17, 1965, immediate deployment of the 173rd Airborne Brigade was ordered.

Finally in a Rose Garden speech on July 14, 1965, President Johnson proclaimed that "our national honor is at stake in Southeast Asia. And we are going to protect it." (Goldstein: 206)

Plei Me and the Ia Drang Campaign

In late July 1965 the President announced that he was increasing American combat strength in Vietnam by 100 thousand to a level of over 179 thousand. Shortly afterward, the 1st Cavalry Division was ordered to Vietnam, eventually to be located at a base camp at An Khe, about half way between Pleiku in the highlands and Qui Nhon on the coast.

Brigadier General Chu Huy Man of the People's Army of Vietnam (PAVN) was tasked with drawing the American air cavalry into battle, to learn about its fighting capabilities, and then circulate the information among the PAVN and National Liberation commanders after battles.

Coe's team became aware that something might happen at Plei Me around mid-October when it was noted by Vietnamese agents and confirmed by patrols conducted by Duc Co that Viet Cong elements were leaving the Duc Co area and moving east towards Plei Me, another special forces camp forty kilometers south of Pleiku. Patrols from Plei Me also reported increasing contact with VC elements.

General Man ordered the 33rd NVA regiment to seize the camp at Plei Me at 1930 hours on October 19, 1965, while the 32nd Regiment would move into position to ambush reinforcements, repeating tactics successfully used against the French. The attack began by bombarding the camp followed by repeated infantry assaults, initially overrunning a twenty-man outpost, but the remaining defenders repelled the PAVN, and a siege situation developed.

At first light the next morning, 250 Army of the Republic of Vietnam (ARVN) airborne rangers led by Maj. Charles "Charging Charlie" Beckwith arrived by helicopter at the camp. Later in his career, Beckwith became known for his role in the organization of the Delta Force and his command of the failed effort to rescue the hostages in Iran during President Carter's administration.

Typical of South Vietnamese generals through much of the war, II Corps commander General Vinh Loc procrastinated over what action to conduct. Vinh Loc tried to persuade General Westmoreland through senior U.S. advisors to commit elements of the 1st Cavalry Division to relieve Plei Me. General Westmoreland agreed to use the division to defend Pleiku, but required that the relief force be ARVN. Vinh Loc, under intense pressure by the Americans, finally agreed to send a force of a thousand men including armored personnel carriers led by tanks. During this battle Lieutenant Coe flew air cover, monitored communications from the ground units, and relayed information back to his headquarters.

The enemy attack was beaten back with accurate U.S. artillery and air support. Also, the guns of the tanks were loaded with canisters of small shot which mowed down the surrounding bush to stubble, plastering dozens of enemy bodies to tree trunks. The relief column arrived at the Plei Me camp on October 25, 1965, and the U.S. 1st Cavalry Division arrived on the 27th, thus ending the siege. U.S. President Lyndon Johnson called Beckwith during the siege to congratulate him.

Lieutenant Coe was attached as a liaison from Pleiku Sector to an artillery unit of the 1st Cavalry Division and the unit moved to a location known to be heavily mined. He pointed this out to the battery commander who did not seem concerned. They moved by road and as they occupied the destination, mines randomly began exploding. Several soldiers were injured by the evening. That evening Coe found a shovel and began digging a foxhole. One of the officers asked him what he was doing. He told him that when the mortars began raining in at around two in the morning they would understand. Shortly afterwards, he noticed that everyone was digging foxholes. Apparently, his credibility as a person with local knowledge had increased and "incoming" was a new term learned by the newly-arrived troops.

COMBAT LEADERSHIP LESSON #2: Upon assuming a new command, listen to advice from experienced people who have been there before you. *Always* dig in and after dark change to new dug-in positions.

In the spring of 1966, Coe's team began to wind down. The team's effort began from the backwash of the triple ambush on June 1, 1965, when the provincial staff and its American advisory team were in shambles and looking at possible disaster with the buildup of enemy troops in the Central Highlands. American troops increased security in the Pleiku area and the focus of the war shifted from reconstruction to search and destroy. However, success at search and destroy operations actually improved success at reconstruction. No one listened to Senator Humphrey's advice.

Lieutenant Gary Coe briefing results of Pleiku Sector military operation, spring 1966.

Aftermath

Later in his military career Colonel Coe commanded a Hawk missile air defense artillery battalion in Germany, attended Harvard University for a year on a National Security Fellowship, and eventually retired from the army following several years service at the Pentagon.

In 2006 Coe received an email from a Michael Dibbert of Dallas, Texas. He gave Michael a call and learned that he was the son of the Lt. Col. Bernard Dibbert who was killed in the Viet Cong ambush on the 1st of June 1965. Young Michael wanted to know how his father had died. Someone gave him Coe's name as one who might be able to tell him what he wanted to know about his father's death.

Gary Coe told Michael what he knew. The detail that he was able to provide young Dibbert seemed to complete the search he had undertaken. He told Gary that he had given him more information in ten minutes than he had been able to find out over ten years of searching. Coe hopes that he was able to help provide him the closure for which he was looking. In parting Michael encouraged Colonel Coe to write about his life for his children and grandchildren. Michael assured him that they will want to know. It was a tremendous sense of satisfaction to Colonel Coe that he was able to talk to young Michael forty-one years after the death of his father. Many of the children of our warriors killed in action never are able to obtain that closure.

In May 1966, Lt. Col. Hank "Gunfighter" Emerson, a battalion commander from the 101st Airborne Division, was at Coe's headquarters planning an operation near Dak To, a special forces camp north of Kontum. This became an intensively-fought operation. Lieutenant Coe returned to the United States. in the summer of 1966 when Captain Ron Brown was commanding "Attack" Company in Colonel Emerson's battalion.

As the siege of Plei Me terminated, the 1st Cavalry Division began planning its movement into the Ia (means "river" in Jarai) Drang Valley. The Ia Drang campaign lasted from October 28 thru November 25, 1965. Captain Tony Nadal would command Alpha Company of the 1st Battalion, 7th Cavalry, in the historic battle at the Ia Drang and LZ X-Ray. Captain Joel Sugdinis would command Alpha Company of the 2nd Battalion, 7th Cavalry, at LZs X-Ray and Albany. The Ia Drang campaign caused a distinct reduction in VC and NVA operations in the province. There were fewer incidents where VC intimidated villages, collected taxes, or cut roads.

CHAPTER 4

Garry Owen (LZs X-Ray and Albany)

CAPTAIN RAMON A. "TONY" NADAL, II, USA
(LZ X-RAY 1965)

CAPTAIN JOEL E. SUGDINIS, II, USA
(LZ ALBANY 1965)

March to the sound of the guns.—The Duke of York, 1793,
to his commanders during the Dunkirk campaign

EARLY U.S. GROUND COMBAT

The first major combat operations by deployed U.S. ground forces took place in the Ia Drang Valley of the Central Highlands in November 1965, where elements of the newly arrived 1st Cavalry Division (Airmobile) encountered substantial North Vietnamese Army forces in a fierce but inconclusive battle. The 1st Cavalry Division was the embodiment of a new concept of air mobility which emphasized rapid deployment of infantry units by helicopter, then resupply and reinforcement of them by the same means. This battle was an early test of the war of attrition approach to conduct of the war and, inasmuch as far higher casualties were inflicted on the enemy than those suffered by U.S. units, General William C. Westmoreland, Commander of the U.S. Military Assistance Command, Vietnam, concluded that the results validated his approach. Over time, though, that judgment was increasingly called into question. The North Vietnamese replaced their casualties, while American support for continuation of the war was undermined by the mounting numbers of U.S. deaths.

Battle in the Ia Drang Valley

The *New York Times* bestseller book, *We Were Soldiers Once . . . and Young,* coauthored by Lieutenant General Harold G. Moore, USA (Ret.), and Joseph L. Galloway, the movie starring Mel Gibson, and at least five television specials have related extensive reports of this historic 1965 battle, the first major combat operation of American troops in Vietnam. One company commander in then Lieutenant Colonel Moore's battalion at LZ X-Ray was Captain Ramon "Tony" Nadal, commanding officer of Alpha Company, 1st Battalion, 7th Cavalry.

Another company commander in the Ia Drang campaign was Captain Joel Sugdinis, commanding officer of Alpha Company, 2nd Battalion, 7th Cavalry, at LZs X-Ray and Albany. The following are their highly personalized stories of a ferocious, intense, and trying four days in combat against determined and significantly larger enemy forces in two areas that were only two miles apart.

Marching To the Sound of the Guns

Captains Nadal (West Point 1958) and Sugdinis (West Point 1960) had always marched to the sound of the guns as airborne ranger infantry officers. Joel Sugdinis had unknowingly prepped for West Point by attending LaSalle Military Academy on Long Island. He had been in Vietnam for a previous tour as an advisor. These two were dedicated Americans whose be all and end all of existence revolved around commitment to America through military service on the front lines of combat action.

In the spring of 1965 the United States made the decision to begin to send large American troop units to Vietnam. The 1st Cavalry Division had trained together for almost two years at Ft. Benning, which proved to be extraordinarily beneficial for their success on the battlefield as the first full Army division to be deployed. Staff Sergeant Southern Hewitt, one of Captain Nadal's squad leaders in Vietnam, commented that this time together was invaluable as the unit members got to know each other very well because they had trained and socialized together for so long. Very simply stated, in Hewitt's words they were "a tight unit." Nadal said that Colonel Moore had created a unit with tremendous cohesion.

The Enemy Strategy

In November 1964 the plans in Hanoi were for the North Vietnamese Army to cut South Vietnam in half along Route 14 between Pleiku and Qui Nhon in the Central Highlands. During 1965 they would move two divisions from North Vietnam into the Central Highlands of South Vietnam. The NVA launched the offensive with a tactic that the Viet Minh had often used against the French: attacking a critical outpost or fortification in order to ambush the relief column sent to rescue the beleaguered outpost.

When the NVA began their campaign in the Central Highlands, the 1st Cavalry Division, with its four hundred helicopters, had just arrived in South Vietnam in August 1965 and established their base camp at An Khe, halfway between Pleiku and Qui Nhon, astride Highway 14. In late October the NVA attacked Plei Me special forces camp, located southwest of Pleiku. The assault surprised both ARVN and the Americans; ARVN asked for American help in protecting the relief column that was being sent to the camp. This battle evolved somewhat like Japanese theatre; both sides knew what the other was going to do. The wild card, however, and unknown to the NVA, was the ability of the 1st Cavalry to quickly move its infantry and artillery over long distances by helicopter. When the NVA ambushed the relief column, which was approaching on the only road to the camp, an American artillery battalion deployed by CH-47 helicopters provided extensive fire support as along with 1st Cavalry helicopter gunships and U.S. Air Force fighters. The ambush was defeated and the enemy withdrew. With his forces primed and ready, 1st Cavalry Division commander Maj. Gen. Harry W.O. Kinnard Jr. received permission to pursue the enemy and the division's 1st Brigade deployed to search for the enemy.

Warning Order Received

On November 10, the Cav's 3rd Brigade, which included the 1st and 2nd battalions of the 7th Cavalry and the 2nd Battalion, 5th Cavalry, relieved the 1st Brigade and began to aggressively patrol, locate, and destroy the enemy force. These three battalions, as well as five others in the division, were light infantry units capable of deploying rapidly by helicopter. From the time Nadal's battalion arrived in the area of operations (AO) until November 14, the battalion conducted platoon-size saturation patrolling without enemy contact. Late in the day on the 13th the line companies received a warning order from Colonel Moore to prepare to air assault to a new location. Nadal had been involved in several previous air assaults with only scant enemy contact thus far, so the next day's operation did not overly concern him. Even though intelligence reports indicated probable enemy in the area, he believed that any enemy contact would be limited to a light skirmish.

Hal Moore, a highly professional, superb battalion commander, was aggressive, tough, and smart, with a low tolerance for BS. He also truly cared about his soldiers. Captain Nadal knew that if he were going to war, he could not go with a better CO. The entire battalion had great faith in Colonel Moore, a fact that would become very important in the days ahead because the survival of 1st of the 7th Cavalry would ultimately depend on his cool leadership and intellect.

Lieutenant Colonel Harold Moore (left) and Capt. Tony Nadal (right) on combat operation near Bong Son, South Vietnam, 1966.

Day One LZ X-Ray

November 14, 1965, began as a pleasant, clear day in the Ia Drang Valley with tolerable temperature. Later in the day it would become much hotter. The battalion had been scheduled to be pulled out of the area the following day, but the day before Moore issued orders directing his battalion to air assault into Landing Zone X-Ray, a clearing located next to the large, jungle-covered mountain named Chu Pong, a massif which straddled the border of South Vietnam and Cambodia. Sketchy intelligence indicated that this might be an enemy base camp. Nadal's Alpha Company was scheduled to be the second company into the LZ where it would relieve Bravo Company, commanded by Captain John Herren, Nadal's West Point classmate, of their security mission on the landing zone so Bravo Company could scout the local area. Due to a scarcity of helicopters—even the 1st Cavalry Division's four hundred choppers did not allow enough lift for all of its heliborne assaults to take place simultaneously in one flight—it took three round trips of about twenty minutes each way for the lift unit to move Nadal's company into the LZ. The landing began at 1120 hours. The company's present-for-duty strength on that day was 5 officers and 115 enlisted men, but several of the enlisted remained at An Khe. The authorized strength was one hundred sixty four enlisted men, but malaria and rotations back home had reduced the company's strength. The enlisted soldiers were both draftees and regulars (volunteers) and several only had a few weeks left on their time in Vietnam before they would return home at the end of their enlistment.

Landing Zone X-Ray was a clearing approximately two hundred by one hundred yards with a clump of trees and a large termite hill near the middle and a dry creek bed which began on the slopes of Chu Pong Mountain running along the LZ's western side. The creek bed, which varied from two to five feet deep, would play a major role in Alpha Company's battle during the next two days as it was a natural avenue of approach into the landing zone for the enemy as well as a good improvised defensive position for Nadal's company to defend the western part of the landing zone. The LZ was covered with dry grass from one to three feet high. The terrain immediately surrounding the landing zone was covered with small trees thirty to fifty feet high, spaced several feet apart. There were large termite hills, some fifteen feet across at the base and over ten feet high that were scattered through the area; these mounds provided good cover for the enemy. The grass extended throughout the area and visibility for anyone standing was good for a hundred meters or so. However, when Nadal's soldiers "went to ground" in the grass, their visibility was reduced to zero and they became isolated and difficult to control in a fight as they were visually separated from their leaders.

Hitting the Ground
When the first helicopter carrying Alpha Company arrived, Captain Nadal

reported at the LZ to Colonel Moore, who informed him that Bravo Company had already captured an NVA prisoner who had stated that he was part of a much larger force located on the edge of the mountain whose mission was to kill Americans. Moore directed Nadal to begin deploying his company along the creek bed to Bravo's left. He had landed with his 1st Platoon landed and it immediately moved to deploy along the creek bed with one squad out of the creek bed facing south towards the mountain. The mountain, which was heavily covered by jungle, loomed above them, rising steeply 150–200 yards from their position.

Awaiting the arrival of his other platoons, Nadal remained at the battalion command post (CP) adjacent to the landing zone. When Alpha's 2nd Platoon arrived Colonel Moore directed Herren's Bravo Company to move forward of the creek bed to make contact with the enemy and develop the situation. Nadal told his 2nd Platoon to keep contact with Bravo company and cover its left flank. When 2nd Platoon arrived, a firefight had started in s 1st Platoon sector. Hearing the increasing volume of fire, but receiving no radio reports from the platoon, as soon as his 3rd Platoon landed Nadal moved to the 1st Platoon sector to check it out. After his last platoon landed and was in position, Nadal crossed the open grassy LZ area, followed by his radio operators (RTOs). One of them was Sgt. Jackie Gell, Alpha Company's communications sergeant, who was acting as one of the company commander's RTOs; the other was Spec. John Clark. Both were excellent. RTOs were unsung heroes of infantry platoons and companies in combat because their job carrying the radio targets them by the enemy and their responsibility to be accessible to their CO keeps them in the field of fire.

Approaching the creek bed Nadal ran into the 1st Platoon's platoon sergeant, Korean War veteran Sfc. Lorenzo Nathan who told him, "You'd better get down or you're going to get killed." Although the volume of fire was growing, at this time Nadal recalled little sense of personal danger.

Leading From the Front

Nadal asked the platoon sergeant, "Where's Lieutenant Taft?" the platoon leader. "Lieutenant Taft is dead. He's in the creek bed," Nathan answered. After the initial bloody encounter, 1st Platoon had pulled back from the creek bed with their platoon leader left on the battlefield. Impulsively Nadal responded, "Damn, we can't leave him there, let's get him back." Turning to his communications sergeant, Sergeant Gell, who was still acting as one of his RTOs, he said, "Let's go get Lieutenant Taft." Nadal and Gell moved forward to the creek bed and found the lieutenant's body. They were now in a portion of the creek bed that was a no-man's land with the NVA now on the edge of the creek bed, but not yet occupying. As Nadal and Gell struggled with Lieutenant Taft's body, enemy soldiers were throwing hand grenades in their direction, but fortunately they either failed to explode or went off with relatively harmless puffs of black smoke along the edge of the creek bed. The grenades did not seem to have much shrapnel effect, but Nadal was well aware of their explosions. The lieutenant's body was brought to the platoon's lines, where Nadal directed that someone take him back to the command post. On the way back with Lieutenant Taft they came across a wounded soldier so they started back for the wounded soldier. This time some soldiers provided covering fire as they ran back to the creek bed and again grenades were thrown their way, but no damage was done. They recovered the wounded soldier, who survived the battle, and someone carried him back to the aid station.

Company commander Tony Nadal had just taken extraordinary risks in recovering his two men. When questioned about it afterward he responded with several reasons. In the first place, Colonel Moore had told the battalion at Ft. Benning that no member of the battalion would ever be left on the battlefield. The dead and wounded would always be brought back. Nadal heartily concurred with this because it is important for your soldiers to know that if they become casualties they will not be left forgotten on the battlefield. Of equal importance to Nadal, who had been in command of the company for only a little over a month, was his belief that with this being their first major engagement, he had to personally demonstrate to his soldiers that he had the courage to lead them competently. As a soldier of Puerto Rican heritage, it had always been important to him to prove without any doubt to his men that he was worthy of leading them. Obviously, he proved himself.

While Nadal and Gell were recovering Taft and the wounded soldier the enemy was pouring down the mountainside. As was eventually discovered, Moore's battalion had landed next to a full NVA regiment, resting after the battle for the special forces camp at Plei Me, and parts of another regiment that had recently arrived in South Vietnam. The creek bed was the enemy's best avenue of approach into the battalion's defensive position, so Alpha Company's 1st Platoon initially bore the brunt of the attack. A machine gun team, comprised of Spec. Bill Beck and Spec. Russell Adams, who were best friends, performed heroic service throughout the day with their fire denying the enemy entrance into the perimeter. While Beck was bandaging a wounded officer, Adams took a hit to his head through his helmet. (Moore and Galloway: 101) Beck said he had never been as scared as when he saw his friend wounded, so he fervently prayed, repeating the Lord's Prayer. Enemy soldiers were everywhere and Beck asked to be able to live. Immediately calmness overcame him and he not only survived, but left the battle unwounded. His best friend Adams survived his wounds. Heavy fighting continued into the afternoon.

Nadal was unaware of the passage of time. He was so involved that until the battle was reconstructed some months later he had no idea of how long this phase lasted. At approximately 1530 hours there was a lull in the battle. The dead and wounded were evacuated and the soldiers began preparing defensive positions and ammunition was redistributed. The biggest problem became a lack of water. Combat is thirsty work. One of the results of adrenaline pumping through the body is thirst and the troops' canteens were empty. In *Gunga Din*, Rudyard Kipling's poem about a water bearer serving British soldiers in India, he wrote, "But if it comes to slaughter, you will do your work on water and you'll lick the bloomin' boots of 'im that's got it."

At around 1600 hours, Nadal received a radio call from Moore ordering Alpha and Bravo companies to launch another assault to recover a platoon missing since early in the fight. After quick coordination with Bravo Company, Nadal prepared to lead the assault. This second assault of the day is best described by some of Captain Nadal's men. Pfc. Carmen Miceli was one of Nadal's "grunts." He remembers Nadal gathering his men together and saying, "Men, we've got an American platoon cut off out there and we're going after them. Garry Owen [the 7th Cavalry motto]." SSgt. Southern Hewitt, one of the squad leaders remembers Nadal ordering, "Fix bayonets."

The troops responded enthusiastically and they prepared to move out in an echelon left formation that would provide firepower to their left from where the enemy was coming. The assault was to launch at 1620 hours. At the time Nadal felt some trepidation because it was late in the day and he feared that they would be caught at night in the middle of the woods unprepared to defend themselves. Artillery support was lacking, as well. But, with or without supporting fires now was the time to launch the assault.

The Rescue

In a scene reminiscent of World War I and Civil War charges, Alpha's Company executive officer Lieutenant George Jennings reported what happened next, "Captain Nadal was the first one out of the creek bed, yelling 'Let's go!'"

The troops followed Nadal and moved out towards what was believed to be the missing platoon's location. They charged forward from twenty to a hundred yards when all hell broke loose. Unbeknownst to the American defenders, during the lull in the fighting the NVA had been moving forward through the grass on the other side of the creek bed in preparation for an assault on the Alpha company position. The opposing forces met in what was literally hand-to-hand combat for some of the soldiers: as they say on TV, "up close and personal." The 2nd and 3rd platoons, which were leading the charge, began to take casualties. Everyone went to ground except Nadal's five man command group. On Nadal's left Sgt. Johnnie Rangel killed an NVA soldier with his bayonet. Grenades flew through the air, rifles were fired in deafening volume, and an enemy machine gun opened its deadly fire on the command group. To Nadal's immediate right Lt. Timothy Blake, his artillery forward observer (FO), to whom he was speaking was shot dead as was his recon sergeant Floyd Reed. Meanwhile, to Nadal's left commo sergeant and acting RTO Jackie Gell was shot through the chest and killed. (Moore and Galloway: 123) Only the other RTO, John Clark, who was partially behind him, and Nadal were spared. Dropping down to remove the radio from Sergeant Gell, the company commander grabbed Spec. Johnny E. Reynolds, who was lying nearby, and told him that he was now Nadal's RTO. (Tanner had been the RTO for Sgt. Steve Hansen, the mortar FO.) Nadal then tried to contact his platoons. Both his remaining platoon leaders, 3rd Platoon's Lt. George Johnston and Lt. Walter Marm of 2nd Platoon, were already wounded. Marm had been hit in the jaw as he charged across open terrain after firing a light antitank weapon (LAW) at a termite hill that was providing cover for an NVA machine gun that was raking his platoon. He reached the hill, threw a grenade over its top and then assaulted, firing his M16 rifle. Marm killed the machine gun crew, relieving the pressure on the right flank. The wounded platoon leader was medevaced from the battle. For his valorous action Lt. Walter Marm subsequently received the Medal of Honor.

Some enlisted men and NCOs were killed as they attempted to rescue their wounded comrades. They all learned a bitter lesson from this, their first fight: the best and first thing you do for a wounded buddy is to kill the SOB who shot him. Otherwise, you also may be killed in trying to rescue him. Nadal recalled warning Sergeant Floyd not to go after one of his men who had been wounded because he suspected that whoever shot him was still covering the area. Sergeant Floyd yelled back, "He's one of my men", went after him, and they both died.

The Battle Continued

Trying to gain control of the battle, Captain Nadal moved his 1st Platoon, which had been in reserve along the left rear, forward and around the NVA soldiers. They advanced only a short distance when they also become entangled in the enemy. As darkness approached, it was evident to the Alpha company commander that they could not advance against the superior numbers of enemy, that the Americans would continue to lose men if they remained where they were, and that their current positions were undefendable. Reinforcements from Capt. Myron Diduryk's B/2/7 Cavalry began to arrive.

Captain Nadal radioed Colonel Moore and requested permission to pull back to the creek bed. Bravo company commander Captain Herren concurred. Nadal decided to use artillery smoke to cover the withdrawal. His artillery FO, Lieutenant Blake, was KIA and Blake's radio destroyed, so Nadal called in the fire mission through the Battalion S3 (operations officer) on the battalion command net. Smoke generally doesn't cause casualties, so he called the mission right on top of the fight. With the Americans mixed up with the enemy there was no point in placing it elsewhere. As it turned out, the artillery battery had no smoke rounds, but it did have white phosphorous (WP or Willie Pete) shells, which create a tremendous amount of smoke, but also can cause terrible injuries as the phosphorous sets everything it hits on fire. Not knowing that Nadal had called the fire mission on top of his own positions, Moore authorized the battery to fire the white phosphorus. The WP burst in the middle of the unit. Miraculously, no one was hurt. Initially Nadal was surprised because he wasn't expecting WP. The Willie Pete shells, however, created a much thicker cloud of white smoke than a normal smoke round would, so he radioed his platoons to begin their withdrawal. After the men in the company began their withdrawal, Captain Nadal remained alone on the battlefield to provide covering fire for his men.

Remarkably, Nadal and his radio operator John Clark had remained unwounded thus far. Clark described Captain Nadal as, "Very cool and collected." The only time he ever observed Nadal as even the least bit ruffled was when the white phosphorus shells were exploding over his men, and the company commander was very concerned about the casualties he expected the WP rounds to cause among his men. Clark reflected on the fact that he and Nadal were untouched throughout all the heavy action and he attributed it, as did Nadal, to "Divine intervention."

When they returned to the creek bed, Nadal was emotionally and physically exhausted. During the battle he remembers that he was not afraid, but now, thirsty and worn out, he was drained of energy. He wanted to sleep, but his troops were looking to him for guidance and orders. They then began the process of preparing a defensive position. He kept the bulk of the company in the creek bed with the exception of his 1st Platoon, which bent back out of the bed toward Charlie Company, which had helicoptered in that morning immediately after Nadal's company and defended the southern edge of the battalion perimeter. Water arrived, ammo and rations were passed around and he coordinated the platoon's locations and fires. Alpha Company's executive officer, Lt. George Jennings, was of enormous help during this process, as he had been during the fight in handling the KIAs and WIAs.

Although the two-company assault did not achieve its objective to recover the lost platoon, it probably saved the battalion. Had Alpha and Bravo companies not assaulted when they did and engaged the enemy in the grass beyond the creek bed, shortly thereafter they would have received a battalion-sized assault, launched from their immediate front, against which they were unprepared to defend. Shortly before dark, a platoon from B/2/7 Cavalry, led by Lt. Rick Rescorla, an outstanding leader, was attached to Nadal's company and the platoon was placed to the left of Alpha's 1st Platoon, now the left-most company element, adjacent to Charlie Company. (Lieutenant Rescorla survived the Ia Drang and the war. Ultimately he died a hero while evacuating employees from one of the World Trade Center's towers on September 11, 2001.) That first night UPI reporter Joseph L. Galloway finally was able to hitch a ride into X-Ray.

Several men in Alpha Company reminisced about the battle and their commanding officer. John Clark said, "Captain Nadal made a big difference in the company due to his prior SF tour in Vietnam"; George Jennings, "Our company was prepared because of their experienced CO who demanded excellence"; Joe Marm, "He was a very good company commander"; Carmen Miceli, "He was very cool, organized, a damn good leader. Thank God for his leadership"; Southern Hewitt, "He was a leader who said, 'Let's go, not *you* go'"; Steve Hansen, "He had the right temperament for combat, never panicked. Nadal was the personification of a company commander in combat with his courage, decisiveness, judgment and tactical proficiency."

Night Falls on Day One
As night fell American infantrymen continued the process of redistributing ammunition, coordinating fires and, this time, using the radio of Sergeant Steve Hansen, the mortar platoon FO, successfully requesting artillery fire

missions. As the day had progressed, they enjoyed an increasing amount of fire support. The air force pulled all the plugs in providing close air support while additional field artillery batteries were moved to be in range. By evening they were well protected by friendly fires. They had air force close air support during most of the day. When the ordnance was delivered by the old, propeller-driven A-1E Skyraider, the support was very effective, but the fast-moving jets could not deliver the ordnance close enough to their positions to be very helpful. The continuous, all-night firing by the artillery saved them. During the night the air force provided support from AC-47s with suppressive fires from their side-mounted miniguns and with illumination flares until 0200 hours when their flare supply ran out. The sudden, eerie darkness increased the troopers' sense of danger.

During that first night they received a couple of attacks on their left flank, but the combination of artillery, mortars, machine guns and Claymores convinced the NVA that they had best call it a night. Nadal mentioned the heroic support provided by the pilots of the lift choppers who evacuated their wounded during the day and brought ammunition and water to the troops. Years later, in 2007 and 2001 respectively, two pilots, Major Bruce Crandall and Captain Ed Freeman, received the Medal of Honor for their extraordinary efforts in flying repeatedly into LZ X-Ray while under intense enemy fire.

That first night, November 14, Captain Sugdinis's company (A/2/7 Cavalry) was alerted to be ready to air assault into LZ X-Ray to support the fighting there.

Day Two

Before daylight, early the next morning of November 15th, a fierce attack was launched on Capt. Bob Edwards's Charlie Company. The attack continued into daylight and almost overran the company. Most of Charlie Company's soldiers were either killed or wounded and the enemy did overrun a number of their foxholes. Faced with the possibility of having the perimeter broken and the entire LZ overwhelmed, Colonel Moore directed Nadal to send a platoon to Edwards's assistance. Nadal selected his 2nd Platoon and ordered them to move across the LZ. They started across and were quickly taken under fire from Charlie Company positions that were now occupied by the NVA. One of his men was killed and several wounded. The platoon hit the dirt and returned fire across the LZ, helping to prevent the enemy from crossing the landing zone. Shortly thereafter, under tremendous pounding from artillery and air support, the NVA gave up the attack on Charlie Company with the survivors withdrawing back up Chu Pong Mountain.

Captain Sugdinis and his company were airlifted in early on the morning of November 15th to X-Ray. Sugdinis traveled on the seemingly ever-present Major Crandall's chopper, which had to circle before landing due to constant enemy ground fire. During the day there were several human-wave attacks on Sugdinis's positions. He remembers, "My men performed admirably all day," adding that his executive officer, Lt. Larry Gwin, a Yale University Distinguished Military Graduate, could not have been a better XO. The artillery support was "amazing." The NVA tried another assault that night, but his men repulsed the attack. Sugdinis admits he was plenty scared. Lieutenant Colonel Robert Tully's 2nd Battalion, 5th Cavalry, also arrived as reinforcements on the second day.

Captain Joel Sugdinis (left) and Lt. Col. Harold Moore (right) at LZ X-Ray, November 15, 1965.

Day Three

Early on the morning of the 16th, the NVA tried one more attack, this time on the positions manned by B/2/7 Cavalry. Most of the previous day Capt. Myron Diduryk's company had been able to develop strong defensive positions and the enemy assault was easily repulsed with the NVA leaving twenty-six dead on the battlefield while Bravo Company had suffered only three wounded.

That day, starting at about noon, 1st Battalion was transported from the Landing Zone X-Ray back to their base camp. Prior to their departure, all the companies walked over the battlefield and found stacks and stacks of dead NVA bodies that had been hidden behind the termite hills. The Alpha Company soldiers discovered that some of the enemy KIA were actually still alive. These wounded NVA soldiers were medevaced from the battlefield. The bugles were now silent, but Tony Nadal had once again marched to the sound of the guns.

COMBAT LEADERSHIP LESSONS
FROM LZ X-RAY PER TONY NADAL

- Unit cohesion derived from mutual respect, rigorous training, and lengthy interactions among all ranks are essential to survival and effectiveness under combat conditions.
- Soldiers will do almost anything for leaders they trust. Trust will be derived when competence and proficiency are exhibited by military leaders.
- Individual soldier rotation in combat debilitates units. Unit integrity should always be maintained to every degree possible.
- Fear is often overcome by commanders during battle due to their activity and mental engagement while their subordinates are awaiting orders. The leader must reflect calmness at all times.
- Loyalty to your leadership in the military is solidified when the soldiers believe that their leaders will always return them home dead or alive and not abandon them on the battlefield.
- Troops must be briefed and drilled as to what they should do when their fellow warriors become casualties so they do not add themselves to the casualty count.
- A true leader must lead from the front to establish credentials for trust and faith. The leader must be first in and last out.
- The psychological impact of a tough battle needs to be discussed

with young leaders. A unit is vulnerable after a tough engagement because leaders and troops are physically and emotionally fatigued. The natural inclination is to rest and reduce alert levels, but the leaders must continue with the tasks of preparation for further combat action.

- Noncommissioned officers are critical to a unit's success. At LZ X-Ray, the men followed their sergeants.
- Never underestimate your enemy. Dedication, ideological commitment, or fanaticism may outweigh weapons and technological superiority.

On November 16th Sugdinis's company experienced several enemy probes. His men were already severely sleep deprived. Beginning at 0930 the rest of the 2nd battalion, including the attached Alpha Company, First Battalion, Fifth Cavalry, walked from LZ Columbus, three miles east, entering X-Ray at noon that day.

Among those who walked in to X-Ray that day was 2nd Lt. L.J. "Bud" Alley, the second battalion communications officer. He began working the 2nd Battalion radios and was next to Colonel Moore when reporters, brought in by a Chinook at noon, swarmed over the battlefield. In the ensuing conversation with the reporters, Bud Alley remembers, "Colonel Moore was fierce, charismatic, and emotional as he spoke of the valor and courage of his men."

B-52 bombing strikes were planned on the Chu Pong Massif the next morning, so Lieutenant Colonel McDade's battalion (2/7 Cav) and Lieutenant Colonel Tully's battalion (2/5 Cav) were ordered to move by foot on the 17th to LZ Columbus (for Tully) and LZ Albany (for McDade), which were far enough away from the bombing strike to be safe. McDade's battalion, less Diduryk's Bravo Company and Sugdinis's third platoon, which had departed the day before with 1/7 Cav, plus A/1/5 were to be airlifted from Albany back to base camp after the helicopters received necessary repairs. In the column was Captain Roger A. Knopf (USAF), 2nd Battalion's air controller.

The March to LZ Albany

Initially the march to LZ Albany was relatively uneventful. However, the men had been without sleep for three days, were hungry, and carried equipment that felt heavier and heavier in the 110 degree heat. Both battalions

Second Lieutenant Bud Alley before convoying to Catecka Plantation and then on to LZ X-Ray, November 14, 1965.

originally headed northeast from X-Ray for two miles, then McDade's battalion turned northwest on a route that would take them two more miles to the Albany pickup zone. Tully's battalion continued marching northeast to Landing Zone Columbus. Captain Sugdinis's Alpha Company led the 2nd Battalion with his two remaining platoons and the battalion reconnaissance platoon, which had been attached to him. Just after the turn to the northwest B-52 vapor trails could be seen high overhead and the ground shook under the battalion as their bombs impacted back at Chung Pong Massif.

From later reports Lt. Larry Gwin, Alpha Company's executive officer, learned that they walked in between two enemy battalion-sized units of approximately 600 men each. McDade's battalion had approximately 350 men. The odds were greater than three to one against the Americans. Both NVA units were well rested; neither had been in the fight at X-Ray.

The Battle Begins

Advancing eventually to only two hundred yards east of LZ Albany, Sugdi-

Lieutenant Larry Gwin at An Khe Pass with Highway 19 to Qui Nhon in background.

nis's company was positioned in a triangle formation with the Recon Platoon forward, 1st Platoon to the right and 2nd Platoon to the left. Just as Sugdinis reached the high ground a little east of their objective, LZ Albany, Lieutenant Gwin, who was about fifty feet in front of his company commander, radioed that the Recon Platoon, under the command of Lieutenant Pat Payne, had captured two NVA prisoners. If the enemy didn't already know where they were due to lack of noise discipline of the Americans, they certainly would now. Sugdinis moved to his recon platoon and informed McDade about the POWs. McDade began to move from the Headquarters Company area farther back in the battalion column and ordered all his company commanders to join him at the head of the column. Behind A Company, throughout the now-stalled column, after almost sixty hours without sleep and four hours on the march, except for some security flankers, the men tended to fall out and relax.

Shortly afterward Sugdinis spotted what might be enemy activity nearby. He ordered the company to move to the west and get battle ready. The Recon

Platoon was to move to the far west side of a clearing that was assumed to be Albany while 1st Platoon was to move to the north side of the clearing and the 2nd Platoon to the south side. Recon Platoon angled south to avoid moving straight across the clearing and hit a clump of trees that allowed them to see another larger, unmapped clearing, which was the actual Albany landing zone, even farther to the west. Then, as company XO Larry Gwin recalls, "all hell broke loose. . . . As if on cue, the entire jungle suddenly seemed to explode in an incredible crescendo of small arms fire, as if everyone had opened up around us with every weapon they had." (Gwin: 133) Capt. George Forrest, CO of A/1/5 Cavalry, having arrived near the head of the column with the other company commanders, turned around and raced back to his company, which was behind 2nd Battalion's Headquarters Company. Sugdinis immediately took steps to establish a defensive perimeter in the island of trees where the Recon Platoon had positioned itself. Shortly thereafter the battalion command group, including CO McDade and XO Maj. Frank Henry arrived inside the perimeter, after moving forward through the column after the two enemy soldiers were captured. "The most savage one-day battle of the Vietnam War had just begun." (Moore and Galloway: 229) The company was engaged in hand-to-hand fighting from approximately 1300 to 1630. On the company's left flank Lt. Gordon Grove's second platoon was virtually annihilated. Gwin reported, "I saw Gordy Grove coming across the field with two wounded men. They were the only ones left of his platoon who could move." (Moore and Galloway: 236) Later Sugdinis was on the radio to Gordon's platoon sergeant, William A. Ferrell, when he heard the sergeant say he had been hit and his platoon was being overrun. Then, Sugdinis was totally stunned to hear nothing but Vietnamese over the radio; the push to talk button had become jammed. Ferrell's body was recovered later.

Initially the enemy attacks were by individuals, but soon moved to large groups. The NVA soldiers would stand up and charge across open areas toward the American perimeter, and then be repulsed. Eventually, Capt. Joe Price, the battalion's artillery forward observer, and Major Henry got connected for air and artillery support. The situation was desperate. Henry told Sugdinis he could call in napalm air strikes. Sugdinis believed an enemy assault from where his second platoon had been hit so horrifically could be in such overwhelming strength that it would annihilate the rest of the men in his company and even the battalion. And, although he couldn't be sure, he also figured that there probably were no survivors left in Gordon's second platoon. Under extraordinary pressure, with immediate action required Sugdinis alone made the hard but calculated decision that they had to call in napalm bombs on 2nd Platoon's position. He called in two napalm air strikes. Later Major Henry called in more napalm strikes, bombing runs, and artillery barrages.

❖ ❖ ❖

At a reunion of the battalion in 2010 to his great amazement and relief Sugdinis learned that wounded 2nd Platoon survivors and other members of the battalion actually thanked him for calling in the napalm strikes. Remarkably, several of the few survivors were only splattered with liquid napalm, which hadn't ignited. More importantly, however, the strikes killed many NVA soldiers who otherwise would have swept through their position and killed the remaining 2nd Platoon wounded as well as assaulting the company's defensive perimeter. The day following the battle when a sweep through the second platoon area was made, one of the survivors was Sgt. John Eade, a fire team leader, sitting up against a tree. Sergeant Eade struggled to his feet, called out "Garry Owen," and immediately collapsed. He survived despite eight wounds, a minor napalm burn, and loss of one eye. The other three members of his fire team had been killed. (In 2011 the three members of Sergeant Eade's fire team posthumously awarded Silver Stars.

The Center of the Battalion Column

Farther back in the battalion the men had been marching in two columns a hundred yards apart. Shortly after Recon Platoon captured the two prisoners, the columns' forward movement stopped; very few of the soldiers were particularly alert. Lieutenant Bud Alley, the battalion commo officer, was near the front of Headquarters Company, just ahead of Captain Forrest's A/1/5 Cav, the battalion's trail element, when the heavy attack started forward of his position. As calls for medics rang out, the battalion medical platoon leader, Lt. John Howard, moved ahead of Alley with his medics. Here the attack came from the west in a pincer movement with the enemy blocking on the east.

Alley and the men around him were in the middle of firefights all afternoon. He and another soldier were pinned down by an enemy machine gun. As they attempted to silence the gun, the other soldier took an enemy round in the head, but before he died, he pulled the pin on his grenade and threw it toward the enemy.

Eventually Alley moved along with several other soldiers, all of whom were wounded except for Alley toward the sound of the American artillery being fired from LZ Columbus, two miles away. He and the other survivors were taken into the Columbus perimeter after first light the following morning.

The Battalion Rear

Air controller Roger Knopf was with the battalion's headquarters company. They could barely see ahead because of the high grass. Knopf remembers that they had no food since the day before. When the prisoners were captured at the front of the column, the interpreter was called forward, and the column stopped, but the company did not set up defensive positions.

When they heard firing ahead, Knopf said it was originally reported as our troops firing by mistake on each other. In fact, however, it was the sound of the NVA attacks. The men in his area began taking AK-47 and mortar rounds. He became an infantryman and did not call in any air strikes because he did not know where to direct them. Eventually Knopf was in a group of fifteen men and after several became casualties, he attempted to call in medevac choppers, but ground fire and a small landing zone, kept them from landing. They established a small perimeter and were joined by several others. The group moved away back toward the point at which they had made their turn to the northwest. The air force officer was carrying a radio and helping to carry wounded. By nightfall they had managed to evacuate some of the wounded, but other wounded men had to spend the night on the ground.

Back at the Forward Perimeter

On the afternoon of the 17th things were still hot and heavy at the Albany perimeter. Another napalm run had decimated a hidden enemy force that had been preparing an assault. At one time Sugdinis spotted an enemy soldier with another enemy on his back. When Sugdinis realized the enemy was shooting our wounded, he shot him dead.

Just before dark on November 17, as Lieutenant Alley and his group were sometimes literally crawling toward LZ Columbus and Captain Knopf and his group were digging in for the night south of the Albany perimeter, reinforcements from Camp Holloway helicoptered into the Alpha Company perimeter. The battalion's hardy and spirited Bravo Company, led by Captain Myron Diduryk, again rode to the rescue, assaulting under intense enemy fire.

❖ ❖ ❖

The next morning Captain Knopf moved forward to LZ Albany with Capt. George Forrest's company and Capt. Walter Tully's relief company (B/1/5 Cav), which had marched overland the afternoon of the 17th from LZ Columbus. Knopf passed many KIAs, both American and NVA. He saw several dead Americans whose wounds had been bandaged, but apparently had been found later and executed by the NVA. He spent the afternoon helping bring our KIAs to the landing zone. He spent the next day, the 19th, scouring the kill zone and discovered more dead and wounded. In retrospect Knopf regrets he was not with the battalion commander, who had moved up to Alpha Company when the prisoners were captured, where he would have been able to call in air strikes himself. The two biggest lessons he learned are that the air controller should always be with the battalion commander and

Air Force Capt. Roger Knopf in tall grass on November 18, 1965, the day after the battle at LZ Albany.

air support should always be in the vicinity when a column is moving on the ground.

All day on the 18th and into the 19th the battlefield was combed to retrieve our KIAs and some isolated wounded who had spent the night before very quietly so as not to alert the NVA, who had spent the night retrieving their dead and wounded.

Of Sugdinis's company of 110 men, including Recon Platoon and the battalion command group, who defended the perimeter at LZ Albany, 34 were killed in action and 20 were wounded, roughly 50 percent casualties. Sugdinis himself received only a minor wound. He believes that enemy KIA totaled 400 to 500. Charlie Company suffered 91 casualties out of their 100 man strength. The almost 350 man battalion suffered casualties of, 155 killed and 124 wounded. Only 70 remained ready for further action.

On the 18th, Sugdinis had one further emotional story to relate. Very near the perimeter three dead NVA were found behind an anthill. Sugdinis personally opened the pocket of one of them and found a picture of the NVA soldier with his wife and two children. As he replaced the picture wrapped in plastic in the enemy's pocket he reflected, "They may be the enemy, but they also are fathers and husbands." This battle was over and Captain Joel Sugdinis had lived to fight another day. Larry Gwin said of him, "He was an outstanding combat company commander."

They were all brothers in the Garry Owen outfit. King Henry in William Shakespeare's *King Henry the Fifth* (1599) put it in words that will last forever: "We few, we happy few, we band of brothers; for he today that sheds his blood with me shall be my brother."

Meanwhile Back at the White House

In November 1965 the 1st Cavalry Division's action in the battles of the Ia Drang was an indication of what was to come: "Although heralded at the time as a major U.S. victory, the Ia Drang battle foreshadowed the future course of the war. Communist troops suffered losses dramatically disproportionate to those absorbed by the United States. Yet they were not intimidated by the American show of strength, their commitment to the war remained undiluted." (Goldstein: 225)

The advice of General Douglas MacArthur (not to engage in a ground war in Asia) and French President de Gaulle (that fighting in this part of the world would be very challenging) was not given serious consideration.

America was in the war!

Aftermath

In 1993 after he retired from active duty, Colonel Tony Nadal had the opportunity to return to Vietnam with Lieutenant General Hal Moore and several of the officers who fought at Landing Zone X-Ray as part of a one-hour television special produced and aired by ABC News. They flew into Hanoi and, on the second day there, they were introduced to the NVA officers that had commanded the units they had fought against at X-Ray. They also had the opportunity to meet General Vo Nguyen Giap, the famed Vietnamese war hero and victor in 1954 against the French at Dien Bien Phu. For the next ten days they were together with these Vietnamese officers and eventually rode a decrepit Russian helicopter back to LZ X-Ray, their long ago battleground. The ability to share their experiences with these officers and to gain an insight into their thinking was truly amazing and revealing. They communicated through very competent interpreters provided by the Vietnamese Foreign Office.

Over the course of the ten days Colonel Nadal developed some rapport with a Colonel Thuc, who had spent the two days attacking the left flank of his unit in the battle. Colonel Thuc had joined the Viet Minh at age sixteen, led a squad as a sergeant in the final assault in the battle of Dien Bien Phu, and then remained in the North Vietnamese Army. By 1964 he was a captain and was ordered with his company to march south from Hanoi to the Pleiku area. He remained in South Vietnam for the next ten years. During that time he received only one or two letters per year from his family, was wounded eight times, was once left for dead and suffered from hunger and cold in the Central Highlands. Although he had no artillery or air support, Thuc never gave up, never quit, and all the time believed he was uniting his country and driving out the occupiers. It became evident to Nadal that these officers viewed themselves in the same manner as our American patriots who fought at Valley Forge must have viewed themselves.

The rewards of leading troops in battle are in the binding relationships that are formed. John Clark, Nadal's former RTO and a very successful business man today, and Nadal are very close with a bond forged on a battlefield where they almost died together. Both of them and a large part of Alpha Company have reconnected over the years and they join the other members of their battalion who fought at LZ X-Ray at an annual reunion where they remember their dead, play golf, laugh, and enjoy each other's company. Not many

Vietnam units have this rapport or close relationship. It is one of the treasures of Colonel Nadal's life.

Then Pfc. Carmen Miceli, who retired as a battalion fire chief in North Bergen, New Jersey, said that his world in the battle was a very narrow twelve-foot square, but this volunteer draftee had a very broad view of what he, our military, and our other Vietnam veterans accomplished. About his time in the two day battle, very simply, but succinctly, he concludes, "This is what we do! Someone has to do it! Most people do not know what we do!"

The stories of Alpha Company at LZ X-Ray and 2nd Battalion at LZ Albany are just two of many that could be told. Both Nadal and Sugdinis are aware and respectful of the many outstanding officers and NCOs who led from the front, experienced great dangers and hardships, took care of their men, and in some cases gave their lives. Over three million of our military served in Southeast Asia during the war. Their courageous, honorable, and dedicated service and their willingness to answer their nation's call, was their gift to America.

The members of Lt. Col. Hal Moore's battalion who fought at the battle at X-Ray will join together each year until they are all gone, but in the words of Douglas MacArthur, "Old soldiers never die; they just fade away." The sacrifice, honor, and valor of Nadal, Sugdinis, their men, and all who supported them to bring about this victory, will never fade away.

The First Reunion of the Second Battalion
Battalion commo officer Bud Alley remembers when the battalion's survivors arrived at An Khe on Sunday, November 21, 1965:

> We sat out there in the sun all day waiting on movement orders . . . we were all hoping that we would fly back to An Khe . . . but finally at about 5:00 PM we were loaded into deuce-and-a-halfs, and we drove back to An Khe . . . as we entered the perimeter, it was dusk . . . the men from all round the perimeter stopped beside the road and stared at us . . . when we arrived in the battalion area, the division band was there and it played Garry Owen. The colors were there also and it was the first time I saw the colors or heard the song Garry Owen. Within minutes of our arrival, it was dark and we officers sat around a lantern having a drink . . . the men had gone to their EM club tent for beer . . . about 10 minutes later, the troops came out en masse to where we were and thanked us for our leadership and asked

if we would have a drink with them . . . now you know the protocol of the army back then . . . so it was quite a bold step on their part and we were honored to have been asked...as leaders, we all felt we had let them down . . . but the men didn't see it that way . . . what an honor to receive . . . needless to say, many beers were consumed that night by all as we hugged, and sang, and generally drowned our misery together that night . . . for we all knew that dawn would bring us the reality of dealing with the effects of our wounded and dead.

The second battalion has had three additional reunions since that first and is planning on having more.

Tony Nadal retired from the army and after a successful civilian second career, retired to Williamsburg, Virginia. After his army service and a successful civilian career, Joel Sugdinis retired to a quiet life in Eastham, Massachusetts on Cape Cod. Bud Alley has organized three reunions. He lives in Brentwood, Tennessee where he plans to teach and write. Roger Knopf went on to fly eighty-eight combat missions in F-4s over Laos and the Ho Chi Minh Trail. He retired from the air force and lives in Norton Shores, Michigan. Larry Gwin is retired on the shore north of Boston and writes everyday. He wrote a highly successful book titled *Baptism: A Vietnam Memoir* that was published in 1999 and continues in print today, thirteen years later. Both Captains Nadal and Sugdinis and many other members of both battalions received Silver Stars.

❖ ❖ ❖

After this battle, as expected, the North Vietnamese Army with their South Vietnamese Viet Cong allies continued their struggle in the Central Highlands. The next summer Captain Ron Brown of the 101st Airborne Division fought the enemy farther north near Dak To in the Toumorong.

CHAPTER 5

The Unlonesome End Story

CAPTAIN RON BROWN, USA
(BATTLE OF THE TOUMORONG, 1966)

Spartans do not ask how many but where they are.
—Agis II, King of Sparta, 427 B.C.

BATTLES ON THE BORDERS

During the early years of U.S. ground combat in Vietnam the most pressing tasks were finding the enemy and engaging him in decisive combat. Many of the battles at that stage involved multi-battalion and sometimes even multi-division operations conducted in the deep jungle along South Vietnam's western border with Laos and Cambodia. Enemy forces had established a series of bases west of those borders, along with their major access routes out of North Vietnamese down through the Laotian panhandle and into Cambodia along the network known as the Ho Chi Minh Trail. Since U.S. forces were at this stage prohibited from crossing the border, enemy forces could break contact and move westward into their sanctuaries, there to rest and refit, in the process controlling the level of casualties they would experience. This situation was extremely frustrating to U.S. units and commanders, who spent long hard days thrashing about in the jungle trying to locate the enemy and then—when he could be located—fighting him on ground of his own choosing, and then only so long as it suited the enemy to continue the engagement.

Destined To Be A Soldier
Ron Brown was dedicated to soldiering after watching a movie at age eight about the two West Point Heisman Trophy winners in the mid-1940s, Doc

Blanchard and Glenn Davis. West Point was his only college choice from then forward. He attended McCallie Military School in Tennessee on the western slope of Missionary Ridge, the site of an important Civil War battle outside Chattanooga. He was honored twice to be awarded by the Military Academy Association of Graduates for being first in his class, which graduated in 1962, in military aptitude and leadership.

Meanwhile Back at the White House

McGeorge Bundy left his position as President Johnson's national security advisor in March 1966. By the 1990s he had begun to seriously reflect on the war and his part in the decisions made in the summer of 1965:

> As he immersed himself in the essential decisions of Vietnam more than thirty years after the Americanization of war, Bundy arrived at three conclusions at variance with his advocacy as national security adviser. He dismissed the notion that there was a geopolitical imperative to fight the war, a conviction he had fervently held in the White House. He rejected the premise that there was ever any possibility that the North Vietnamese would relent in their drive to unify the country or would negotiate a compromise settlement with the United States, a potential outcome he postulated in 1965. And he acknowledged that the massive military deployments initiated in 1965 were doomed to fail and held no plausible expectation for a military solution to the conflict. (Goldstein: 222)

It is always easier to look back decades later with more wisdom, insight, and knowledge, but we were committed by early 1966 with no turning back and our warriors began to acquit themselves very valiantly and courageously to fulfill the diplomatic, policy, and political decisions promulgated by *The Best and the Brightest* gathered safely about the presidents in the hallowed halls and conference rooms of the White House.

Ron Brown and Bill Carpenter at West Point

On a beautiful Saturday afternoon in September 1958 Ron Brown attended his first football game as a plebe (freshman) at the United States Military Academy at West Point. To both his amazement and, the entire sporting world as news of the novel formation spread, when the Army football team huddled to call its first offensive play of the game, one player was standing twenty or more yards from the huddle. It was the birth of what became known as the "Lonesome End." All-American Bill Carpenter was the lonesome end and it certainly never occurred to Brown on that fall afternoon that almost eight years later, in June 1966, the lonesome end would need company—a lot of company—if he and his men were going to survive. This is Ron Brown's story of that battle and the leadership lessons he learned from it.

Lonesome end Bill Carpenter, class of 1960, and Ron Brown, class of 1962: they met for the first time since their cadet days in Vietnam in 1966 where Bill commanded C Company and Ron commanded A Company of the 1st Battalion, 502nd Infantry, 101st Airborne Division. During a major campaign in the Central Highlands near Dak To, Carpenter's company had been ambushed by a North Vietnamese regiment numbering fifteen hundred to two thousand men and he was forced to call napalm on his position in order to save his company. Brown's company had been providing security for an engineer unit that was building an airstrip about seventy kilometers south of Dak To at Ban Me Thuot, but this "quiet" mission had turned into a real firefight when the Viet Cong attempted to overrun the engineers. In the middle of this action Ron was directed by Lt. Col. Henry "Gunfighter" Emerson, the battalion commander of 1/502 Infantry, to return by helicopter immediately. When he arrived at Dak To, Emerson briefed him on Carpenter's desperate situation and gave him the order to link up and reinforce Captain Carpenter's beleaguered company.

COMBAT LEADERSHIP LESSON #1:

• CIRCUMSTANCE: A Company had been involved in a tough combat situation for over a month and the men thought they were returning to the battalion base at Dak To where they would get well-deserved showers, medical attention, and hot food.

• LESSON: A leader must quickly recognize the attitudes and feelings of his men and immediately propose a situation that makes their current desires and expectations seem insignificant to something more important.

• SOLUTION: He immediately called together the officer and NCO leaders of his company and told them about the gravity of Charlie Company's situation. He directed them to brief their men, stressing and emphasizing the critical condition of Carpenter's company. They needed to get their soldier's minds off hot food and hot showers and on to the needs of their fellow troopers.

After meeting with the battalion commander and receiving the intelligence reports and maneuver plans from the battalion staff: Alpha Company was to move three thousand meters at night through dense, treacherous jungle terrain, battle their way through the North Vietnamese Army Regiment that was threatening to overrun Carpenter's company, and link up with and reinforce their fellow Screaming Eagles. Of course after successfully accomplishing this extremely dangerous and high-risk mission, the 170 men of Alpha Company along with the survivors of Charlie Company would then be surrounded by the NVA Regiment, as well.

This mission was going to be a tough sell to Brown's men.

COMBAT LEADERSHIP LESSON #2:

• CIRCUMSTANCE: His men viewed this as a "Mission Impossible" situation and recognized that success meant fighting their way through and in order to become surrounded by an enemy force more than ten times their size.

• LESSON: A leader must be able to give academy award-winning performances in front of his men. In order to demonstrate his own confidence in the mission, he must show them why he exudes such confidence by his knowledge of the situation, prior experiences in similar occurrences, thorough planning that helps insure success, and his absolute confidence in his men's ability to accomplish the mission.

• SOLUTION: After the platoon leaders met with their men, the company commander assembled the entire unit together and briefed them how critical it was to rescue their fellow Screaming Eagles. He told them about his thorough reconnaissance by helicopter and how he had selected a route through six to eight-foot tall jungle grass that would keep them out of sight, and out of the fire of their enemy. Ron emphasized that the dark of night along with the rain that was falling were their biggest assets and would greatly facilitate mission success. He also stated that the Gunfighter—their battalion commander had already begun to be a legend in his own time—had told him that they were the only company in the entire United States Army that he would select for this mission, and Captain Brown had responded to his CO that he, Brown, already knew that. Ron's closing statement to his men was that he had asked Colonel Emerson to wait a few days so the NVA could send in some reinforcements because with only ten to-one odds against Alpha Company, it just didn't seem like a fair fight for the NVA. The Alpha Company troopers totally and loudly agreed, and Brown knew they were ready for the mission.

Movement to the Toumorong

Just before his company moved out, Captain Brown pulled Colonel Emerson aside and asked him about contingency plans in case they encountered a situation that made it impossible for him to accomplish the mission. Emerson looked at him with steely eyes and replied, "Bulldog", either reinforce Carpenter or let them bring your dead body back." Mission failure just wasn't an option with the Gunfighter. Ron remembers walking away from Emerson with this thought running through his mind: "Tis not for me to reason why, tis only for me to do or die."

Navigating through three thousand meters of mountainous and treacherous jungle terrain on a sunny day would be very difficult, but during a pitch black night with rain falling in monsoon torrents would have been impossible if Sgt. "Hawk" Hawthorne, an Apache Indian, had not been in their company. Hawk had the ability to find the correct route in any type of terrain. Sergeant Hawthorne was posted at the head of the formation and Brown told him, "Hawk, take us to Charlie Company." Hawthorne selected a route utilizing the high elephant grass that Brown had seen during his reconnaissance flight and the company soon learned that indeed the darkness and rain were their greatest assets. Progress was slow but steady as they maneuvered around pockets of NVA soldiers who could be heard talking and moving all around them. The Alpha Company troopers literally had to hold on to the men in front of them in order to stay together in such adverse conditions. Occasionally machine-gun and small-arms fire would open up, but the elephant grass and defilade position of Hawk's route kept the company out of the line of fire. Their luck ran out, however, when they hit an open area just before climbing the final ridge that separated them from Charlie Company. Two machine guns began placing intense fire on Brown's troopers and he immediately realized that they could not proceed without taking out the enemy machine guns, so he ordered everyone down and not to return fire as it would only give away their position. He took a squad of ten men and proceeded to move under cover to the flank of the machine-gun emplacements. When they reached a good attack location Ron told the squad to wait until he crawled close enough to throw a grenade into the enemy position. When the grenade exploded the squad was to attack the machine guns. As he was crawling towards the machine guns with a grenade in his hand, for some reason his mind flashed back to his childhood days when he had "practiced" this very act while playing soldier in his back yard. However, when the machine guns started firing again, he immediately returned to reality. The noise from the guns actually allowed him to get close enough to be within throwing range. When the grenade exploded behind the guns, the assault fire from the squad riddled the area. Brown shot two NVA soldiers who ran directly towards him and the squad killed the remaining six.

COMBAT LEADERSHIP LESSON #3:

- **CIRCUMSTANCE:** The sighting and firing of the NVA machine-gun positions greatly endangered the success of the company's mission. The guns blocked them from their route to Charlie Company's position. A prolonged firefight would have allowed the machine guns to be reinforced by additional enemy soldiers.
- **LESSON:** A leader must recognize and evaluate the situation and initiate an immediate action plan that must be executed immediately and vigorously to save both time and lives. A leader must know to lead by example to instill the confidence and belief in him with his men.
- **ACTION:** Captain Brown immediately reduced the danger to the company by not allowing them to return fire, thereby keeping their exact location unknown to the NVA gunners. He quickly led the squad to the machine-gun position, crawled within hand-grenade range and assaulted the position. Ron acted as a commander of his men; he didn't ask them to do anything he was not prepared to do.

After eliminating the machine guns, the troopers threw caution to the wind and moved very quickly to get out of this area and up and over the ridge to Charlie Company's beleaguered position. The enemy now knew they were there and Brown did not want to give them opportunity to hit his men when they were this vulnerable. After over nine hours of movement he knew they were near Carpenter's company, but with the wind, rain, and darkness it still would be very difficult to link up safely with them. He radioed Carpenter to fire a flare but the jungle canopy was too thick for it to be seen. Brown's men started firing in the air and shouting "strike force"—the 502nd was known as the Strike Force—which resounded through the jungle. Link up was accomplished. As Alpha company entered Charlie's position, the company CO had a feeling of total satisfaction and fulfillment. "Mission Impossible" had been accomplished without the loss of a single one of Brown's men. These feelings were short lived, however, because as the last man, Pfc. John Deisher, was entering the perimeter he was hit in the back by a heavy volley of gunfire from some NVA soldiers who had followed them. Without even thinking, Brown ran thirty yards down the hill to Deisher and dragged his body into the perimeter. Brown was absolutely deflated: in his mind total success had turned to total failure.

COMBAT LEADERSHIP LESSON #4:

• **CIRCUMSTANCE:** The elation of complete success of an extremely difficult mission was devastated at the very last moment by the death of one of Ron's men. The emotional bonds that develop between warriors, especially between leaders and their men, in life-and-death combat are like no other. There is no way to describe the depth of this feeling without personally experiencing it in combat.

• **LESSON:** A leader must be emotionally prepared to accept the loss of his men. Because he felt so close to his men and considered his most important duty as a leader was to keep them alive, the most difficult aspect of being a company commander for Ron Brown was living with their deaths in combat.

• **SOLUTION:** As Ron cradled Deisher's body feeling the man's blood run down his arms, he had to go beyond his personal, human strength and revert to his spiritual, religious strength in order to ask God to strengthen him. He assembled his men around Deisher's body and used his death to inspire and build up emotions against the enemy who had killed him. Ron knew his men were going to need every possible inspiration to survive this difficult situation in the coming days, and he had to use every means possible to provide it to them.

Arrival at Carpenter's Position

Arriving at Charlie Company's position was an emotional, roller-coaster high because of hope on their faces, and an emotional low because the smell of burnt flesh permeating the entire area. Carpenter, although the senior of the two commanders, put Brown in charge of the perimeter because he had more men. Carpenter's company had been at full strength with 168 men, but had suffered 41 casualties, 26 alone from the earlier aerial napalm strike. The next four hours were spent reinforcing and digging in the position. By now, Brown had been almost forty hours without sleep, but was too busy even to think about resting.

The next two days were dominated by fighting off repeated probes and attacks by the NVA. Over the next thirty hours Captain Brown continuously exposed himself to enemy fire while carry ammunition, calling in air strikes, and adjusting artillery fire. The position on the ridge proved to be an almost fortress-like position for the defenders. However, the longer they were there the weaker the wounded and napalm-burned troopers were becoming; many were beginning to go into shock. Brown admired the medics because they were the bravest, most dedicated and unselfish soldiers that he had ever known. They performed unbelievable acts to help and keep the wounded troopers alive in every combat situation. His admiration for the burned and wounded troopers is indescribable because throughout their enduring pain and suffering they never complained, inspiring the rest of the men. Brown realized that they couldn't hold out much longer. Emerson had informed him that he had assembled additional reinforcements and they would move towards the surrounded troopers. Twenty stretchers had been dropped by helicopter, but there were twenty-six litter cases that needed to be evacuated. Following the policy that they would never leave any of their comrades behind, dead or alive, Brown made plans to reach an evacuation point a thousand yards away carrying the dead as well as the wounded.

The troopers waited until the torrential rain started up again to move out. Although this would make moving the litters and the six other wounded men who were being back-carried much more difficult, Brown hoped the NVA would think that no one in their right mind would try to move wounded under such severe conditions. The hilly terrain was so difficult and slippery that the troopers had to use their entrenching tools (small fold-up shovels that were part of the soldiers' basic gear) to dig footholds for the litter bearers. Ron Brown still swells with pride and admiration today as he remembers those brave, courageous, never give-up, exhausted men carrying their fellow wounded and dead troopers. Often a litter bearer would just collapse from sheer exhaustion, but another soldier would immediately take his place. Only when they had cleared the final ridge before the evacuation point and started moving across the grassy plain did the NVA realize what had occurred. They attacked the rear of the column but did not have enough force to overrun it. Brown ran to the rear to direct the effort to fight off the attack and was totally amazed that, after stopping the enemy in their tracks, his troopers were now chomping at the bit to counterattack the NVA. (Revenge is a first-class motivator.) During that part of the action Brown was wounded by grenade shrapnel, but still was able to order the charge that overran the enemy position.

Back into the Fight

After the Alpha-Charlie company column reached the reinforcements from their battalion, and their dead and wounded were evacuated, Brown sat down on a log and began picking grenade fragments out of his arm. He was now exhausted; all he could think of was food, a shower, and sleep. Now, after all he had been through Ron suddenly realized it was his twenty-sixth birthday. Bringing the wounded and unwounded men from both companies back alive was his greatest birthday gift ever. Colonel Emerson walked up and told him that Charlie Company was being moved to the rear to get replacements and that Brown's company was going to be airlifted back to the same mountainous area the next morning to follow up on a B-52 bombing strike on the NVA regiment.

COMBAT LEADERSHIP LESSON #5:

• **CIRCUMSTANCE:** After successfully accomplishing their missions above and beyond the call of duty and enduring indescribable and exhausting hardships, Alpha Company was now being sent back into combat while Charlie Company was being moved to the rear.

• **LESSON:** Life in combat is not fair; orders are orders. The higher headquarters that make decisions often know little about the condition or morale of subordinate units. The maneuver companies are pins on a map, but the combat leader must accept this and make the best of the circumstances. Hopefully, should he become a senior commander or staff officer he will remember this lesson.

• **SOLUTION:** Captain Brown assembled the company and once again gave an academy-award performance. First, he congratulated them on their outstanding accomplishments. With a big smile on his face, he told them that now it was their turn to have some combat *fun*. He informed them that he had demanded (a total fabrication) that the Gunfighter give Alpha Company the mission of going back to mop up after the massive B-52 raid that was planned on the NVA.

Ron played the "getting our revenge card" to the max, hard selling it to his men.

❖ ❖ ❖

Sitting in the lead helicopter the next morning and feeling the vibrations from the s 2,000 lb.-bomb explosions funneling down the valley, Brown looked at the faces of his men, which said to him, "Now our fun has begun." Bomb craters were used as their LZs and when Brown jumped off the Huey into a bomb crater, his hands were burned by the still steaming ground. NVA soldiers who had not been blown to kingdom come by the massive bombs were staggering around stupefied from the shock waves. Alpha Company killed them like flies. Although many NVA soldiers were still alive, the B-52 raid had left many of them dazed. For the next five days Brown's men annihilated the remnants of the NVA regiment As the days passed the stench from decaying bodies became so strong and pungent that the troopers became nauseated. For Brown's men it was a glorious five days of mopping up and pursuit. In this case, revenge was absolutely wonderful!

Aftermath
For his actions in this battle Captain Ron Brown received the Distinguished Service Cross (DSC). In part the citation reads:

> During the assault, Captain Brown charged a [machine gun] emplacement and personally killed three Viet Cong . . . one trooper fell seriously wounded. Captain Brown immediately raced 30 meters down the slope to the wounded trooper and carried him to safety . . . Despite the fact that he was wounded by a grenade explosion, Captain Brown ordered a charge that overran the insurgent position."

In 1968, shortly before Ron Brown resigned from the army, he was invited to dinner at the Fort Belvoir, Virginia, quarters of Lt. Gen. Harry W. O. Kinnard Jr., who at the time was head of Combat Development Command. Kinnard had a noted military historian as a house guest: retired army Brig. Gen. S. L. A. Marshall, the author of *Battles in the Monsoon*, a history of campaigns in Vietnam's Central Highlands in the summer of 1966, and many other books on World War II, Korea, and Vietnam. Brown and Marshall had become good friends since the battle in the Toumorong. Marshall handed Kinnard a copy of Brown's DSC citation and Kinnard wrote across

General Creighton
Abrams presenting
Distinguished
Service Cross to
Capt. Ron Brown
for his heroic action
at the Battle of the
Toumorong in
June 1966.

it, "Should have been Medal of Honor." It probably would have been had
Brown been killed in one of his innumerable exposures to enemy fire.)

❖ ❖ ❖

Ron Brown eventually received a PhD in business administration from the
University of California. Later, after holding numerous senior executive positions, Doctor Brown retired as the executive vice president and managing
consultant of the DBM company.

Parting words from Ron Brown:

> I end this story with an absolute thankfulness and gratitude in
> my heart that I had the distinct pleasure and privilege to lead out-
> standing fellow Americans in combat. To me there is no honor or
> responsibility higher than having men follow you in life-and-death
> combat. I studied "Leadership" in my curriculum at West Point
> where leadership was defined as the art of influencing human behav-
> ior. However, I later read a better definition of combat leadership

which I said to myself every day in combat before starting a mission: "Every American soldier is willing to shed his last drop of blood for his country. It's getting him to shed the first drop that requires leadership."

My hope and prayer is that my leadership made my men willing to shed that first drop, but my real leadership made them not to have to shed it. God bless you all real good.

In January 1967, during convalescence from his wounds Captain Brown was reassigned to General Westmoreland's staff at MACV headquarters while his classmate Marshall Carter was in heavy action as a marine in I Corps.

CHAPTER 6

Take the High Risk, High Reward Route

CAPTAIN MARSHALL N. CARTER, USMC
(1ST MARINE DIVISION 1966–1967)

HOW IS IT POSSIBLE to vanquish the enemy except by a blow over the head? And for this it is necessary to attack him, to spring upon him. This was known to army leaders in biblical times.
—Leon Trotsky, 1922, *Military Writings*, 1969

MARINE AREA OF OPERATIONS

U.S. Marines were deeply involved in Vietnam from the earliest days of deploying ground combat units. Marine battalions landed in Da Nang in what was known as the I Corps region of South Vietnam (the group of five provinces farthest north and closest to the DMZ) in March 1965, and marines continued to carry the bulk of the load in fierce fighting there for the next several years. A source of some controversy (but also some learning) was that senior marine leaders on the ground favored using small marine units formed as what were called combined action platoons to work with South Vietnamese in and around the villages, an early approach to pacification. General Westmoreland was thus continually pushing the marines to conduct more search and destroy operations in furtherance of his preference for a war of attrition, a dispute that was never really resolved despite Westmoreland's nominal command authority over the marines.

The Family Business

The U.S. Army, West Point, and Virginia Military Institute (VMI) were all part of the "family business" for Marshall Carter. His grandfather, Brig. Gen. Clifton C. Carter, graduated from West Point in the class of 1899 and served as a professor at West Point for twenty-five years. The family tradition at VMI was also carried by the mother's side of Marsh's family. His father was a distinguished army general who graduated from West Point in 1931. Marsh says he had to be *sent* to West Point by his parents, as his first choice had been to become a geophysical engineer and attend the Colorado School of Mines. Backed by substantial family tradition and influence he entered the Military Academy and graduated in 1962 the same year his father Marshall S. Carter, who by then was a three-star general, was appointed deputy director of the Central Intelligence Agency. Later, from 1965 to 1969 his father served the United States as director of the National Security Agency. With such deep army roots, you would have expected Marsh to be a *natural* as an officer with a successful army career following his graduation from West Point. Showing a decided degree of early independence he chose not to enter the *family business*. Instead he chose to be commissioned in the Marine Corps so he could escape one of the family traditions.

Kit Carson Scouts

The Marine Corps combat forces landed in I Corps at Da Nang in March 1965. By September they realized the intelligence value provided by Viet Cong (VC) defectors to whom the South Vietnamese government offered an amnesty through the *Chieu Hoi* (Open Arms) program. Historically, information gained from prisoners, defectors, and disenchanted guerrillas has proven invaluable. (Carter: 31) The Republic of Vietnam's President Ngo Dinh Diem had started the amnesty program in 1963, gaining seventeen thousand defectors in the first year. (Westmoreland: 101) Many *Chieu Hoi* were employed by the American military as what were called Kit Carson Scouts. They wore the same uniforms as the Americans with whom they served and were paid forty-four dollars a month. (Randal)

The marines in I Corps were achieving great success in capitalizing on information provided by the turncoat VC. A major challenge faced by all Americans was determining who were the real bad guys in the villages where by day everyone seemed friendly while at night some would venture out as guerrilla fighters. Kit Carson Scouts were able to identify loyal villagers from the bad actors.

One Kit Carson Scout provided information that led to the January 10, 1967, ambush of an enemy platoon, which resulted in thirteen enemy killed in action (KIA). The real value of the operation was in the papers found on an enemy courier who had been killed in the ambush. The papers indicated that four days later there was to be a meeting of fifty to a hundred enemy leaders at a Buddhist temple in the hamlet of Ban Lanh, five miles southeast of the province capital of Hoi An. (Carter: 32). Ben Lanh was one of more than a hundred hamlets in the hundred square mile area between Hoi An and Da Nang, twenty-five miles to the north. (Randal)

Subsequent to the meeting the group of VC leaders would travel to nearby mountains for explosives training. The marine intelligence officers and chain of command had in their hands a combat leader's dream: the opportunity to annihilate the enemy's leadership in the area. The decision was made to conduct a quick raid into the hamlet at exactly noon, when the meeting was to convene. Captain Marshall Carter's Company C, 1st Battalion, 1st Marines, was assigned the mission for a heliborne raid.

Their mission was to kill or capture the Viet Cong leaders. A major element of the plan recognized that the hamlet was in an area in which there was little governmental influence. It was likely that at least a battalion of main force Viet Cong would provide security for the meeting. It would have to be a quick strike and finish up before dark so the marines would not be risk becoming surrounded after dark. The planning for this operation focused on three factors of marine doctrine: enemy ability to introduce reinforcements, the raiding party's ability to hold off those reinforcements until the raid was completed, and isolation of the battle/attack area by supporting air and fire support. (Carter: 32)

Carter's company of 176 marines could be quickly introduced by helicopters into the target area, but Carter knew his company might be in a firefight for as long as six hours and a reinforcing infantry company had to be ready also to assault into the hamlet either to reinforce the attack or to assist in the extraction of his company. The plan for the operation was made by the lower level commands. Carter was the principal officer involved since he was the commander of the unit that would assault the village.

COMBAT LEADERSHIP LESSON #1: Actual plans must be made by the executing units and not higher echelons that have not been charged with execution of the mission. (Carter: 32)

As they didn't want to arouse suspicion with out of the ordinary flights over the village, Carter and the reinforcing company commander only managed to get a general view of the landing zone and objective area by taking a regularly-scheduled courier run by a helicopter. Due to the small amount of time available before the VC meeting they could not practice in depth rehearsals, but Captain Carter supervised briefings on large-scale maps of the objectives in the hamlet. Each man in Carter's company was individually briefed on the plan of attack and planned backup contingencies. They would wear flak jackets and carry two days of ammunition, and demolition charges, as well. (Carter: 33) Planning for this seemingly uncomplicated operation encompassed all possible support elements including airborne air tactical controllers, aerial observers, helicopter flight leaders, and battalion staff officers.

The appointed day, January 14, arrived and fixed-wing air strikes placed suppressing fire f on the areas occupied by the enemy adjacent to the landing zone to facilitate a clear landing. The fixed-wing were all USMC A-4 Skyhawks and F-4 Phantoms. They were armed with napalm and self-retarding bombs (called "snake eyes"), 500 or 750 pound bombs that could be dropped at as low an altitude as five hundred feet, and attacked in two-plane flights. At noon, as the Company C marines began landing—it would take two waves of six Ch-46 helicopters each to transport the entire company— two Skyhawks used under-wing mounted smoke generators to lay down a heavy smoke screen both to shield the landing zone from possible enemy observers in the nearby mountains as well as to create a diversion: the VC security forces might think it was a chemical agent meant to delay them from heading to the hamlet. Helicopter gunships and fixed-wing aircraft conducted strikes on targets of opportunity during the assault and prevented enemy units from attacking the marines on the flanks.

Carter maintained full and complete operational authority as the ground (assault) commander even though the battalion commander and operations officer hovered just over the objective in a command-and-control helo.

COMBAT LEADERSHIP LESSON #2: In small unit operations tactical decisions should be left to the ground commander and no attempts should be made by commanders or staff officers hovering overhead to impose their decisions on the ground commander.

In the planning, Carter requested eight CH-46 Sea Knight troop helicopters. (The Sea Knight is similar in design to the army's Ch-47 Chinook, but smaller with the Sea Knight measuring about forty-five feet long while the Chinook is just under a hundred feet long. Ch-46s can carry from twelve to fifteen combat-loaded marines). Six of the helos would be used for the initial assault, and return to pick up the marines in the second wave; the other two helicopters would be backups. Captain Carter requested the two extra aircraft because he knew this could be a potentially "hot zone" as marines had operated in this area only sparingly before, the villages were fortified, and it was outside the 1st Marine Division's normal area of operations. He wanted to be prepared for any contingency.

As the first wave approached the landing zone, Captain Carter's helo, which carried half of the company's command team, was struck by heavy caliber machine gun fire, killing one of his marines and severely damaging the aircraft. They barely made it back to the pickup zone where they transferred to one of the two spare helos. Actually, most of the helos took fire. It took Carter, the company commander, twenty minutes or so to get back into action, but the attack had not been delayed since his platoon commanders knew their missions and had proceeded without him.

The 1st Platoon secured the landing zone for the assault platoons, who immediately encountered intense enemy fire and an impassable obstacle of water, a large pond about thirty feet across. It was hidden under bamboo trees and couldn't be seen from above or from aerial photographs. It was not unusual for villages like this to have such a pond. If one of the two attacking platoons was held up by a physical barrier it would reinforce the other platoon. Carter ran over to the water barrier to confirm that it was impassable—there was also barbed wire around it—probably to keep animals . . . and attackers out, so it became necessary for the attacking force to skirt around its edges.

COMBAT LEADERSHIP LESSON #3: Rehearse contingency plans as diligently as the principal plan.

Within an hour the assault platoon was approaching the pagoda, the supposed meeting location. An enemy company began fighting a delaying action to cover the withdrawal of other enemy units, which began to take fire from the orbiting helicopter gunships and fixed-wing aircraft. Within two hours after the marines' initial landing the VC had redeployed and their resistance stiffened with the Americans receiving automatic weapons fire from camouflaged positions. Carter had established his company-level fire support coordination group after the first wave landed at the edge of the landing zone near the village under his operations/gunnery sergeant. The company commander moved between the attacking platoons with only two radio operators, one for the battalion net and one for company net. Company C did not have an executive officer assigned, so the company's gunnery sergeant, Tom Thompson, filled in. Gunnery Sergeant Thompson was a highly experienced Marine Corps veteran who by that time had served sixteen of his eighteen years on active duty in marine infantry companies. At the company command post (CP) Thompson oversaw and directed three 60mm mortar crews, an artillery forward observer, a marine first lieutenant F-4 Phantom pilot assigned as forward air controller for this mission by the air wing, and a 3.5-inch rocket launcher team that used white phosphorus rounds to mark air targets for the air support. (In later wars laser devices have proven much more accurate as wind has a tendency to misdirect the smoke signals.) Before the operation Carter had planned and authorized blanket firing clearance outside the landing zone and hamlet area.

COMBAT LEADERSHIP LESSON #4: Preplan and prearrange all air support and ordnance delivery.

By the three hour mark the assault platoon had reached the pagoda, but not until fighting its way through heavy enemy resistance. At this time Carter was behind the attacking platoon as they reached the center of the village at the Buddhist pagoda. The VC leaders either had never been in the pagoda or had rapidly dispersed and were nowhere to be found. Some were killed as they exited a tunnel or underground bunker near the pond. Throughout the war the enemy made extensive use of underground tunnels. Enemy casualties at this time were twenty-six KIAs. Extraction of Company C from the landing zone was ordered, but was delayed due to the need to recover a dead marine who was on a path that was raked by enemy fire; several marines had already been wounded attempting to retrieve his body.

Company Commander Marshall Carter personally retrieved the dead marine and one other casualty. As Carter was moving from the platoon stopped by the pond to the attacking platoon, he came upon Jack Sutton. Corporal Sutton had been firing a machine gun to provide cover for the attack, but was badly wounded and could not move his legs. Carter carried him to a safe area where Sutton died a few minutes later. The other KIA marine, Cpl. Jim Cannington, had been shot and his body was lying on a narrow trail that was covered by enemy machine gun fire, which prevented his platoon from retrieving his body. It was not known at that time that Cannington was already dead; rather it was believed that he was only badly wounded. Carter realized that if Cannington was not brought back the whole movement back to the landing zone would stall, so he decided to do it himself and crawled out under the fire and pulled Cannington's body back. He then acquired a dozen or so grenades from other marines,(since he only carried two himself, to throw to create a diversion so the platoon could move to be extracted by the helicopters.

COMBAT LEADERSHIP LESSON #5: The leader must be prepared to take charge and personally accomplish any action that maintains mission momentum.

Corporals Cannington and Sutton, who were killed leading their men, had both been squad leaders. Three other squad leaders and a platoon commander were seriously wounded in action. The night before the raid one of the elements of contingency planning was leadership succession. Therefore, in all these instances the next senior marine in the squads or the platoon took charge.

COMBAT LEADERSHIP LESSON #6: Plan for subordinate leadership succession in the event of casualties.

The company's navy corpsmen were kept busy tending to the wounded, but amazingly enough none were wounded themselves. (Marine infantry companies had between twelve and sixteen corpsmen on their muster roll.) The enemy firing had been so intense they could not evacuate their casualties until the end of the afternoon so most of the causalities were removed only when the company was lifted out at the end of the day in the first wave of returning Sea Knights. The operation was not delayed for a medevac. A medevac did save a fixed-wing pilot who was hit by heavy machine-gun fire and had to eject just after his bomb run, but the medevac helicopter followed him down in his chute and picked him up right away with covering fire provided by the nearby helicopter gunships. The enemy was so well-hidden that one marine reported, "They were so well-camouflaged I never saw a Viet Cong in six hours." (Randal)

The assault platoons eventually fought their way back to where the helicopters would pull them out and were extracted under hot LZ conditions with the enemy quickly surrounding the withdrawing marines. Air and gunship strikes delivered heavy support for the extraction. As the company's senior leader Captain Carter left on the final helo after popping a flare to mark his position. (The flare reminded him of another extraction before Vietnam when he had been in a reconnaissance unit that operated off submarines, mine sweepers, and rubber boats. Each team member taped a day-night flare, red smoke for day use and red flare for night use, to their K-bar knives.) All of Company C except for about six men, including Captain Carter, had been extracted and a final helicopter was on the way. The pilot and crew could not locate Carter and his men as it was almost 1800 and getting dark. The final CH-46 was circling and searching about a thousand meters away. Carter popped the night side of the flare and they were spotted.

Captain Marshall Carter (USMC) examining captured North Vietnamese Army weapons in I Corps, 1967.

Confirmed enemy body count for the assault company was sixty-one KIA and an estimated seventy-five additional VC KIAs from air strikes. Carter's company suffered five killed and twenty-one wounded. One enemy cadre member, a woman, was captured. She was not interrogated at the village, but was turned over to the intelligence people at the end of the mission. She had grabbed a baby when the landing into the village occurred because the VC knew that a mother carrying a baby wouldn't be bothered by the

Americans. Her cover was busted, however, because she wasn't wearing native village clothing—black pajamas and conical hat—but instead was dressed like a city dweller; it turned out she was from Saigon.

Radio intercepts a few days later indicated that, once the VC saw that only two waves of helicopters had invaded their area, they immediately dispatched battalion and regimental size units to counterattack. One of the reasons only a one company raid rather than an all out assault operation was planned was because the Americans knew the enemy had regimental-size reinforcements in the mountains, two to three hours from the area. This meant an enemy force of massive size could be on the scene very quickly. At about 1700, when the operation was finishing up and Company C was trying to disengage and move back to the extraction site, it was clear that the enemy in the village had been reinforced and the marines were heavily outnumbered. Unless a massive infusion of combat troops was contemplated, which was not the case, it always had to be a quick, small-unit raid with limited tactical objectives.

Aftermath

As is normal for Americans, the marines always recovered their KIAs, and many battalions conducted memorial services in Vietnam, but due to the tempo of the battalion's ongoing operations a memorial service was not held for the Company C KIAs. The next morning Carter went to a press briefing in Da Nang and the company immediately returned into the field under the command of one of his lieutenants who wasn't wounded. Carter's company was constantly on operations and once went ninety-eight days without a hot meal: just C-rations. Gunnery Sergeant Thompson later died from lung cancer possibly caused by Agent Orange defoliant exposure.

This operation was conducted very near to a Vietnamese town named Hoi An which a 1997 guide book described as "Perhaps the most unique town in Vietnam . . . Unscathed by the Vietnam War . . . Narrow streets flanked by buildings that have remained virtually unchanged for 200 years . . . a beautiful ancient Vietnamese town . . . that will seem to you like a time machine. . . . Hoi An was probably inhabited as early as 2,000 years or more ago, and also has the distinction of being, by most accounts, the first place in Vietnam where Christianity was introduced. . . . There are more than a whopping 840 structures in Hoi An that have been deemed as historical structures." (Dulles: 391–393) Before, during and after the war the inhabitants went on with their simple lives.

In retrospect, it was known the area was seriously hot, but the marines had not expected to run into battalion size units. At the time in this mountainous area in I Corps, however, Marine units had to expect major enemy units to be operating. After all was said and done, the Hoi An operation proved that a combined air-ground team could insert units into the heart of enemy country and with supporting arms and air support operate effectively and successfully.

When the company landed, about sixty to seventy-five people fled the village in the opposite direction; they were probably the high level cadre. Many of them, however, were struck by air and helicopter gunship fire, so in conclusion, although no one but the woman was captured, much of the enemy leadership was believed to have been eliminated.

Captain Carter was wounded later in the spring of 1967 and received a Purple Heart. For his valorous action in this raid he was awarded the Navy Cross, our country's second highest combat decoration. (The army and air force equivalent is the Distinguished Service Cross.) In part, the citation reads: "During the withdrawal to the landing zone for reembarkation, one platoon was pinned down by rapidly increasing Viet Cong forces. Appreciating the significance of a delay on the success of the operation, Captain Carter moved immediately to the point of crisis. Efforts to evacuate the body of a fallen comrade under intense enemy fire prevented the platoon from being withdrawn. With complete disregard for his own safety, Captain Carter exposed himself to the heavy volume of enemy fire by crawling forward and bringing the fallen Marine to a point where he could be further evacuated. Captain Carter then covered the withdrawal of the platoon to the reembarkation site by single-handedly hurling grenades at the enemy in close combat." Dedicated combat leaders who place the safety of their men before their own are signally represented by Marshall Carter.

After fourteen years on active duty Carter entered the private sector, but remained in the Marine Corps Reserves. He never became a geophysical engineer, but had a very successful career in banking and investments. For nine years he served as chairman and CEO of State Street Bank in Boston, a Fortune 500 company, and in 2011 was Chairman, New York Stock Exchange Group.

❖ ❖ ❖

Meanwhile there was an air war that was fought every day north of I Corps along the coast and installations of enemy North Vietnam.

CHAPTER 7

The Air War and Incredible Rescues

LIEUTENANT ROBERT "BREV" MOORE, USN
(MARCH 17, 1967)

CAPTAIN JOHN A. CORDER, USAF
(FEB. 8, 1968)

The advent of air power, which can go straight to the vital centers and either neutralize or destroy them, has put a completely new complexion on the old system of making war. —Brigadier General William "Billy" Mitchell, Skyways: A Book on Modern Aeronautics, *1930*

THE AIR WAR

All services—U.S. Army, Air Force, Navy, and Marine Corps—made highly significant contributions to conduct of the air war in all its modes and manifestations, from counter-guerrilla and counterinsurgency operations to full-scale conventional combat. B-52 Stratofortress bombers had multiple roles, from interdicting traffic on the Ho Chi Minh Trail to close-in support of tactical operations at such places as Khe Sanh during Tet 1968 and An Loc in the Easter Offensive to strategic bombing of Hanoi. Interrogation of enemy prisoners established the B-52 as the weapon system they feared most. Tactical fighter aircraft—operating from ground bases in or adjacent to South Vietnam or from aircraft carriers in the South China Sea—were also an essential component of almost every battle, providing vital close air support to engaged units on the ground. Meanwhile the helicopter, newly introduced to the battlefield on a grand scale during this conflict, was both omnipresent and extraordinarily versatile. Gunships, command and control ships, logistical ships, troop carriers, and heavy lift aircraft were indispensable in giving ground forces, and air assault units in particular, the battlefield mobility that made them so effective and in sustaining them once they were deployed and on the ground.

Soldiers and marines, though, both of U.S. forces and the South Vietnamese, admired above all others the inspiring courage and devotion of Dustoff pilots and crews manning the medical evacuation ships that so often made the difference between life and death for wounded warriors.

Destiny: Naval Aviation for Lieutenant "Brev" Moore

Moore was destined for a career flying off the deck of aircraft carriers as a naval aviator. Graduating in 1963, he was the second generation of Naval Academy graduates to become a naval aviator. His father (USNA '32) became a rear admiral and originally flew catapult-launched observation aircraft off battleships. His maternal grandfather, also a naval aviator, commanded the World War II aircraft carrier USS *Franklin*, which was badly damaged off the coast of Japan toward the end of the war. Two uncles were naval aviators. It ran in the family. By 1956, following an eight-day visit to a jeep carrier commanded by his father, there was probably no turning back for Robert.

Navy Lt. Brev Moore standing beside an A-1 "Spad" Skyraider on the aircraft carrier USS *Kitty Hawk* before a mission in 1966.

Destination: Yankee Station off North Vietnam in the Gulf of Tonkin
Moore trained to fly the A-1 Skyraider propeller-driven attack aircraft and
in late 1965 he steamed to the waters off Vietnam on the USS *Kitty Hawk*
for his first six month deployment to Southeast Asia. During this tour he
conducted attack missions in both South and North Vietnam, Laos, especially along the Ho Chi Minh Trail, and supported ground operations for
army and marine units.

On his second tour in the war he flew off the USS *Hancock*, an old Essex-
class carrier built for World War II. Prior to March 16, 1967, on his second
six-month deployment, he had flown a total of approximately 150 combat
missions. Most of his fellow pilots in the squadron were also experienced
attack aviators from the previous *Kitty Hawk* cruise.

Into the Shadow of Death in the Deep
Lieutenant Moore was an aviator in the attack aircraft squadron VA 115,
nicknamed the Arabs, flying the A1H/J Skyraider aircraft. On March 16,
1967, he was part of a four plane flight off the USS *Hancock* (CVA-19) supporting destroyer shelling of targets along the coast of North Vietnam. Immediately after takeoff the flight split into two sections: the squadron Skipper,
Hank Bailey, and his wingman, Gene Goeden, flew off to meet a destroyer
farther north while Moore and his wingman, Lt. Comdr. Arnie Henderson,
flew south to meet their assigned destroyer.

After checking in with the destroyer and circling overhead for almost
two hours, spotting gunfire from the destroyer, it was time to return to their
carrier. The destroyer had been unable to hit the logistics craft berthed at
Dong Hoi so Moore led his two-plane section in an aerial attack to complete
the mission. Upon descending below the cloud cover, Moore and his wingman, Lieutenant Commander Henderson, were immediately overwhelmed
with antiaircraft fire. Moore banked hard left to escape the AA fire and
headed to safety over water. On the way out, however, he was hit with multiple 12.7mm machine-gunfire. Smoke filled his cockpit and he considered
bailing out, but he was too low. As he quickly reviewed his options, the smoke
cleared and miraculously his engine kept working! However, all of his radios
and major instruments were out of action, which would make it difficult for
him to return to the *Hancock*. Circling near the destroyer, Lieutenant Moore
waited for his wingman to come up beside him, but he waited in vain. It had
become quite dark by this time and he decided to take a dead reckoning back
to his carrier, which he knew to be fifty-five miles northeast.

The radar on the *Hancock* didn't pick him up, and having been flying for five to six hours, he knew his fuel level was becoming dangerously low. At this time he had no idea of his location so he prepared to ditch. The moon was fairly full which helped him prepare for what he planned to be a controlled crash into the ocean. Moore "blew open" his canopy to prevent it from closing upon impact and began to slow down his airspeed for descent and turned into the wind. He placed his landing gear handle UP and flaps handle DOWN. In the darkness and with the indicators out of operation he couldn't tell whether his gear and flaps were actually up or down. Moore doesn't recall seeing the flaps go down at all. He had seen a squadron mate ditch alongside his ship with his plane floating for some amount of time so he thought he would have some time during that float-period to deploy his life raft and settle himself into the water. The water would be 86 degrees, bathtub temperature, so he wasn't concerned about hypothermia. Thoughts of his Dilbert Dunker training flashed across his mind as he kept descending, two thousand feet, fifteen hundred, one thousand.

He was wearing an air force LPU (life preserver unit) that he had acquired so he wouldn't have to wear the navy-issued World War II Mae West life preserver, which was heavier and rubbed his neck. The air force life preserver was designed to be like having a water wing under each armpit. Moore's life raft was packed with his parachute, which was stored in the seat pan upon which he sat. He had been told it was going to float so he assumed there would not be a problem with it. Passing through five hundred feet above the ocean, into the wind, at good 90-knot airspeed, he checked that his shoulder harness and seatbelt were locked and then . . . splashdown! He was immediately inundated by water as the aircraft began to sink; there was no float-period for Lieutenant Moore this night. He unhooked his seatbelt and shoulder harness and reached up for his canopy crossbar to pull himself from his plane into the deep and dark water of the Tonkin Gulf.

Naturally, his first instinct was to inflate his life preserver. Between his life preserver, parachute, flare pistol, and vest packed with survival gear and additional flares, however, his weight made it a struggle to remain above water level just to breathe. His first challenge was to locate the toggles to inflate his LPU. As he felt around with his hands while trying to locate the toggles, he began to sink and then had to "dog paddle" madly to reach the surface again where he gasped for air, and then again reached for the LPU toggles. Still not finding them, he started to wonder if he had forgotten to wear his LPU. Meanwhile, he realized that the life raft, which was hooked up to the parachute, was *not* floating to provide buoyancy and instead was dragging him down into the water. Therefore, he unhooked all except for one of the buckles attaching him to the life raft and parachute and again began to swim vigorously to the surface. By now he was desperate in the realization he was drowning from swallowing so much sea water. He knew he had only one choice to save his life and that was to release the parachute and raft. Taking what he imagined could be his last gasp of air, Moore curled up his body as much as he could and reached around behind himself where he *finally* found his life preserver toggles. (The force of the impact had forced the LPU around his body to his backside.) The brick-shaped water wings inflated, floating him on the surface. This was a major relief!

At last he could take a deep breath and evaluate his situation. The lieutenant watched as his plane slowly sank out of sight nose first. Suddenly, it was very quiet. He was alone in the South China Sea. He swam over to retrieve his flight helmet, which was floating nearby. He had also removed it to help cut down his weight. If only it was his raft. He pulled out his survival radio, turned on the switch, and tried transmitting, but got no response. This was not surprising since it was ten at night and he assumed there would be no search attempted until it was light the next day. Up to his armpits in the water, Moore turned off his radio to await the morning.

By this time he could see the stars quite well and was aware of the extraordinary quietness. Bobbing up and down in the water, he began to think about if and when he would be rescued. The young officer began to think about his fiancée and his family, wondering if he would ever see them again. After a few hours he saw what he thought was a ship's light on the horizon. After waiting a little while he pulled out his pencil flares in case he decided to signal the ship. It seemed very far off and, of course, it could have been an enemy ship. He decided to take the risk and fired off two flares, one after the other. The ship did not appear to be coming any closer and then the "ship's light" washed over his face! All along a small piece of phosphorescent plankton had been in the water a foot or two away from him and his eyes had played tricks on him as he wanted to believe he was seeing a ship.

By this time the water was beginning to feel really cold. The difference between its 86 degrees and his 98 degrees was starting to affect him: Moore's body was having its heat sucked out of it. He was losing more heat than his system could produce, so he crossed his legs to try to conserve as much heat as possible. The decision to abandon his life raft was becoming a significant life-and-death issue. After a while he began to shiver uncontrollably.

Thankfully the swells of the ocean were gentle as he continued to float when, to his surprise, he saw the lights of another ship. He said to himself, "I'm not going to be fooled again." As he continued shivering and bobbing up and down like a cork, however, he decided to risk signaling and fired two more flares. As the lights came closer and closer he knew it was a ship. Whether friend or foe remained to be seen. Moore had expended all his flares and as the vessel came closer and closer he began to wave his helmet, which was covered with reflective tape. The ship's searchlight began to scan the water and to his great relief, he heard instructions blaring from the ship in English. His ordeal was about to be over because his rescue by an American ship was imminent.

The flight helmet's reflection was spotted by the searchlight and a life boat was on its way to pluck him from the water. Although Lieutenant Moore had been in the water for seven hours and was very cold, he managed to walk up a stepladder to the main deck of his rescue ship, the navy oiler USS *Ponchatoula* (AO148), where he was greeted and escorted to the sick bay for observation. The ship's captain, Howard E. Greer, future commander of Naval Air Forces Atlantic, loaned him some clothes and then he rested. Later that morning a helicopter flew him back to his ship. Ever since he has been grateful to St. Patrick as it was March 17th, St. Patrick's Day.

His original four plane flight on March 16, 1967 was certainly ill-fated. All four ditched for one reason or another and Gene Goeden, the skipper's wingman, did not survive. After his rescue, Moore flew another forty missions.

Brev Moore served a total of twenty-four years in the navy before retiring in 1987 and started a second career as a defense contractor. His son, Robert Brevard Moore III, followed in the footsteps of his grandfather and father and also graduated from the Naval Academy, and becoming, of course, a naval aviator.

And the woman he thought about so fervently as he floated in those cold ocean waters, his fiancée: forty-four years ago he and Virginia were married.

Flying High Above the Flat Farms of West Texas

Growing up in the flat lands of West Texas, John Corder would gaze into the sky to watch the planes from Reese Air Force Base flying over his family farm. When he plowed the fields, the sky above beckoned. Following high school, and only nineteen years old, he was accepted into the air force's Aviation Cadet program in 1959. He was one of the last young Americans to become an air force officer through this program. He began his United States Air Force career as a navigator on B-52 crews based at Carswell AFB in Ft. Worth, Texas.

John Corder's First War: the Cold War

During the Cold War American B-52s maintained patrols on the periphery of the Soviet Union and Corder logged over two thousand hours as a navigator. He flew forty-three nuclear patrol missions in Strategic Air Command B-52s skirting Russia as a deterrent to their ICBM threat. Each B-52 round trip lasted twenty six and a half hours.

During the 1962 Cuban Missile Crisis, four of Corder's B-52 nuclear patrol missions skirted the Russian northern coastline by about three hundred miles. These four missions were the closest to Russia ever flown and were visible on Russian radar, but outside the range of their fighter jets. Perhaps these air force bombers on station off the USSR prompted Soviet Union leader Premier Khrushchev to back down on basing his missiles in Cuba.

Having worked in the targeting office of his B-52 wing, Corder had become familiar with and highly-experienced in the penetration of the heavily-defended areas of the USSR. He focused his attention on becoming proficient in radar navigation and bombing, which would serve him in good stead in his second war, which became a very "hot war."

In March 1964, John began pilot training and was eventually assigned as an F-4 Phantom jet fighter pilot at Eglin AFB, Florida. At this time air force tactics relied on "clear weather" flying operations; the pilot needed to be able see and visually attack enemy installations on the ground. Radar was only used to target enemy aircraft.

Corder's Second Air War

In late 1966 six months before the deployment of his fighter squadron (twenty-four F-4s) to the 8th Tactical Fighter Wing at Ubon, Thailand, Corder responded to the urgent need for the air force, and especially his soon-to-be-deployed squadron, to develop an all-weather radar-bombing capability against North Vietnam military targets. His extensive experience as a Cold War B-52 Stratofortress navigator made him more than ready to help the wing develop the ability to use radar targeting. In addition to his ninety-three combat missions over North Vietnam, Corder's B-52 experience in prepared him for the additional duty of radar bombing officer in the 8th Wing's fighter tactics branch. Most of his fellow fighter pilots showed no interest in this new development.

In May 1967, when the wing arrived in Thailand, the weather was good, but Corder began to train his fellow pilots in the use of radar navigation and bombing for times to come when the weather over North Vietnam would not be quite so favorable. By the beginning of 1968, the northeast monsoon season began. This resulted in clouds over North Vietnam frequently extending from three hundred to twenty-five thousand feet. Their targets could not be visually recognized, but pressure for daily bombing missions came down through the chain of command all the way from the top: President Johnson's White House.

North Vietnam's Bombing Capability

By January, 21, 1968, the Marine Corps Combat Base at Khe Sanh, located in the northwest corner of South Vietnam on the Laotian border, was surrounded and cut off by NVA forces. The situation echoed that of the French at Dien Bien Phu in 1954. January 30 marked the beginning of the Tet Offensive, which involved American forces throughout South Vietnam and severely limited their ability to relieve Khe Sanh. Ultimately, the siege would not be over until the summer.

At 1430 hours, February 7, 1968, an aircraft from 7th Air Force Headquarters in Saigon landed at Ubon. The air force major general who was the 7th Air Force director of operations was visiting Ubon to coordinate a special combat mission into North Vietnam that was planned to counter what was seen as an alarming new capability in North Vietnamese offensive aviation.

On February 6 the American air defense system detected an attempted bombing mission by three North Vietnamese bombers on Khe Sanh. Never before had the North's air force demonstrated the ability to conduct bombing raids on the South. Even though the enemy's navigation was atrocious—because the three bombers missed Khe Sanh by twenty miles—the 7th Air Force commanding general was incensed that the NVAF would even dare a bombing mission to the South. He demanded an immediate strike on the bombers, which had returned to the Phuc Yen MiG base just northwest of Hanoi. The enemy bombers were Russian-built IL-28 Beagles that had come into North Vietnam from China. The nationality of their crews was unknown. This new enemy threat was not yet known to the media and the United States was desperately trying to avoid comparisons between besieged marines of Khe Sanh and the French disaster at fourteen years earlier at Dien Bien Phu.

The 8th Tactical Fighter Wing had been chosen to make the response and Corder was one of several in planning meeting with the visiting general from Saigon. The meeting kicked off with a discussion of whether a two-aircraft mission could penetrate the high cloud cover over the North Vietnamese air base by flying at three hundred feet off the ground to destroy the three Beagle bombers at Phuc Yen. The wing was tasked to plan such a mission and present the plan in Saigon later that day. Captain Corder planned the mission and flew out that evening for a 2000 hours meeting in Saigon with the 7th Air Force commanding general who asked Corder what the odds were for the survival of the two F-4s being planned for the mission. Corder replied, "The airfield has over one hundred 37mm gun batteries as air defense and the odds are 100 percent that one F-4 will be shot down on the mission and it may be that neither will survive." John then presented a Plan B as an option to Plan A's probable suicidal results.

Corder had flown previous combat missions targeting airfields, industrial areas, and transportation lines of communications in North Vietnam. His Plan B consisted of three flights of four planes each loaded with cluster bomb units, which would be dropped through the cloud cover to saturate bomb the Phuc Yen Air Base. Support from other aircraft for refueling would be needed and F-105 Wild Weasels would fly ahead of the F-4s to detect and destroy the enemy surface-to-air (SAM) missile sites. Other F-4 combat air patrol aircraft would be provided to counter any enemy MiG fighter activity. Plan B would be quite an operation and every aspect had to be planned in short order because Corder would return immediately from Saigon to lead the strike force now scheduled to take off at half past three on the morning of February 8, 1968.

The strike force was airborne when the advance elements reported that cloud cover rose all the way to twenty-five thousand feet, leaving no "visible room" to maneuver away from enemy SAMs. Corder aborted the mission and everyone returned to Ubon. At 0930 hours, after about one hour of sleep out of the past twenty-four, Captain Corder was awakened and informed that Plan A had been ordered! Corder with one other F-4 was directed to fly to Phuc Yen airfield, penetrate below the 300' cloud cover, and find and destroy the three enemy Beagles. They would enter North Vietnam's air space naked with no other fighter protection.

Captain Corder's plane with its weapons systems officer, Captain Tracey Dorsett, and the other F-4 took off on what could only be defined as a mission for which there was a low percentage of return at all, but off they flew into what was the most heavily-defended area of North Vietnam. Eventually, about fifteen miles from Phuc Yen they were streaking over rice paddies at 600 knots, *thirty feet above the ground*; they would be on target in ninety seconds. It was 1400 hours. In the distance they could see the tracers from eight to ten antiaircraft guns providing close-in defense for the base. It was an incredible barrage coming up at them and into their path.

One minute out from target, Corder's plane was hit! A chunk of the left wing was shot off and the right engine stopped; his airspeed dropped from 600 to 180 knots in only six seconds. Both fire lights came on. They spotted one Beagle, but their air speed was too slow for their cluster bombs to be effective. His wingmen raced past at 600 knots and inadvertently pulled up into the clouds.

Their first instinct was to jettison all outboard weapons and hope to damage the one bomber. Their second instinct, made in a split second, was to jettison only the left outboard weapons in an attempt to have them hit the parked bomber. They made a wide left turning arc to egress the area and continued to receive heavy ground fire which hit his plane again and then he lucked out! They were still over the base and luckily spotted the second Beagle. They jettisoned their remaining weapons, racks and sparrow missiles on the second bomber at 180 knots and 40 feet above the ground, believing they did heavy damage to it. They continued heading for Laos and slowly began climbing to get over the mountains they were approaching. It took an hour to go the approximately 180 miles to get to clear weather in Laos where a rescue might be possible. By this time, he realized there was a hole in the bottom of his cockpit and his foot had been hit by shrapnel, but John does not remember feeling pain from the wound.

The Phantom was met by an emergency tanker, but could not connect due to battle damage and shortly afterwards Captains Corder and Dorsett bailed out. The Jolly Green rescue helicopters were ready to pick them up and Air Force A-1E Skyraiders and more F-4s were in the area to protect them when they hit the ground.

They were rescued, but not before another harrowing experience on the ground. Corder heard obviously enemy voices on two sides of him. Two enemy soldiers approached him with AK-47s, but when they threatened him he shot them both with his .38 caliber pistol. He had to wait one and a half hours more while the A-1Es kept pressure on the enemy in the area to make it safe for the rescue Jolly Green. Eventually a tree penetrator line was lowered and up he went. An official Air Force photographer captured a very

happy and relieved Captain Corder after he was hoisted inside the rescue
helicopter.

Captain John Corder (USAF) photographed immediately after his rescue by
Jolly Green Giant on February 8, 1968. *U.S. Air Force photo*

Aftermath

That was only mission ninety-four for Captain Corder and he flew six more
during the month, completing the one hundred missions that allowed his
return to the United States where he rejoined his wife, three-year-old daughter, and a son born during his combat tour. All four pilots received the Air
Force Cross, which along with the Navy Cross and the army's Distinguished
Service Cross is America's second highest award for valor. Salient points of
his citation read, "Captain Corder led two aircraft against one of the largest,
most important, and most heavily defended airfields in North Vietnam.
Despite inclement weather, Captain Corder descended to extremely low altitude for a visual high-speed run across the airfield. Although faced with a
barrage of withering anti-aircraft artillery fire which severely crippled his
aircraft, Captain Corder resolutely and skillfully pressed his attack against
the target, damaging and destroying several aircraft on the ground. . . . As a
result of his actions, Captain Corder was successful in neutralizing a threat
to Free World forces in Southeast Asia."

Air War Number Three

In 1990 and 1991 now Major General John Corder was the director of air combat operations for Desert Shield/Desert Storm and planned and oversaw two to three thousand air sorties per day during his third war. He retired in 1992 and is currently the president and CEO for CymSTAR, LLC, an aircraft simulator modification and repair company based in Broken Arrow, Oklahoma. He and his wife, Willene, live in North Texas.

The Rest of the Story

Two hours after Captain Corder's attack on the two Beagle bombers he saw at Phuc Yen it was reported that only a single Il-28 hightailed it back to China. Never again during the Vietnam War did North Vietnam dare any bombing attacks on American or Allied ground troops in South Vietnam. Captain John Corder performed a mission impossible!

Meanwhile back in South Vietnam, many miles from the area of air war rescue operations, Spec. Robert Fleming, who was in deep trouble at the Tri-Border areas, was not sure he would ever be rescued.

CHAPTER 8

Surrounded on Three Sides!

SPECIALIST FOURTH CLASS ROBERT FLEMING, USA,
173RD AIRBORNE (HILL 875, 1967)

*War is an ugly thing, but not the ugliest of things. The decayed and
degraded state of moral and patriotic feeling which thinks that nothing is
worth war is much worse. The person who has nothing for which he is
willing to fight, nothing which is more important than his own personal
safety, is a miserable creature and has no chance of being free unless made
and kept so by the exertions of better men than himself.*— John Stuart
Mill

HEAVY U.S. CAUSALITIES
*Many commentators on the Vietnam War have made the assertion that the United
States never lost a battle. While that may be true in the technical or literal sense,
many battles involved heavy fighting and comparably heavy U.S. casualties, leading to speculation as to who really lost or won under such circumstances. As it turned
out, even though in the aggregate allied forces imposed far greater casualties on the
North Vietnamese Army and the Viet Cong than they suffered themselves, the
American people were not tolerant of even those casualty levels among their sons
sent to battle.*

Introduction to War
Quite simply, Robert Fleming enlisted in the army because he believed he
would eventually be drafted anyway. His first duty assignment was at Ft.
Campbell, Kentucky where he was eventually joined his brother Jack, a paratrooper returning from Vietnam. On June 22, 1967, Bob arrived in Vietnam

and was immediately assigned to the 173rd Airborne Brigade, which was based outside Saigon at Bien Hoa. The same day, on Hill 1338 south of the Dak To special forces camp, about 250 miles north of the capital, the brigade's Alpha Company, 2nd Battalion. 503rd Parachute Infantry Regiment, commanded by Lt. Col. Edward A. Partain, was in a horrendous battle. Out of 137 soldiers in the company, 76 men were killed and 23 were wounded. "Of the dead, forty-three suffered fatal, close-range head wounds." (Murphy: 84) This meant the enemy swept through the position and put bullets in the heads of any wounded.

In Country

Alpha Company needed replacements fast and its nickname after the disaster became "No DEROS Alpha."(DEROS, date expected return from overseas, was soldier shorthand for the date he expected to leave Vietnam and return home to the United States.) Bob Fleming was rudely awakened as he and friend Jimmy Camarote were rushed through in processing and a jungle school refresher course. The two young men were then assigned to Alpha Company as replacements and transported to Dak To. When the aircraft's ramp went down in the semi-dark of monsoon rain, both soldiers said the same thing, "We are dead." Robert had never before experienced the darkness and malevolence that seemed to permeate the very air and environment of this Central Highlands outpost.

Bob's company commander was Captain Ken Smith and the first sergeant was Michael Deeb. Patrolling through the jungle constantly gave Fleming a feeling of impending doom. At first he became an M60 machine gunner and then later a platoon radioman, believing this to be a good job because he was able to stay better informed than the other grunts in the platoon. When the battalion added a fourth line company, (D/2/503 PIR) Captain Smith and First Sergeant Deeb moved over as the leaders of Delta Company. Captain Smith picked Fleming to be the company radio operator for the battalion net.

A mission at Tuy Hoa on the South China Sea took the Delta Company Sky Soldiers out of the Central Highlands and lasted through October. (Back in the states this month "saw America's largest anti-war demonstrations, when tens of thousands of demonstrators marched on the Pentagon." (Murphy: 134) The contrast between the sacrifice of America's soldiers in Vietnam, volunteers and draftees alike, and the mood at home, particularly among draft-age students, was becoming increasingly stark.) On November 6 Delta

Company flew back to Dak To making no one happy. With Captain Smith moving on to a new assignment, 1st Lt. Bart O'Leary became the commanding officer (CO). Times were tough at Dak To, but things really started to go downhill November 14 when Bravo Company was hit hard. Fleming's company rushed to support Bravo, but by the time they arrived it was too late. They found bodies of Bravo Company troopers strewn all over the place. Delta Company stayed long enough to clean up the battlefield. The enemy dead were all NVA. One of the dead NVA was on his knees and erect as if he were praying, holding on to a vine with his hands, his face ashen. In front of the enemy soldier was a dead Bravo Company trooper. Beside the right knee of the NVA was a pile of wallets, watches, and other personal effects taken from the dead Americans.

❖ ❖ ❖

Second Battalion's chaplain, Maj. Charles Watters, was often with Fleming's company. "If there was any one man who was universally loved in the 173rd, it was Chaplain Watters . . . he had completed paratrooper training and joined the 173rd in South Vietnam in June 1966."(Murphy: 56) Catholic Chaplain Watters was forty and when he was assigned to Fleming's battalion the chaplain was in an extended second year of service in Vietnam. Bob talked to him several times and respectfully told Watters he should get on a chopper and get out of danger because it was getting worse every day and the chaplain didn't have to be out here with the line companies away from the relative safety of the battalion headquarters. Bob was concerned for Watters's safety and had mixed emotions about it. On one hand he knew Watters was a big help because he would help guys carry mortar baseplates and ammo. On the other hand he could get killed and being a chaplain did not require that he put himself in danger. Watters replied, "I want to stay with you guys."

From June through November 1967 probably the longest continuous fighting of the entire war was conducted from Dak To west to the Triborder area. Since November 12–13 Fleming's battalion, "had been in the field, pursuing the forces that had chewed up its Bravo Company. . . . Not only did they discover a number of enemy corpses . . . but on 17 November the column . . . stumbled upon an abandoned enemy base camp." (Murphy: 254) The camp had housed as many as one thousand NVA and included caves used as medical facilities. Fleming's company was searching the camp when Bob's radio barked. He already knew what battalion was going to say. He had been listening when the special forces Mike Force out of Dak To made contact on the south slope of Hill 875. He did not know exactly where Hill 875 was located, but he knew it was close since he could hear gunfire not very far away. Specialist Fleming was right. Delta Company immediately turned around and walked back up the hill they had just come down. The NVA had been thoughtful enough to provide them with steps and railings. When they reached the hilltop they found a ridgeline that would take them directly to the northern end of Hill 875. While en route he spotted a group of pith-helmeted NVA troops running thru an open area, but in a flash they were gone.

In the late afternoon of November 18, Alpha, Charlie and Delta Companies were at the northern end of 875 on a small circular knob that had a large bomb crater between it and Hill 875 proper. The enemy let the companies dig in and spend the night without incident. To this day, everyone who was there finds this remarkable.

On Sunday, November 19 the Sky Soldiers awoke to a beautiful morning, expecting to be attacked. They knew that the enemy was nearby and in strength. But again, nothing. While the hill was being prepped by air and artillery fire, Father Watters conducted Mass for Catholics and other interested soldiers next to the D Company command post. Quite a few guys attended. Others cleaned weapons, getting ready for the assault up Hill 875 that was coming. While he monitored the battalion net, Fleming wondered what the day would bring. He had been in country almost five months, but remembers thinking that if he could have magically gone home before the walk up that hill, it would be a fine thing.

The troopers started up the hill. Delta Company was leading on the left column. Charlie Company, commanded by Capt. Harold Kaufman, leading the right column. Alpha Company, commanded by Capt. Michael Kiley, was split and trailed at the rear of both columns. Delta Company's CP (command post) was in its normal position between the lead platoon and whatever platoon was scheduled to be second that day. Every day the lead platoon changed. They had been advancing for what seemed to be only minutes when Bob heard several bursts of automatic weapons fire. Their lead platoon was in contact. The CP moved up to the sound of the fire and at some point put down their packs and disconnected the radios from the rucks. Fleming and others then moved up close to the bunker from which the NVA firing was coming.

Battalion had already been notified of the contact and artillery fire was being called in by forward observer (FO) Sgt. Randall Tenney. The 173rd men were on a narrow ridge covered by very tall trees. The NVA were dug in and the U.S. companies were not. There was no way to maneuver except straight into the enemy bunkers or to retreat back down the hill. One of the men in the lead platoon was standing up in front of the bunker, obviously wounded. He was wobbling, but would not go down. Specialist Richard Kimball dropped his equipment and ran to get him. A burst of machine-gun fire killed Kimball. At one point Father Watters went out and grabbed the trooper, threw him over his shoulder, and brought him back into the perimeter. Fleming said it was hard remembering the sequence. The American artillery fire was getting close; the NVA were firing machine guns, rockets, and mortars. The NVA mortar fire had to have been preregistered; it was too accurate not to have been. Helicopters were called in and then shot up by the NVA when they arrived.

After pinning down the lead elements of the 2nd Battalion attack, the NVA launched an assault down the side of the hill where Alpha Company was attempting to cut a landing zone. The NVA were trying to cut the companies apart from each other. The gunfire at the rear was as bad as at the forward point of contact. Delta's CP was behind a fallen log and Bob heard a large explosion behind him. Then he felt a sensation like a cold spoon was being placed on his lower back. It was the strangest sensation. He shivered for half a second and twisted to look on his lower back. Bob started to say, "Hey, I think I'm hit." By the time "hit" left his mouth he *knew* he was hit. He looked behind himself and watched a stream of blood spurt straight up about a foot from his rear and then fall back down. The FO, Randall Tenney, started yelling "check fire" into the radio. Fleming knows the time: it was exactly 1117 hours.(He read it later from a radio log.) Sergeant Tenney took his knife and cut Fleming's trousers completely off. While he was tanned from the waist up from hours of filling sand bags with his shirt off, Bob was pale white from the waist down. The shrapnel was so hot it cauterized the wound and stopped the bleeding. Everything on the battlefield was green, brown and earth shades, and here Bob was this pasty-white target. That's all he could think about. "Was I so visible that the NVA could see me?" Shortly thereafter Charlie company's CO, Captain Kaufman, called for the units to disengage and move back. The enemy fire had been so intense that to stand up was to die. During the afternoon, "1st Sgt. Michael Deeb finally identified the bunker from which the shots came that had killed Jacobson (the company point man) . . . to their surprise rifle fire now struck them down from the rear, pinning them down. Unknown to the paratroopers, tunnels connected many of the enemy positions. Bunkers they thought were destroyed suddenly came alive with new fire. Some sky soldiers were being fired on from three directions." (Murphy: 263)

The rear of Alpha Company had been overwhelmingly attacked causing them to move up the hill to join with Charlie and Delta. Everyone knew they were in deep trouble. The Charlie and Delta company CPs were grouped together about a hundred feet back from the first bunker, near a huge tree. Alpha's CO, Captain Kiley, had been killed at the rear when the NVA swept thru their position. Private First Class Carlos Lozada, whom Bob knew when he had been in Alpha Company, stopped the NVA attack for which he later received the Medal of Honor. Alpha had dozens of wounded. Their medical supplies and water were running low. The wounded were brought in near the CP. All day long the shooting continued. Supporting air and artillery continued. Aerial support had been flying east-to-west passes across the top of the hill.

That same horrifying day, at 1858 hours as it started to get dark, a Marine Corps fighter-bomber flew a north to south pass centered on the ridge and dropped two bombs. One of them tree-burst almost directly above the command post where the Charlie and Delta Company command sections were located along with most of the wounded.

Fleming was sitting down in a shallow hole. He had told Private First Class Ellerbrook to get out of the hole and replace Bob on the radio because Ellerbrook was winded and not digging fast enough. Fleming felt the first nanosecond of the blast as the flame wrapped around his face. Then nothing. The bomb killed forty-two and wounded forty-five of the Sky Soldiers.

When Bob began to regain consciousness he had no idea how long he had been out. His eardrums were ruptured. His first sensations were of being burned. His shirt was smoldering and his bare legs had burning debris falling onto them. He was still so stunned that he could not move. So he just sat there feeling excruciating pain. As badly as he wanted to, he couldn't move. He was choking from breathing the hot ash in the air. As he came to he felt more and more pain. His ribs felt like they had been kicked in. Blood ran into his eyes from the top of his head. His nose, ears, and mouth were bleeding. He was deaf except for a high-pitched squeal in his ears. Time seemed suspended before he could find the strength to move again. He didn't know what his actual condition was following this, his second wounding of the day.

After what seemed like forever Bob finally was able to move a little. Eventually he wanted to stand up; why, he didn't know . . . he had no idea what had happened. All he knew was he was in extreme pain. As he struggled to stand, he fell down several times before finally standing up. He looked through his blood-filled eyes and saw flames everywhere. Equipment was burning and the CP was lit up as well. He was standing there shaking so much that a feather in the wind could have knocked him over.

Bob was totally confused. The light from the burning equipment and other fires disturbed him and he started to yell: "Put out the fires, they can see us. We are backlit, someone on the perimeter help put out the fires." Now if you had asked him who *they* were he probably couldn't have told you. Charlie Company's CO Captain Harold Kaufman and his command section had been at the six o'clock position at the big tree. They were now all dead. There were bodies and parts everywhere.

Fleming climbed out of the hole and was immediately grabbed around his bare ankle by an attached engineer, who had been near his shallow hole receiving an IV administered by Sergeant Tenney. Now the engineer was completely missing one leg. His second leg was almost completely off and one arm was missing. The engineer was screaming for help. Fleming knew that he couldn't do very much and asked him to let him go so that he could at least find some bandages. The engineer wouldn't let go. It took both of Fleming's hands to pry the one hand off his leg. Fleming is still bothered that he still could not do anything for him. Now he knows the true meaning of *death grip*.

Next Jesse Sanchez was screaming for someone to get a tree off him. Sanchez was Sergeant Tenney's radio operator and was about four or five feet from the hole Fleming had been digging. Sitting next to him had been Father Watters. When Bob got to Sanchez he was lying on his back with a tree across his mid section that was about a foot in diameter and more than ten feet long. Fleming tried lifting the tree. Jesse was getting upset at his lack of progress so Fleming finally got down on his knees and dug dirt out with his bare hands from underneath his trapped comrade.

This was virgin jungle topsoil so Bob was able to make a hole that Jesse could drop into. Then Fleming slid him out. The tree had crushed him and apparently Jesse was bleeding badly internally; there was nothing Fleming could do to help him. Bob held the dying soldier as he bled out. Jesse Sanchez was the nicest guy he knew in Vietnam. He was one of those rare people that you would have to lie to say something bad about. Sanchez and Father Watters were close. Bob always thought that Jesse might have gone on to become a priest after Vietnam. Father Watters lay in pieces next to Sanchez. "The bomb landed almost beside the valiant priest, killing him instantly." (Murphy: 279)

"To those who saw him that day, Father Watters was an inspiring example of coolness under fire. Totally oblivious to the hail of enemy fire, he moved across the battlefield, tending the torn and mangled bodies, giving last rites to the dying. Time after time he advanced to the firing line, pulling the wounded to safety, carrying them to the aid station, and recovering the dead." (Murphy: 271) And now this sainted man of God was also dead. The Medal of Honor was posthumously presented to Chaplain Watters for his valor on Hill 875.

By now the fires were out. People from the perimeter were at the command post helping out, trying to get back in communication with higher headquarters. Everyone still alive at the CP had to scream at each other to be heard. Fleming found Sergeant Tenney, who was wounded badly and got him into a hole. Tenney made Bob get into it, too, and told him not to let him fall asleep. Yeah right; that's all Fleming wanted to do. Fleming's bell had been rung but good. Every part of his body screamed, "Help me." There was no help available, however, and he knew it. That brutal and vicious night of November 19, 1967, was the longest of his life.

The sun came up the next day over a surreal landscape: the body of a dead American was hanging upside down by an ankle in a tree; bodies were piled against the trees in stacks; bodies and body parts were scattered everywhere; there was smoke in the air tainted by the acrid smell of burnt plastic and the sickening odor of human body fluids. The scene etched deeply in Bob Fleming's mind never to depart.

Fleming asked Wambi Cook of Alpha Company where his friend Jimmy Camarote was. "He's dead farther down the hill." Camarote had been right; he wasn't going to make it home alive. You could have hit Fleming with a sledgehammer at that point and he wouldn't have felt it. Jimmy was from Philadelphia and married with two kids.

That day, Monday November 20, the three companies had quit trying to advance because there were so many dead, and most of those left alive were wounded. There were no medics, medical supplies, water, or ammo. Most of the officers and senior NCOs were dead or wounded. They couldn't go forward, couldn't go back, and there was no relief in sight. The survivors were rocketed and mortared by the NVA all day. No choppers got in. Fleming imagined he was developing gangrene in his wounded buttock.

As darkness approached, elements of the 4th Battalion, 503rd PIR, entered the 2nd Battalion perimeter. They came up from the bottom of the hill through the Alpha Company dead. The survivors were a real eye opener for the men of 4th Battalion; the scene would have scared anyone. The 2nd Battalion soldiers hit them up for all the water they had. A 4th Battalion guy gave Fleming a can of C-ration pears. They had been humping through the jungle using artillery as a blocking method to keep from being ambushed. The 4th Battalion essentially took over because they had a command structure that still functioned. Major James R. Steverson, the battalion commander, had not joined his three companies in the assault. He remained high above the action in his command-and-control helicopter. However, most of his headquarters group were with the three companies.

The third day, Tuesday, November 21, it was more of the same: incoming rocket and mortar rounds. There was still no food or water beyond what 4th Battalion had carried with them, and very little medical treatment. The soldiers near the bottom of the hill were trying to carve an LZ out of the triple canopy jungle while constantly dodging incoming enemy mortar fire. Fleming passed in and out of consciousness, awakening to gun or mortar fire, not functioning very well due to dehydration and loss of blood. The gangrene got worse, causing him great concern about how bad his wound could become. He was unaware if any dustoffs (medevac helicopters) were able to land that day. Bob was patient because he knew he had to wait until the more seriously wounded were evacuated; after all, he was still able to walk. The bodies were starting to smell horribly to include his own due to his gangrene.

Wednesday November 22, it was a repeat of the day before. Bob's gangrene was really nasty and he thought that if he did not get out today he might die. At the least he knew that he was looking at a large chunk of his buttock to be removed. He still had function in the leg, but was getting scared. Dustoffs were coming and going . . . under fire, of course. He waited as long as he could before going down to the LZ. Half-naked he climbed up about six feet to get into a medevac chopper that was in a hover pattern, not actually being able to land. He had a poncho liner and wrapped it around himself. The chopper, after being loaded, pulled out under fire from some enemy automatic weapons at the top of the hill. He kept waiting for the helicopter to crash and burn, but it arrived at Dak To safely where an almost full C-130 cargo plane facing east was idling at the end of the airstrip.

When the chopper landed at the western end of Dak To airstrip, Bob climbed out of the chopper and waited for someone to move the wounded trooper who was lying on top of his poncho liner. So Bob stood there wearing nothing but a shirt and a pair of boots while waiting for them to move this badly-wounded soldier. He could have jerked the liner from underneath him, but he was hurt enough, and Bob could wait. He was standing under the helicopter's whirling blade and the sun had just disappeared over the horizon.

While he was waiting he looked around and did not recognize the place. There were hundreds of people at the landing pad. He noticed some big guy walking towards him with a nasty look on his face. By this time Fleming admits he was not playing with a full deck. His lights might have been on, but no one was home. It wasn't what the big guy said. He was wearing shiny silver colonel's eagles on the collars of his clean starched uniform. It was the way, he said it, "Hey soldier, cover yourself up." Normally that would be a reasonable request, if Fleming wasn't covered from head to foot with blood and the blood of a bunch of other people, if he had had more than a canteen of water in four days, or any food, if someone hadn't dropped a bomb on his battalion, if maybe he hadn't been wounded twice. But he had been through all that.

He did what any battle-hardened young paratrooper might do. He told the colonel what to do to himself, along with a mention of his mother. Now, he knew it was wrong, but at the time he was only minutes from being in the middle of the continuing agony that was Hill 875. The colonel was smart. Had he persisted, there would have been a fight. Fleming would have lost physically, but the colonel would have looked real bad kicking the ass of a wounded trooper who looked like Bob did. When he heard what Fleming said, the colonel came to an immediate stop, did an about face and marched off. Bob never heard a word about it. The colonel realized he couldn't court-martial Fleming. Who would have believed it? A minute later he had his poncho liner wrapped around him like a kilt. Ten minutes later he was on the C-130 flying to a hospital in Qui Nhon. He was stuck with tubes everywhere and given fluids by IV and antibiotics for the gangrene. At first the only thing the medical staff examined was his gangrened buttock.

On Thursday, Thanksgiving morning, November 23, Bob found himself lying on a stainless steel operating table, ready to have a large hole cut into him. The black and blue and purple, rotten stinking flesh and shrapnel was removed surgically. He was awake for the procedure. The doctor gave him a spinal so that he wouldn't get sick from general anesthesia, which would let Bob eat some of the Thanksgiving meal. He was able to eat some, but Thanksgiving Day was ruined for him forever. Every year from November 19 to 23, he finds himself still on Hill 875 reliving his experience in what he calls unreal time.

His wound was left open and packed. After the recovery room he was sent back to the ward. There were two wounded NVA prisoners in the ward across from him with a military policeman as their guard. Most of the wounded in this general surgical ward were from the actions at Dak To. Guys were asking the MP to take a walk. He refused. The scared MP knew what would happen if he left. The nurses were a little shook up too. Most of the guys in the ward were still in active-combat alert mode, Bob included. The hospital was mortared while he was there and they were putting mattresses on top of everyone.

After two days he was loaded in a plane and sent to Clark AFB in the Philippines, and then later flown on to Japan. A day or two later they ripped out the dried packing and then sewed his buttock shut. He was not awake for this. By Christmas Bob was up and walking tentatively. Christmas is

January 1968, Spec. 4 Robert Fleming at An Khe base camp upon return from two months hospitalization recovering from wounds.

another time of the year that sends him back. In mid-January 1968, amazingly enough, he was returned to finish his one-year tour in Vietnam, was promoted to Sergeant E-5, and in mid-June 1968 he went home.

> **COMBAT LEADERSHIP LESSON FROM A GRUNT:** Commanders many miles away have little if any grasp of a situation and should leave the tactical decisions to the command structure on the ground. That includes the commanders up about fifteen hundred feet in a slick. It's very easy to make decisions when you are not on the ground in contact. If you are to make potentially life-and-death decisions, feel free to join the grunts on the ground. If the intelligence reports indicate friendly troops may be outnumbered, use B-52s to carpet bomb the area before committing the infantry.

Air power has its limitations and close air support (CAS) should only be used dangerously close when absolutely necessary and only when a forward air control (FAC) is on station and in complete charge of the aircraft doing the bombing . . . and after clearing it with the soldiers on the ground.

Aftermath
Several SOG teams moved into Cambodia due west of the action during the Hill 875 battle and discovered a road through the jungle across which Russian-made trucks carried food and ammunition to the NVA fighting on the hill. "About 4:00 AM the truck returned. This time the cargo at first looked like heaps of tree limbs, but in the stark moonlight Stevens (the SOG leader) got a better glimpse and recognized the protruding forms as arms and legs locked in rigor mortis, whole piles of NVA bodies frozen in death-grim testimony to the 173rd Airborne Brigade's combat effectiveness. . . ." (Plaster: 108-110)

In addition to his medals and wounds Bob Fleming came back with what was later diagnosed as post traumatic stress disorder (PTSD) and traumatic brain injury (TBI). He was finally examined for the TBI by the Veterans Affairs medical people in 2009, forty-two years after the original injury.

Bob returned to his home in Pittsburgh and it was terrible. It was like the world had passed him by. He didn't have a clue as to what to do; his thought processes were erratic at best; he could not compose complete sentences and his emotions were at war with themselves. One day he was in a war zone where for some strange reason it made sense. Since he was a combat veteran, people expected hardness in him. Even the rear echelon troops avoided the grunts when they came in and out of the field back in Vietnam.

He started drinking to ease the pain and was turned down for a job on the railroad where a number of his family members worked. Eventually he worked at the Postal Service and was subjected there to a situation that confronted him as it does many veterans in government work forces. As a benefit of their service in uniform veterans are given a boost in points in the hiring process for governmental employment. Jealousy of those already in the Postal Service who were not veterans and resented his "cutting in line" for employment resulted Bob being the target of harassment by his coworkers.

His grandfather Fleming was a Free Methodist minister and Bob was raised in this tradition, but he was having trouble with the whole spiritual question because he could not understand what happened. "Why me?" Every day he asked himself that question. He knew the answer: there is no answer, at least not while he is alive. But, that doesn't stop him from asking. Following Vietnam, religion was not much help to him. Around this time he met Angela and married her. This is one area where he says that there was an intervention from God because he doesn't think he could have done this well for a wife by only his own efforts.

Fleming ended his story to the author this way: "Please excuse me for the descriptions above. I hope that the pictures that I have painted are not so vivid as to irritate your own memories."

❖ ❖ ❖

Author's note: I was wounded in a mortar attack at the Dak To special forces camp on June 17, 1967, in an enemy attack that precipitated Fleming's Sky Soldiers of the 173rd Airborne Brigade being airlifted to the area. The Army can be really small, especially for us Military Academy graduates. The previous afternoon members of the command group of the 173rd made a visit to my camp. Among them was Lt. Col. Partain, who had been one of my tactics instructors at West Point. We had a short conversation off to the edge of our dining hall and I told him I was under a cover name in my assignment. As I was being medevaced by chopper from Dak To the next morning, I noted the arrival of the C-130s transporting the members of Partain's battalion to engage the NVA.

Fleming's Future
"Hill 875 for me is like having a video tape machine in your head. On this

machine is the event. This machine serves no purpose except to drive you crazy. You don't even have control of the remote. I see the guy in the tree, Sanchez with the tree over his body, the engineer and all the other bodies and horrid scenes that at one time were very real, every day. The memories come back sometimes hourly. I cannot control it. While it may not be as bad as the original event, repetition makes up for it. I suffer constant reminders of my failures, a harassing game of 'what if.' Yeah, what if you had done this, then maybe that would not have happened. You could have called off that plane if you would have been on your radio." Robert Fleming deals with the agony of guilt and self-blame which is the condition and emotion of so many of our warriors. One element our warriors face is "survivor's guilt," why they lived while others died.

When Sergeant Robert Fleming left Vietnam in mid-1968, Marine Corps Capt. David Pickett was beginning his own tour of duty in I Corps, adjacent to North Vietnam.

CHAPTER 9

"Mom, I Am Joining the Marines ... Again"

Captain David Pickett, USMC
(KHE SANH AND OPERATION PHOENIX 1968–1969)

Greater love has no one than this, that he lay down his life for his friends.
John 15:13 (New King James Version)

PHOENIX

Following a change of command that saw General Creighton Abrams replace General Westmoreland as the top U.S. leader in Vietnam, an accompanying change in approach to conduct of the war resulted. A key element of the new strategy was rooting out the covert Communist infrastructure that through terrorism and coercion maintained domination over the populace of South Vietnam's rural hamlets and villages. This, in turn, depended primarily on actionable intelligence, especially identifying and locating members of the cadre, or what became known as the Viet Cong infrastructure (VCI). The mission was to neutralize that infrastructure by killing or capturing its members, or inducing them to rally to the government side. The program to accomplish this was known as in Vietnamese as Phuong Huong, *which roughly translates to Phoenix. From the outset the enemy realized how dangerous this program was and made strenuous efforts to discredit it by characterizing it as an assassination scheme. Such propaganda succeeded to the extent that U.S. congressional investigators were dispatched to Vietnam to inquire into the matter. They concluded (and reported) that of some fifteen thousand VCI neutralized during 1968, 15 percent had been killed (mostly in regular combat operations in which they were taking part), 72 percent had been captured, and 13 percent had rallied to the government. Naturally the incentive was to capture enemy cadre or induce them to rally, since those who had knowledge of the enemy infrastructure and its functioning were invaluable intelligence assets.*

Raised to Serve His Country

Captain David Pickett's upbringing can be characterized as typical "gung ho" Texan. His parents had moved from a country farm to Dallas during the depression. Neither graduated from high school, but what they lacked in formal education they gained in the values inculcated in their only child including a belief in service to country. David's father joined the army in 1942 and deployed with the 1st Cavalry Division to the South Pacific where he was wounded. He returned home in 1945, and never talked about his wartime service.

First Marine Tour

David played college football at Southern Methodist University (SMU). Upon graduation in 1961 he joined the Marine Corps; his father was very proud. Marine Lieutenant Pickett spent an uneventful three-year tour as a at Twenty Nine Palms base in California punctuated by the exciting time when they loaded up for Cuba in the fall of 1962 in response to the Cuban Missile Crisis. He took the law school admission test and scored 715 out of 800, at the time the second highest grade ever for prospective SMU law school student. He admits that no one was more surprised than he himself at his score.

While David was in law school the Vietnam War began to heat up. He had friends who landed at Da Nang in March 1965 when the first contingent of marines came ashore. It began to weigh on his conscience that here he was in law school while his marine friends were in the war so he decided that his obligation was to volunteer again after law school and go to Vietnam. Some of his fellow law students were only in law school to avoid the draft and none of them could understand his decision. His parents knew he would not have to go to the war zone since he was an only child who had already served. The most challenging part of his reentry into the Marines was that he had to tell his mother who had great reservations and anxiety about his decision. David's father supported the decision and his mother's misgivings were eventually overcome.

David rejoined the Marines in May 1967 and didn't reveal his law degree in order to avoid being confined to a desk in some legal position since he vastly preferred a line officer assignment. Amazingly never was he asked, nor did his law degree ever appear on any record in the Marines.

Meanwhile Back at the White House

The Tet offensive by the enemy in February 1968 resulted in President Johnson deciding to forego running for reelection. "Later bitter commentators observed that Tet had proved the domino theory, even though only one domino—Lyndon Johnson—fell as the result of it. (Sorley: 12) President Johnson's wife, Lady Bird, wrote in her diary on Sunday, March 31, 1968, "The President had made the decision that he would not run for another term as president. President Johnson said he had talked to General Westmoreland and had asked how it would affect the morale of the men. Westmoreland told him he did not think it would matter appreciably." (Lady Bird Johnson)

After Tet 1968 General Westmoreland was replaced in Vietnam by General Creighton W. Abrams. Our forces had reached their maximum build up and the home front support for the war continued negatively. As historian Lewis Sorley reported, "Whatever the mood of the country, for those in Vietnam the war still had to be fought, and the new leadership went about doing that with energy and insight." (Sorley: xiii) The war went on without Johnson and Westmoreland and our military continued to slug it out with the enemy.

Khe Sanh

David Pickett arrived at Khe Sanh, which had been under siege for several months in the first week of May 1968. He was assigned to command a two-gun, 8-inch artillery battery that supported the Marine Corps infantry manning outposts on the hills surrounding Khe Sanh. These hills were named according to their elevation: 558, 861, 861A, 881 North and South, and 950. During Pickett's short but intense time at Khe Sanh in which heavy casualties continued to be experienced, he became aware of the horrific conditions experienced by the men who served there during the siege, which continued until his departure on July 5, 1968, after the Seabees destroyed the bunkers and the base was leveled. Several NVA divisions continued to surround the base, there were incoming rounds daily, planes and helicopters rarely landed due to intense fire, defenders lived in bunkers and the doctors worked around the clock in pitiful conditions in underground hospitals. When he left the base on July 5, his truck was blown away by incoming, his radio operator lost a hand, and several of his men were wounded as they began a road march to Dong Ha on Route 9.

When he then returned to his parent unit, the 12th Marine Regiment, as the senior captain he expected to be given command of an 8-inch howitzer battery, but the assignment went to a "regular" officer rather than "reservist" Captain Pickett. Not without justification, David developed a bit of an attitude. He was given command of the regiment's headquarters battery, the administrative unit, which was too far removed from the action for a man like Pickett. To add a little action and excitement to his life David began accompanying marine lieutenants who flew air reconnaissance missions and called in fire missions. This did not go over well with Pickett's regimental commander, a full colonel.

In a rather heated encounter with his boss, Captain Pickett was ordered to cease the joy rides. Pickett told his CO he wanted a new assignment. In an instant he got one! The regimental commander said, "Pack your bags and be at the airstrip at 0600 tomorrow!" Needless to say Pickett spent a fitful night wondering what the next morning would bring.

Operation Phoenix

Getting off the plane in Da Nang he was met by an army colonel in civilian clothes who told him to go to the base exchange and buy civilian clothes before reporting a week later in Saigon for a one week orientation on a new assignment that would definitely fulfill his desire for action. He was joining Phoenix!

In *A Bright Shining Lie* Neil Sheehan described the Phoenix program this way, "In 1967 . . . [Bill Colby] had helped Robert Komer, a former CIA officer . . . to set up the Phoenix Program to kill, jail, or intimidate into surrender the members of the secret Communist-led government the guerrillas had established in the rural areas of the south." (Sheehan: 18)

Vietnam historian Stanley Karnow defined Phoenix like this: "Conceived by the CIA . . . Phoenix was basically another American solution grafted onto a South Vietnamese problem. The Saigon government intelligence services, responsible for uprooting Viet Cong (VC) agents, were typically a tangle of rival groups competing with each other for power and graft . . . By centralizing these factions under sound management, the American theory went, the rural apparatus on which the Viet Cong rallied for recruits, food, money, and asylum could be crushed." (Karnow: 601)

Pickett believes that we went into South Vietnam without learning from the experiences of the French, who failed in Indochina because Ho Chi Minh understood insurgencies and the French did not. Initially, Americans did not understand that a counterinsurgency effort was necessary to successfully oppose the Communist infrastructure in the South.

Asian specialist and intelligence operative Hilaire du Berrier wrote a book published in 1965 which recounted the Communist strategic concept of a "long war." As early as 1957 Ho Chi Minh's Tong Bo (assassination organization) murdered 472 South Vietnamese village leaders. The Republic of Vietnam government never could protect the villages, which appeared government-controlled by day, but were VC-controlled by night. (du Berrier: 165)

The abuses of Ngo Dinh Diem, president of the Republic of Vietnam from 1954 until he was deposed and assassinated in a 1963 coup, were so extreme that they played into the Communist's long war strategy. The Communists conducted nocturnal tribunals in the countryside, gaining control of local hamlets and villages long before they organized the Viet Cong military units in-country or sent regular North Vietnamese Army units down the Ho Chi Minh Trail. (du Berrier: 184)

Pickett believes the United States would have been wise to have adopted the successful counterinsurgency operations of the British in Malaya and of the battle against the Hukbalahaps in the Philippines. Instead we adopted what to that time had been the successful American conventional warfare model of overwhelming military power of artillery, air, and firepower. What was needed in South Vietnam for eventual success, however was a pacification effort to win the local people over to our side. Former South Vietnam Premier and Vice-President Nguyen Cao Ky reflected about our manner of waging the Vietnam War: "You cannot use a steamroller against a shadow. The Americans found themselves pitted against an enemy they could neither understand nor combat." (Ky: 150)

In du Berrier's *Background to Betrayal* the embedded challenge for the Phoenix operatives was described this way: "First a Vietcong unit would move into a village at night, set up a court and try and execute the local administrator and all his aides, under the eyes of their fellow citizens. Automatically the village became not only converted but 'loyal.' The next move was to confiscate identity cards issued by the Diem government. Communists agents used them as passes and the poor (peasant) of the countryside, deprived of his card of identity, had no alternative but to become a Vietcong. The national army with its American equipment was too cumbersome for night chases through the rice paddies, even if so inclined." (du Berrier: 185) This had been occurring for ten years before Phoenix was established to counter it.

In May 1967, MACV commander General William C. Westmoreland approved a program aimed at pacifying the countryside and destroying the Viet Cong infrastructure, who were civilians by day and guerrillas by night. Success would be achieved by what was on the face of it a simple two-part operation: provide security to the villagers and eliminate the Viet Cong. Pacification would be the new buzz word.

The program was named after a mythical Vietnamese bird, the name of which loosely translated as Phoenix. It operated under the auspices of Civil Operations and Revolutionary Development Support (CORDS) and was controlled by the Central Intelligence Agency (CIA).

Westmoreland " ... gave CORDS advisory responsibility for the militia—the Regional and Popular Forces that had the assignment of local security [and] gave CORDS advisory responsibility for PHOENIX, a project aimed at identifying and excising, the VC political infrastructure and run by the South Vietnamese primarily under direction of CIA advisers." (Westmoreland: 216)

Phoenix was authorized on December 20, 1967, but was delayed in starting oper-

Marine Corps Capt. David Pickett on the outskirts of Quang Ngai City during a firefight with Viet Cong in February 1969. He normally wore civilian clothes because he was attached to the Phoenix Program.

ations due to the February '68 Tet offensive. The CIA did not have enough agents to operate the program down to the hamlet level so military officers and NCOs were requisitioned to fill out the program.

When Pickett had the heated exchange with his regimental commander, the colonel probably had just received notice of the need for some of his personnel to be detailed to the program. Pickett's dissatisfaction happened at just the right time for his commander to supply his first officer to Phoenix.

Quang Ngai

Captain Pickett reported into Quang Ngai province south of Chu Lai and lived in the Embassy House, a two-story building where he lived and worked with three American military officers and three CIA officers.

The group depended totally on a twenty-man local Popular Force group for security. The isolated location from which they operated meant they had no hope of American military to support them in case they were attacked. Simply put, their mission was to gather intelligence and interdict Viet Cong attacks in their area.

They had seemingly unlimited budget and could readily procure whatever resources they needed, such as, helicopters, American military C-130s, and CIA Air America aircraft. The grass roots mission was to assist in the self-defense of the villages by providing them advice and weapons.

The Embassy House group had an inexhaustible supply of weapons straight from CIA sources including sawed-off shotguns, M79 grenade launchers, and foreign small arms of all types. Pickett carried a Swedish K submachine gun and a sawed-off shotgun when he made his village rounds with his interpreter, driver, and bodyguard, all of whom were probably destined for execution when America left Vietnam.

His mission had three elements:

- Ensure security for the villages
- Capture and kill Viet Cong insurgents
- Assist the locals with the means to pursue their agricultural needs for feeding their people

Pickett believes that our assistance to the villagers could be considered bribery to keep them on our side by means of food, weapons, and ammunition. A glaring deficiency was that the villagers could be indifferent in providing for themselves when they knew the Americans would do it for them. Premier Nguyen Cao Ky agreed with this especially at the level at which he was an observer when he recounted someone who asked him: "Why should we fight? The Americans are doing it for us. Let's relax." (Ky: 151)

Captain Pickett and other Phoenix operatives were primarily concerned with obtaining intelligence on Viet Cong plans for offensive operations. With the VC working at night, the Phoenix operatives played the game on the enemy's terms and also worked their operations in the dark to find, capture, try to convert VC soldiers to the government side and become what were termed *Chieu Hois* (Open Arms) or as a last resort kill them, if they were so bold as to run when faced with exposure during a Phoenix operation. Pickett was amazed at the creativity shown by the enemy in the caves and underground tunnels they built for concealment.

The cover story for the Phoenix operations in Pickett's area was that they were involved with Revolutionary Development: helping the villagers with their agricultural pursuits so that they could feed themselves. That was their job in the daytime. The nighttime work of Pickett's group became much more dangerous when they would go out five or six at a time and set up ambushes. If they felt that a hamlet was really infested with VC, they would enter, take custody of the inhabitants and destroy the entire hamlet. The villagers would all be brought back and turned over to the South Vietnamese troops for interrogation. Pickett lost track of them after that, but he admitted he had to turn his back many times on the interrogation techniques utilized. He maintains however that in many cases the detained villagers were valuable in revealing enemy plans, personnel, and locations.

Pickett said that the Vietnamese were challenging because they did not have the aggressiveness and drive to which the Americans are accustomed. Their primary loyalty was to their family. If their immediate family was not impacted, they were not interested in endangering themselves or becoming involved.

Tet 1969 brought another Communist offensive, but it was not nearly as widespread as the '68 Tet offensive. Still, February and March 1969 was a very active time all over South Vietnam especially in Pickett's area. The entire country was placed on a 7:00 PM curfew. The friendly militia units in Quang Ngai had active enemy contact practically every night and there were heavy enemy as well as friendly casualties.

On March 14, 1969, reliable information was received that a VC platoon was going to attack Quang Ngai City. Pickett joined army Major Bill Gavan in planning an ambush on the route that was to be taken by this platoon into the city. The Army major, who had graduated from West Point in 1962, was on his third Vietnam tour, had been wounded four times and was awarded a Silver Star." Gavan was very lean and on the short side at 5 feet, 8 inches tall. Because he was bald, his nickname was "Bald Eagle." Pickett held Gavan in the highest professional and personal regard because he truly believed that, if the occasion demanded, the army officer would lay down his life for his marine comrade.

This would be a night operation whose success would be dependent on good prior planning. The major element of the plan was preplanned American artillery fire on the enemy column if the Phoenix ambush did not stop them. Pickett and Gavan left Embassy House after dark with only four Popular Force soldiers. Before the night was over they would have a major surprise.

As expected from the intelligence report, at 0300 hours the enemy column walked right into the ambush and ten of their members were immediately killed by claymore mines, hand grenades, and automatic weapons fire from the six men. The major surprise was that the enemy force was not just a platoon; it was a full company! The preplanned artillery was called in resulting in another fifteen or so enemy KIA, who were pulled back when the VC pulled back after the barrage.

The ambush planned by this Phoenix team saved Quang Ngai City, which would have been in total chaos had the VC company not been intercepted.

COMBAT LEADERSHIP LESSON: Always plan for every possible contingency before an operation.

At a level well above Pickett's operational responsibilities and pay grade there were significant improprieties in the program. "Saigon officialdom saw the glitter of extortionist gold in the Phoenix Program, blackmailing innocents and taking bribes not to arrest those they should have arrested. . . . Thousands died or vanished into Saigon's prisons. Colby was to state in 1971 that 18,000 Viet Cong insurgents (VCI) had been captured in the whole of South Vietnam under the program, 20,000 had been killed and another 17,000 had defected." (Sheehan: 733)

However, even by the enemy the program was reported to have been a success. "To Colonel Bui Tin, a senior officer, it had been a 'devious and cruel' operation that cost 'the loss of thousands of our cadres' (Karnow: 602) It appears that Pickett and others assigned to Phoenix deserved high grades for their performance.

Aftermath

Pickett returned to Dallas, Texas, in the summer of 1969 and went to District Attorney Henry Wade's office to visit John Vance, a marine with a Silver Star and Purple Heart from the Korean War, to remind Vance of his earlier commitment to Pickett of a job upon his return from Vietnam. The offer escaped

Vance's memory and the only opening at the time in the prosecutor's office was for a secretary. Hoping for the best, marine combat veteran David Pickett became a secretary. So much for utilization of the leadership skills of his marine life! Eventually he was assigned to prosecute the flag-burning cases which brought him great satisfaction and his success in this assignment led to full-time prosecutorial duties. He then entered the local political arena, which brought him early successes and election as a Dallas County commissioner.

By 1979, ten years later, Pickett was single, out of politics, and quite frankly bored. He became qualified as a civilian pilot and contacted an old high school buddy who was the chief pilot for the Saudi Arabian bin Laden family and asked him for a job. Thirty days later Pickett was flying right seat in one of ten aircraft in the family's fleet all over the Middle East and Europe. The bin Ladens were a large family with a number of half-brothers, one of whom, Osama, became infamous as the leader of Al Qaeda. During Pickett's time as a pilot for the bin Laden's Osama was only a teenager and they never met.

Pickett remembers "greeting my father on his return from World War II in 1945 when he arrived from overseas with other veterans at the Dallas bus station. He was still in uniform with his 1st Cavalry patch, boots, and Eisenhower jacket. All of us greeted our returning victorious warriors with great festivity and flag-waving. Unfortunately the return of our Vietnam veterans was met with derision and disgust by some segments of our society. My father always was very proud I had become a marine." David concludes, "It was not a question of whether I would serve, only when."

About the time in 1969 that Captain Pickett was completing his Phoenix assignment in I Corps, well-known army ranger Patrick Tadina was roaming the jungles in provinces south of Quang Ngai, causing untold misery for the enemy.

CHAPTER 10

A Ranger's Ranger

STAFF SERGEANT PATRICK TADINA, USA (1965–1970)

What counts is not necessarily the size of the dog in the fight—it's the size of the fight in the dog.— Dwight David Eisenhower

RANGERS

Rangers have a long and illustrious history in the American army as elite infantry. Service during the Vietnam War added to their record of accomplishment and valor, so much so that when General Creighton Abrams returned from Vietnam to become army chief of staff he created a ranger regiment as a means of infusing ranger standards and values throughout the army. So successful was that initiative that, in gratitude for the respect he had shown them, the rangers inducted General Abrams (a tanker) into the Ranger Hall of Fame.

The Elusive Tadina

Several people who were aware of the exploits of a legendary Vietnam warrior named Patrick Tadina suggested that his story should be included in this work. Tadina, however, was nowhere to be found, just as he had proven elusive to the enemy in Vietnam. Someone said one of his company commanders had been a Dick James. Bingo! Dick James is a West Point classmate of mine. Command Sergeant Major Pat "Tad" Tadina, who had retired from the army and was working overseas as a security consultant, was then easily located through James. Eventually I made contact with him and initially he referred me to his record as recounted in a book where his wartime feats on several missions are detailed by Tadina's team member Bill Shanahan, in a book coauthored with John P. Brackin, *Stealth Patrol.* When Tad returned on leave from

148

his overseas assignment I was able to contact him and get his personal story.

Journey to Soldiering

He is half Asian and half Hawaiian from the island of Maui. Pat had some challenges with the law as a juvenile and was sent to a reform school where he got himself into even more trouble. He was sent to another reform school on the island of Molokai that was, as Tad remembers, for hard-core guys. It was unique in that there were no fences or walls, nor was there anywhere to go on the small island but to the mountains or the ocean, so the reform school residents became accustomed to performing hard labor in fighting forest fires, planting trees, and cutting wood. As Tad began to mature he realized that if he did not change his life he could end up dead or in prison. After two years in reform school he had become accustomed to a disciplined life and decided the army would be a good fit for him. In 1962, when he was released, he enlisted in the army and had no problem with military discipline. By 1965, when he returned in uniform to visit his probation officer, Tadina was wearing sergeant stripes,. This was the beginning of an incredible military career for a young man who became a legend among the fraternity of rangers.

A Ranger's Ranger

Tad Tadina began a continuous sixty-months of service in Vietnam beginning with the 1st Infantry Division in Vietnam in 1965 and continuing with the 173rd Airborne Brigade in 1966. With his Asian features, 5 foot, 6inch height, 140 pound weight, dressed in a North Vietnamese Army (NVA) uniform he could pass as a Viet Cong or NVA. He became the quintessential long range reconnaissance patroller (LRRP, pronounced lurp). As the war and his time in Vietnam progressed he began running missions in a ranger company where he became the most experienced and reliable team leader in the company.

Tadina was raised in a fatherless family with four other siblings. An older brother also entered the army when Tad had already been in Vietnam for two years. Tad said that his brother did not have to go to Vietnam since Tad was already assigned there and as the only other male of the family, he would have been given a war-zone exemption. Tadina's brother ended up being killed in Vietnam.

Wherever and however he served, Tad was the absolute best at what he did: a leader of small teams infiltrating enemy country. He never lost a single man under his command in action. "Normally he was one of the most laid-back guys on the base. He wasn't one of those hard-core, roughneck types who liked to get in fistfights and drink a lot of beer—he was just a really nice, quiet type of guy. And that's why everybody liked him." (Shanahan: 130) He was a study in contrasts, around the base, a quiet, unassuming man yet a consummate warrior with many enemy kills. He was a natural warrior, well-suited for his combat missions.

Ranger Training

Tad led long range reconnaissance patrols whose mission was to gather intelligence on the enemy. He enjoyed an amazing reputation in that none of his team members had ever even been wounded although over his five years in combat Tad was wounded three times himself. He was admired for always bringing his men home safely. A superb trainer, he teamed with MSgt. Roy Boatman in training the ranger company LRRP teams. Tadina and Boatman became a mutual admiration society and a study in physical contrasts; Boatman's six foot five inch height towered over Tadina. Together they developed a break-contact drill that involved one man throwing grenades and as the soldier behind him laid down a base of fire; the grenade thrower moved behind the shooter and the process was repeated until contact with the enemy was broken or they succeeded in significantly reducing the enemy fire sufficiently for the LRRPs to move away out of danger. Training with this drill scenario became a ranger company requirement before a LRRP team began a mission. Each team would perform several dry-fire drills and conclude with a live-fire exercise in the thick jungle nearby.

Once, a visiting general observed the training being conducted by Tadina and Boatman and remarked that it was one of the most unsafe things he had ever witnessed in combat but, since the men would be relying initially on only themselves in isolated locations, the professional manner in which it was executed meant it was excellent and should be exported to other ranger companies. For any mission Tad began with fully analyzing all available intelligence. Then he constantly rehearsed with his team what their reactions would be for any action that they could foresee occurring. He was an exacting and demanding trainer, no matter how dangerous the training was. This helps to explain why he always brought his team members home safely. When asked why he remained in Vietnam so long, continuing to extend his tours, Tadina said he believed he could train his team members well and, as he became ever more experienced, the more successful he would be in keeping his fellow warriors alive.

Dak To Missions

Beginning in June 1967 the 173rd Airborne Brigade was deployed to the area east of the tri-border point (the spot where the boundaries of South Vietnam, Laos and Cambodia meet) near the Dak To special forces camp. On June 22, 1967, just south of Dak To on Hill 1338 there was a disastrous battle for a U.S. rifle company. In the "Battle of the Slopes" Alpha Company, 2nd Battalion, 503rd Parachute Infantry Regiment (PIR), was attacked by a superior force of NVA and took extremely heavy casualties: 76 killed and 23 wounded out of the 137 Alpha Company Sky Soldiers. (Murphy: 84) Tad was on a mission in the general area during the battle and possesses an audio tape of the last radio transmission of the A/2/503rd radio operator. He transmitted, "They are coming, they are coming", before the transmission ceased. After the battle it was discovered that "many of Alpha's men had been executed [by the NVA]; a large number of the bodies bore ghastly exit wounds in their faces. Other corpses had been mutilated, their features destroyed, ring fingers cut off, and ears removed." (Murphy: 83) Tad's team arrived at the scene of the battle just after the NVA had left. Despite the conditions of the majority of the dead, he was absolutely stunned to see a grouping of a dozen or so of the American dead laid out in a line, covered with ponchos, without mutilation, and with their dog tags intact.

Within hours Tad and his team performed a prisoner snatch of an NVA senior NCO who was a member of the unit that had overrun the Alpha Company. When Tad asked him why some of the American dead had been treated with such dignity, his prisoner said, "My unit is a regular NVA unit and we are professional soldiers, not the rag-tag VC." Tad commented the NVA unit wore black berets and he has one as a souvenir. It is very puzzling that some members of this battalion were truly animals, but Tad encountered a soldier who appeared to have some standards of professionalism and decency. Tad and his team continued to track the NCO's battalion and called in air strikes on the enemy soldiers as they returned to their base camps.

An example of an action for which Tadina received an award for valor was a mission in the Dak To area of operations on August 6-7, 1967. Hiding himself exceptionally well, only ten meters from a group of twenty five enemy soldiers who moved past him, he called artillery in on them. They knew someone was observing them to be able to call that artillery fire, so they pursued and surrounded Sergeant Tadina and his team on three sides. With their

U.S. Army SSgt. Patrick Tadina near Dak To in 1967. Tadina frequently impersonated enemy soldiers and lured them into ambushes.

well-honed ability to move quietly, unobserved through the jungle, Tadina's team was able to escape the trap through the open side and continued their mission. (Bronze Star for Valor citation)

During the Dak To campaign Tad ran constant missions and sometimes ended up in Laos. After the Hill 875 battle in late November 1967 he and his team rappelled from a hovering helicopter into the jungle and called in air strikes as the NVA assault units began returning to their base camps in Laos and Cambodia after heavy fighting against the Americans.

Bong Son Operations

One of the missions on which Shanahan served with Tadina consisted of infiltration of Suoi Ca Valley to establish an observation post and perhaps conduct an ambush. Although it was just a simple trail watch, LRRP missions were always dangerous. They were southwest of Bong Son where the terrain was significantly more open than in many areas of the Central Highlands. All of a sudden an American infantry company came into view. The risk for Tad's team was that the Americans would mistake Tad's team for the enemy. The one hundred-man company began setting up their campsite about three hundred yards from Tad's team. A radio call back to the team's headquarters returned a reply that the infantry company would be expecting Tad's team to emerge from hiding into their position where they would be extracted by helicopter. Tad knew Murphy's Law well—if it can go wrong, it will go wrong—so he wanted assurances that all the members of the infantry company knew his team would be entering their perimeter. He requested that they pop a green smoke grenade to signal their understanding Tad and his men would be approaching their perimeter.

As noted earlier, Tad looked like a VC/NVA, and he typically carried the enemy weapon of choice, an AK-47. He usually led his team at the front, but in this case he wanted someone else to lead the way into the American position so some trigger-happy soldier wouldn't figure he was an enemy soldier trying to trick them. Tad was all serious business in the field on his missions and tried to leave nothing to chance.

While awaiting the extraction helicopters a group of NVA actually walked right by the infantry company at a distance of three quarters of a football field. They must have all been newbies (new in country) as not a single man fired at the NVA, one of whom even waved at the Americans. The NVA probably figured by their brazen attention-getting behavior that they could lure the Americans into a pursuit that would have ended up in an ambush. Tad pointed the NVA out to the company commander who said they might be ARVN troops, and was too timid to take any action. Tad and his men left the area by helicopter and hoped for the infantrymen's sake that their alertness would be heightened.

On another surveillance mission Tad's team was ordered to conduct an ambush on a very small group of NVA. On this mission they were in for a huge surprise, because it was not a small group of enemy, but a continuous line of a long column that was moving directly toward Tad's team. It was a battalion of battle-hardened NVA wearing Khaki uniforms with pith helmets and carrying AK-47s, passing only fifteen meters away. Tad's group remained well-hidden while Bill Shanahan counted 140 enemy soldiers before he gave up counting. And still the NVA kept passing their concealed position. (Shanahan: 144) Even though they came as close as five meters away the team remained totally motionless. They observed one Caucasian-appearing man in the column and two NVA officers brought up the rear as the entire unit completed their passage. The team remained quiet and concealed for a further period of time to ensure there was no one deliberately following at a distance. Tad radioed their headquarters at LZ English where the size of the

NVA unit took everyone by surprise. Tad was ordered to remain in the area to continue to attempt an ambush. Soon two NVA moved down the trail in front of them and Tad opened up and fired on them. One was killed immediately, and the other soldier ran away until he collapsed from his wounds. This mission and the large group encountered in the field prompted a lengthy debriefing back at base camp. Between the experience with the American company and the NVA battalion the week had been quite eventful.

The next assignment of Tad's team was in the area called the Fishhook, a very dangerous area northwest of their base camp about twenty-five kilometers on the northern side of Binh Dinh Province just south of Quang Ngai Province. The area received its name because it looked like a fishhook formed by the An Lao river, where there were tall trees that blocked the sunlight. The area was heavily populated by Montagnards, who were threatened by the VC, and as a consequence they became eyes and ears to report any American movement through the area.

A landing zone had been selected and now it was time for an early evening insertion. The team jumped quickly from the chopper whose skids didn't even touch the ground before it was lifting off, leaving them alone as usual with only the jungle animals for company, which was all they ever desired. There was very little growth on the ground so they had little opportunity for concealment. Tad took the point position as usual quietly leading the group and intermittently halting to listen for any out of the ordinary sounds. After stopping for the night, they moved out again, steadily moving to a higher elevation. Eventually they came across a very wide trail, eight-feet across, and obviously a major infiltration route that was totally invisible from the air. They thought they had seen everything, but this was truly startling, even to Tadina.

Tad radioed back what they had found and was ordered to perform an ambush, which Tad was against due to the obvious heavy enemy presence in that area; they could be heavily outnumbered before an extraction could be effected. They were told they could be extracted by a McGuire Rig which was a rope dropped through the trees on which the members of the team would be carried away dangling from the choppers. Tadina communicated that an ambush and extraction by the McGuire rig was not viable. Fortunately, his reasoning won the day and the ambush was cancelled.

At another time and place (December 13, 1968) Tadina decided to carry out an ambush. When two enemy soldiers were spotted, he exposed himself to their fire as they chased him for a good distance while his team prepared an ambush site. Eventually he drew the two of the enemy into his team's kill zone and they didn't have a chance. (Silver Star for Gallantry in Action citation)

After another insertion the team was moving down a trail when Tad halted and whispered back that he thought they had been spotted. With all his experience Tad was amazing; it was like he had a special sense to detect enemy presence in an area. He felt someone was following them and sure enough, a Montagnard tribesman was tracking them. When the Montagnard knew he was discovered, he broke off and disappeared. They observed the same wide trail they discovered previously and heard noises at night which indicated heavy movement along the trail. Except for sniper fire their helicopter extraction was uneventful.

Captain Dick James, West Point class of 1963, became Tad's company commander in December 1968. In his book *Stealth Patrol* Bill Shanahan described James saying, "he pushed us hard to fulfill our various responsibilities. But he was also a conscientious leader, and he sought to balance that

Lieutenant John Lawton was an advisor to ARVN's 41st Ranger Battalion in the Mekong Delta (IV Corps) from 1965 to 1966. He is pictured here with the battalion's commander.

broader military perspective with the need to protect his men and look out for our safety." (Shanahan: 172) The company commander who replaced Captain James in late 1969, was Captain John Lawton, whose previous responsibilities in Vietnam included command of a rifle company in the Separate Brigade of the 101st Airborne Division and an advisory position with the Vietnamese 41st Ranger Battalion in the Delta. Shanahan described him as "a tough guy who had won several medals prior to joining the company, [Captain Lawton] was a CO who didn't mind getting down in the trenches with the teams—he'd actually put himself out there, at his own personal risk-and as a result the teams often had some pretty remarkable missions." (Shanahan: 172)

❖ ❖ ❖

(Author's note: When I was a political appointee at the Department of Veterans Affairs in Washington, Dick James called me to consider hiring a full colonel, soon to be retiring, by the name of John Lawton. I hired him and he did a superb job, a fine leader in war and peace.)

❖ ❖ ❖

When Captain James took command of the company in December 1968, it had evolved from a Long-Range Reconnaissance Patrol (LRRP) unit to a Long-Range Patrol (LRP) unit. The mission remained oriented on intelligence gathering, but raids and ambushes were periodically ordered to capture prisoners because of the combat expertise of the company. Another change came about on January 1, 1969, when the various LRRP companies became a subunits of the 75th Infantry Regiment. Tad's unit became Company N (Ranger), 75th Infantry Regiment (Ranger). The company was assigned to the 173rd Airborne Brigade. Unlike most of the other ranger companies in Vietnam, it recruited the majority of its solders from the 173rd which resulted in the enlisted men being airborne qualified, but very few were Ranger School graduates. All the NCOs were airborne and some were ranger qualified. All the company officers were airborne and ranger qualified. These backgrounds made the company somewhat better qualified than other ranger companies, but very selective recruiting and rules for weeding out soldiers who were not performing developed a truly outstanding company. John Lawton remembers that there were two Medal of Honor recipients in the company (SSgt. Laszlo Rabel and Sgt. David Dolby) and at least four of his NCOs completed their army service and retired as command sergeants major, one of whom was

Tadina. The transition to ranger companies occurred early in 1969, just at the time they were expecting another Tet offensive, so there was heightened interest in sending out ranger patrols to detect enemy movements.

Tadina said that Captains James and Lawton were his only company commanders who had actually accompanied him on any of his missions. Under Captain James, 450 missions were run and only six of his men were killed in action.

On June 8, 1969, during a two-team mission Tadina first called in an artillery barrage and then prepared an ambush. Firing on a group of enemy soldiers who fled the teams' ambush, he led the pursuit and wounded one enemy soldier. His second Silver Star citation for this action reads in part, "The enemy returned fire and fled into the thick underbrush and rocks . . . toward a suspected base camp. The teams reached a clearing which had to be crossed in order to gain access to the suspected base camp. With continued disregard for his personal safety, Sergeant Tadina . . . crossed alone [and] spotted two enemy in ambush positions. . . . He then initiated contact instantly wounding two of the enemy. Fire was returned by an estimated ten to twenty enemy personnel. Although seriously wounded and completely exposed in the clearing, Sergeant Tadina continued to silence the enemy attack by delivering large volumes of suppressive fire. . . . He refused medical aid and continued to command until the enemy had withdrawn. (Silver Star for Gallantry in Action citation)

The 173rd's ranger company was trained to rappel-in by ropes on which they would slide down from helicopters hovering overhead. This was not a preferred method and was only used in triple canopy jungle. It was very risky, especially when there was no knowledge of the situation on the ground beneath the canopy of the trees

The team could be extracted by a device called a McGuire rig, ropes with snap links at the end for soldiers to attach themselves to that could be lowered to the ground through an opening in the jungle canopy. The rangers on the ground could hook-in and be pulled out through the jungle; it was a tricky and dangerous operation. This was not a normal extraction technique. Over the course of his assignment with N Company, Staff Sergeant Tadina's team only had to be extracted by McGuire rig twice. During a McGuire-rig extraction, the helicopter was extremely vulnerable, especially if it began taking fire because the team had been spotted. When this happened, the rangers understood they might be cut off to save the helicopter and crew. On his first experience with McGuire-rig extraction in combat, Tadina and other rangers who were hooked up to the extraction ropes which were cut off, fell about twenty feet. Then they "evaded" through heavy enemy territory. This experience did not endear Tad to this extraction method.

On one occasionCaptain Lawton was with Tadina when his team was detected by the enemy. They fought their way to the top of a ridgeline and called for extraction and gunship support. Although two lifts were required to extract everyone on the ground, only a single helicopter was available, so it would have to make two separate lifts; the first group was lifted out under light enemy fire. While Tad and Lawton waited for the second extraction flight with one other team member, they were constantly threatened by NVA trying to make it up a steep incline to attack them. Tad told Lawton he didn't want to risk another McGuire rig extraction. It was a heated conversation, but Tadina was convinced it would be safer for him to exfiltrate on foot. When the ropes were dropped, all the captain and the other soldier hooked up and Lawton held out Tad's rope, shouting to him that this was his last chance because the NVA had surrounded them. Lawton told Tadina he wouldn't make it out on the ground and that he was going to order all three of them to be pulled up on the rig so very reluctantly Tadina hooked up and the three men were successfully extracted.

Hospital Raid Background

One of the unusual operations for which Tad seemed to be a magnet was in the fall of 1969: to infiltrate an NVA hospital to mark it for a raid. The genesis of the raid was from information gathered from the interrogation of several prisoners from different sources both inside and outside the brigade as well as radio intercepts. Earlier an N Company team led by Staff Sergeant Santos-Matos captured an enemy soldier sick with malaria who was on his way to an NVA hospital for treatment. Matos's team had been out on a routine intelligence gathering mission. As the team was walking on a minor trail they crossed a well-used trail and Staff Sergeant Matos immediately sent his team to reconnoiter along the main trail while he searched the immediate area of the intersecting trails for a good spot to set up an ambush/prisoner snatch. When the rest of the team returned, Matos began setting up the ambush site. Suddenly, coming down the main trail towards them was an NVA with his weapon slung over his shoulder, very relaxed and walking with an unsteady, weaving gait. Matos jumped off the trail and just as this NVA was crossing directly in front of him, the team leader grabbed him. Almost immediately five or six NVA were sighted coming down the smaller trail and the two groups of soldiers spotted each other simultaneously. Matos wrapped his arm around his prisoner in order to restrain him and with his free hand leveled his weapon and fired on the approaching NVA. Two or three NVA were killed and the others fled. The ranger team called for immediate extraction and returned to base with their prisoner, who came to be known as "Ranger Sam." Sam was grateful that Staff Sergeant Santos-Matos hadn't killed him and for the humane treatment he had received from the rangers and the medical personnel at the landing zone. There was also an element of hero-worship for SSgt. Santos-Matos by an appreciative Sam who was turned over to the brigade intelligence section for interrogation.

Ranger Raid Planning

For the raid Lawton was called to the brigade operations/intelligence staff group to discuss raiding the suspected enemy hospital to capture prisoners; this could be a goldmine of POWs. If the raid were successful, the brigade would be able to interrogate NVA from a variety of enemy units in the Sky Soldiers' area of operations. Lawton was briefed on the intelligence collected thus far—Ranger Sam was one of the sources—and the question was posed to Lawton, "How soon can you launch an operation?"

Lawton reminded the headquarters staffers and brass that the ranger company was organized around six-man teams who were trained to operate clandestinely, from insertion to extraction, for intelligence-gathering missions, not offensive combat missions like the proposed raid. He explained that he wasn't attempting to avoid the mission, but any of the brigade's rifle companies was better organized, trained, and equipped for a raid like this. Countering the case made by Lawton, brigade commander Brig. Gen. Hubert Cunningham pointed out that the ranger company was small, had outstanding NCOs, and hand-picked troops who could pinpoint the hospital better than other brigade troopers. A rifle company would be on standby and inserted by helicopter once Lawton's rangers located the hospital. It would be a complex mission as the area was mountainous with triple-canopied jungle, thick vegetation, and even worse, a paucity of landing zones in the suspected vicinity of the hospital.

The Raid

In planning the operation Lawton realized there were only two or three experienced teams available because all the rest were deployed in the field on operations, on R&R, or in training. Staff Sergeant Tadina's team was one that was ready for the mission. Eventually Lawton organized a dozen or so personnel including Staff Sergeant Tadina's team, a few other handpicked rangers from other teams, and some combat engineers who would bring rucksacks(backpacks) loaded with C4 to blow down enough trees and create a one-helicopter landing zone for use by the standby rifle company because, if it was needed, it would be needed quickly. Due to the importance of this operation, the size of the team, and its diverse composition, Captain Lawton was going to accompany Tadina and his men on the operation.

Tadina's augmented team was inserted without any complications in part due to artillery being fired into the insertion area, which masked the noise of the helicopters carrying the team. Now the challenge was to reach the hospital undetected. With typical ranger creativity and innovation the plan was for Tad—dressed up, as he often had in previous missions, in typical VC garb of black pajamas, Ho Chi Minh sandals, and rumpled hat, carrying an AK-47 his weapon of choice—to enter the hospital perimeter accompanied by Ranger Sam. On past missions when he dressed up as an enemy, Tad had been known to walk down a trail with his team following him and when a NVA soldier, believing Tad to be one of his own, would call out to greet him, it would be his last words because Tad or one of his team members would level him. For the hospital infiltration Tad added a checkered scarf around his neck. Ranger Sam, with his new-found loyalty to the Americans, agreed to accompany Tad and lead him to the hospital. To carry out the deception leaving as little to chance as possible, Sam was even outfitted with a rifle with the firing pin removed.

Many of Tad's missions had been prisoner snatches, and he brought those enemy soldiers back to his base camp and had long discussions with them to learn as much as he could. For three years a Kit Carson Scout, a former enemy soldier who had defected, had been a regular member of his team. Tad learned much from him, but never fully trusted him and as a consequence, assigned his assistant team leader (ATL), who brought up the rear on every mission, to have the additional responsibility of keeping his eye on the scout. The scout was motivated to be loyal on the patrols because he knew what would happen to him if he were ever captured. Tad instructed his ATL to kill the scout if he ever showed any signs of disloyalty.

Tad was so experienced that it seemed he had learned everything about the enemy, the signals they made to each other, punji stake locations, and which trails to use or not to walk on. He could sense nearby enemy. One of the major giveaway of nearby enemy was the smell from the *nuoc mam* fish sauce they consumed. It had an incredibly strong smell that was recognizable over long distances.

Following the insertion the team moved out toward the hospital. A well-traveled trail was found running along a ridge line. Well in front Tad led the group. After a couple of hours, the team heard noises just above them. Lawton sent out a ranger to scout the higher ground. About twenty feet higher up and parallel to the trail they were on was a cleared road that appeared to be in regular use. Unreal! Looking down the far side of the ridgeline toward the noise, about two hundred meters away they saw a well-constructed, but lightly-occupied camp with a few fires burning. It had to be the hospital they were looking for. Farther up the trail three NVA approached Tad and Ranger Sam, and as he planned to quietly overcome them, a soldier in Lawton's main party fired on them. The hospital was alerted; the raid was no longer a surprise. They radioed for gunships to close on the area and provide fire support, but the jungle canopy was too thick. Tad popped smoke to mark his position, which the AH-1 Cobra gunships could not make out, resulting in the raiding team taking friendly rocket fire. The Kit Carson Scout was wounded. This friendly fire stalled their advance to the hospital. By this time the hospital security force was reacting. In order not to be overwhelmed by this much larger force they had to give up the raid and called for extraction. Another team later entered the camp, but it had been abandoned.

Staff Sergeant Tadina was without peer in prisoner snatches. On January 22, 1969, his patrol came under continuous enemy fire. Despite this, Tadina left a secure and safe position and chased down an enemy soldier, bringing him back to base camp as a prisoner. (Bronze Star for Valor citation) On November 14, 1969, he was on a reconnaissance patrol when he located two enemy soldiers in some underbrush. After twenty minutes of trying to obtain their surrender by "conversation" he decided to get more aggressive and moved forward armed with only a knife to apprehend them. They were also brought back as prisoners. (Bronze Star for Valor citation)

If Tad's team captured a wounded NVA, he would require his newest team member to perform the first aid care on the enemy for practice in case one of his own team members might later need help with a wound. Another reason to show compassion to an enemy by saving his life was that he might later be compassionate to an American.

There was a definite distinction in Tad's mind between NVA and VC soldiers. He believed the NVA were more professional, somewhat like our regular army soldiers. In contrast, he considered the Viet Cong to be little more than terrorists. The VC had a reputation of extraordinary brutality; Tad had heard about a man who was captured by the VC who cut off his hands. You can draw your own conclusion about what Tad meant when he said, "I cut no slack with the VC."

Bill Shanahan, who knew Tad intimately from serving with Tad as a team member, said there were many men of great valor in their unit but Tad was exceptional. "I saw him risk his life over and over, far beyond the call of duty, but in a lot of ways his heart and his character were the company's heart and the company's character. He embodied the ranger ideal: committed to the company and loyal to his men." (Shanahan: 263)

Shanahan believes that the Communist soldiers were bound together by a political motivation whereas Americans were bound together by devotion to each other. The enemy had never been defeated after decades of fighting: first the Japanese, then the French, and now the Americans. It was long war that they would patiently fight for control of their homeland. They never gave up; they were a determined opponent; they assumed that eventually we would give up; and they were right. Tadina never gave up, either, he just served tour after tour, ran mission after mission. Each time he extended his tour he was granted a leave, so he did have some relief from combat. Tad's opinion was that a major factor in the motivation of the NVA was that they knew they had to be good and loyal soldiers so that their families back home would be safe.

A 1985 *Stars and Stripes* article called him, "the most decorated enlisted man of the Vietnam War." Again, after accumulating hundreds of missions, Tad maintained his incredible reputation of *never* having one of his team members killed. He always led from the front on all his patrols.

In its summer 2006 issue *Sky Soldier* magazine relates the story of one of Tad's missions:

Eight North Vietnamese soldiers wait patiently in their well-camouflaged ambush position, eagerly anticipating an American patrol that might happen into their killing zone. One NVA soldier motions his comrades for complete silence. They ready their rifles. The soft swish of jungle bush tells them someone is coming. Suddenly, six feet away, a small bronze figure comes into view. He is wearing black pajamas and a floppy hat. He has rubber sandals on his feet. In his hands he carries an AK-47. They relax and hold their fire. One NVA soldier leans out of its concealment to get a better look. SSG Tadina gets off a quick thirty round burst sending the NVA soldier and two of his comrades to their graves. The remainder of the surprised team of NVA soldiers retreat into the thickness of the jungle, but not before sending a few short bursts at their attacker. Hit in both calves, SSG Tadina directs his team's fire into the retreating enemy. Tadina has fooled the NVA again. This small, but giant of a man, patrols either in black PJs or NVA khakis wearing a 60 pound rucksack and a Communist rifle. That day he sent his 111th enemy soldier to his grave.

Tad said that part of his motivation for remaining in Vietnam for so long was in a way to obtain payback for his brother's death. Patrick Tadina eventually had to be ordered out of Vietnam when it was discovered that the enemy had placed a bounty on him. he finally left Vietnam in July 1970.

Aftermath

Over his five years in combat Tadina was cited for valor with two Silver Stars, seven Bronze Stars for valor, two Army Commendation Medals for Valor, and three Purple Hearts. He later was inducted into the Ranger Hall of Fame. Tad continued on active duty through Desert Storm and currently serves as a security consultant on overseas assignments.

His N Company commander John Lawton retired as a full colonel and had been awarded a Distinguished Service Cross during his earlier command of a 101st Airborne Division infantry company. Lawton said, "If I had to go into combat with anyone, I'd like it to be Tad—he is good!" Colonel Lawton is also an inductee into the Ranger Hall of Fame. The Hall of Fame record reported on his DSC-action when he commanded a 101st Airborne Division infantry company near Chu Lai:

[Company Commander Lawton] received word that his second platoon had been heavily attacked in an open rice paddy by an estimated North Vietnamese Army company firing automatic weapons and mortars and had suffered many casualties. Captain Lawton evaluated the situation and led a squad across 50 meters of open ground. He received multiple fragment wounds as he advanced. Disregarding his severe wounds, he continued to crawl to the casualties, only to discover they were all either dead or could not be moved. For a full 45 minutes he single-handedly held the attackers at bay and prevented them from capturing the wounded. He placed suppressive fire on the insurgents until he ran out of ammunition and his position was overrun. With a burst of reserve energy he lunged forward to grab a weapon from one of the enemy, but was wounded a fourth time and left for dead. Through his courageous actions he had delayed the enemy force to such an extent that when the relief force arrived moments later, the attackers were caught in the open and were quickly routed, suffering heavy casualties.

Tadina and Lawton were distinctive warriors characterized by extraordinary feats of repeated acts of valor. It is the author's hope and prayer and should be that of all freedom-loving people throughout the world that America will continue to produce giants such as these two and countless thousands of other warriors who go forth unafraid and committed to fulfilling the missions thrust upon them by our nation.

In 1970, as SSgt. Patrick Tadina's five years of combat service were coming to an end, Wendy Weller's Vietnam service of healing the wounded, maimed, and sick as an army nurse was also coming to an end.

CHAPTER 11

The Real Horrors of War

Captain Marian E. "Wendy" Weller, USA
(NURSE DA NANG 1969-1970)

I realize vividly now that the real horrors of war were to be seen in hospitals, not on the battlefield.—Lieutenant General Sir John Glubb, *Into Battle: A Soldier's Diary of the Great War,* 1978

REAL HEROES

Those who served in Vietnam know there were many heroes, on and off the battlefield, but the two categories universally admired and even loved by combat soldiers are the dustoff (medical evacuation) pilots and military nurses. The pilots flew through hell to rescue the wounded and rush them to the nearest evacuation hospital, where the nurses persevered through incredible trauma and hardship to patch them up and get them on their way home.

The Peace of Her Youth

As the daughter of a U.S. Army Air Corps officer who participated in the D-Day invasion, left active duty after the war but later returned to active military service as an air force officer, interest in military service came naturally to Wendy Weller. In her childhood she was not exposed to violence, but in Vietnam she experienced more than enough for a lifetime. She joined the Army Student Nursing Program (ASNP) in college to obtain a B.S. in nursing and its attendant financial assistance. She was sworn into the army by her father.

Nurse Training

With only minimal educational and civilian nursing experience in gunshot wounds and other violent trauma, Vietnam and battlefield hospital nursing would be a major shock to Wendy. In 1968 at Ft. Sam Houston, Texas, during Medical Field Service School (MFSS), where she actually wore an Army uniform for the first time, the students were required to debride a gunshot wound and perform a tracheotomy on a live goat, which was anesthetized and then shot in all 4 legs, which approximated a war-zone combat wound. Having to perform the tracheotomy while listening to the poor goat trying to breathe, she realized that this was a very realistic way of preparing her for nursing in the war zone. Her first assignment to Walter Reed Army Medical Center in Washington, D.C., lasted four months, just long enough to find out how the army worked. Her duty on Ward 4 (Officers Medical) offered little experience in surgical wounds, although there were some medical emergencies and deaths. Overall, though, she had little experience in shock and trauma before going to Vietnam.

In Country

In February of 1969, a period known to many as "second Tet" or "mini-Tet," Wendy Weller began her trek to Vietnam. While making their approach to land at Long Binh, the pilot announced he was going to maneuver in a way that 747s had not been built to do. He turned the jumbo jet sharply to dodge enemy flak: the overhead-bin doors popped opened and items fell from the overhead compartments while the plane shuddered and shook. Wendy looked out the window and saw fighting on the runway. The plane was diverted farther north up the coast to Cam Ranh Bay Air Force Base where the six nurses on the board were quickly hustled into a bus with bars on the windows and soldiers inside, and driven to a replacement center. At this time nurses were normally in-processed at U.S. Army Vietnam (USARV) headquarters in Long Binh, north of Saigon, so now the nurses ended up without any in-country orders or assignment, many miles distant from the normal USARV in-processing facilities.

Eventually Wendy and her fellow nurses were able to get hops on USAF C130s and C123s on their way to Long Binh. They ended up spending nights at different hospital units in Qui Nhon and Saigon before they finally connected with their chief nurse at Long Binh. On every airbase they saw troops waiting for transport, and engraved in her memory is the look she saw on the faces of these young men. It was a blank stare of desperation, and the waiting soldiers were so quiet, there was little talking among them as if each man was an island unto himself. With around five hundred American women and five hundred thousand American men in country at that time, an American female away from a hospital or Red Cross center was an oddity; sometimes she felt like an alien with two heads from being stared at.

Peace Interrupted

Weller was assigned to the Army's 95th Evacuation Hospital, located in I Corps on a peninsula across from Da Nang. The French had originally landed in Da Nang when they came to Indochina in the nineteenth century and a century later the marines landed there in March 1965. At one end of this strip of land was Monkey Mountain on which was perched a radar and controller site staffed by marines and air force personnel. On the other end was Marble Mountain, where various aviation units such as Marine Air Groups 11 and 16 were based. The hospital was adjacent to the beach, but there was concertina wire separating it from the beach, which was mined to thwart bomb-carrying enemy sappers, so you could see the water but couldn't swim in it, quite unlike the scene shown in the opening shots of the *China Beach* television series (1988–91) that featured Wendy's hospital. Nurses could receive permission to go to the China Beach Rest and Recreation (R&R) center, but they had to be accompanied by armed guards. For these excursions they wore bathing suits under their fatigue uniforms and went to an area far from the troops. But on one beach outing, within minutes of removing their fatigues, a mob of American men started running in their direction, and they hastily left. So much for a few hours in the cool waters of the South China Sea! Wendy doesn't think she had even gotten her combat boots off before the nurses were swarmed. There were many incidents that underscored the gender difference and consequent threats to their safety. Nurses learned early in their tours to always to check under their cots when entering their six foot by six foot hootches (cubicles in wooden barracks) to see if there were any men hiding underneath. They also had to be very selective with whom they hitched rides to the base exchanges at China Beach or Freedom Hill, as some nurses had reported being taken on detours to base camps for several hours instead of to their requested destinations.

There was a whispering male who would stand outside the doors of various nurses; he would talk and sometimes even put his hand thru the screen in the door. Wendy managed to hit his hand with a hammer once and the whisperer didn't bother her again. Although the original hospital staffers had lived in tents, by the time Wendy got to the 95th Evac she was able to live in semi-permanent wooden barracks, partitioned off by plywood into small rooms containing one cot each. The second floor rooms did not have individual ceilings, so there was a decided lack of privacy. The lack of air conditioning was minimally offset by fans. A small TV showed *Gunsmoke* episodes or local Vietnamese stations. The Officer's Club was air-conditioned, which gave relief from the hot, muggy tropical weather. Unsurprisingly, the club's entertainment was heavily weighted toward male preferences. Once she was trying to watch a show performed by Asian showgirls and one of the hospital's doctors who was in her party kept putting his hands over her eyes to shield her, thinking she was too young to view the salacious act. Wendy remembers feeling angry about being treated like this; if she was old enough to be serving in a war zone, she should be able to make her own choices about what she would watch.

Healing of the Wounded at China Beach

The hospital consisted of a series of Quonset huts set on concrete slabs that were put together into long corridors with an A and B wing on each major unit. Patient receiving, pre-op, operating room, lab, X-ray, and the intensive care unit were at the front end of the corridor, followed by the wards. Wendy was assigned to Ward 6A and 6B, the surgical specialty unit, where care was provided for patients who had trauma of the brain, eye, ear, nose, throat, mouth, or urinary system. These injuries often resulted in disfigurement, brain damage, and sometimes sepsis (infection), which was exacerbated by the lack of air conditioning. These metal buildings had only recently been erected, but were a significant improvement over the previous tents. Ward 6A and B patients often had other wounds and burns, as well. There was no separate POW ward at this time and the patients were a mix of Americans, allied personnel, civilian men, women, children, and even infants, plus enemy combatants.

Her interpreter was a former school teacher who spoke Vietnamese and fluent colloquial French, but little English. Finding that she was starting to depend on her high-school and college French, she wrote her mother to send her French textbooks. She could read some of what the man wrote, but her spoken French left a lot to be desired and she was sure she lost much in translation. She made a point of learning the French words for basic medical terms and others about eating, hygiene and pain. There was an eleven-year-old boy with a gunshot wound in his back who had learned English from the marines assigned to Hill 55 near Da Nang, so he served as an unofficial interpreter. The boy proved invaluable in communicating with some of the wounded men and identifying for the staff who was an ARVN soldier (friendly) or a VC or NVA soldier (unfriendly) and who was Laotian (sometimes friendly) or Cambodian from the neighboring countries. The staff kept the Asian casualties who were unidentified in restraints in case they tried to escape or attack the Americans. Because of neurosurgery and brain injuries, many patients were disoriented and combative, yet they could not be heavily sedated as that might mask a change in their neurological condition. Wendy disliked restraining these people, but with limited staff tasked with medical duties she knew it was necessary. Still, she felt like she was torturing the restrained patients. She was also very nervous when working the night shift, as there usually was a corpsman (army medic) on the B side and a nurse and corpsman on the A side with the more acute patients, but when the dinner break came, both corpsmen went to eat together, and the nurses were left alone. It was nerve-racking trying to watch for changes in the patient's conditions as well as watching for escapes or attacks, and during those thirty-some-odd minutes she was hyper-vigilant and very highly stressed. This continued for her entire tour as they worked constantly, twelve hour shifts, six days a week, with very little rest for the weary. The few short lulls when only a few new casualties were admitted brought boredom without the normal intense activity with its attendant adrenaline rushes.

The Horrors Never Subsided

Changing wound dressings could be gross and sometimes complicated. There were screened windows in the walls of the Quonset huts and the nurses learned to have the patient's head face the aisle rather than the wall during dressing changes to help keep dirt and dust raised by incoming and outgoing helicopters from blowing in through the windows onto the patient's head or face wounds. (Ward 6 patients were mostly being treated for brain, eye, ear, nose, and throat trauma.) Again, with her limited surgical and trauma background, Wendy was totally unprepared for the severity of the wounds caused by high-velocity gunshots, grenade, mortar, and artillery shrapnel, and burning white phosphorous and napalm. Infection from punji stakes, which were caused by sharpened wooden stakes that were smeared with dirt and excrement and used in booby traps could be particularly difficult. When the patients came to her unit from the operating room, they were clean and covered with bandages. Within a short time, however, the drainage, the secretions, the sweating, and the bleeding all combined to emit a stench that was almost unbearable. She remembers unrolling the gauze from a casualty's face, and then removing horribly stained and smelly packing from his eye socket . . . and removing and removing and removing. As the packing seemed to go on forever she felt like a magician pulling an endless string of scarves out of hat. Then she had to put fresh packing in the wound. She could not imagine the pain and suffering of the patient and felt guilty for inflicting pain and suffering: patients with head wounds could not be heavily sedated. Every so often Wendy still has nightmares about the packing, seemingly miles of gauze in this poor man's head. She tried to perform this task in a calm, unemotional manner, as the patient intently watched for her reaction to his face. This was so hard to do. Early on she learned to disguise her real feelings and suppress her emotions.

After she became accustomed to dealing with one horror, it seemed that worse one would come along. She remembers a child who was admitted with an infection in his face. The black scab was removed by the doctor, and it was apparent that the bacteria had eaten a huge hole in the toddler's face. It reminded her of looking inside a dollhouse: you could see the child's jaw and gums. She never knew how any of these people recovered from their wounds and she had little closure in dealing with the injuries. Wendy found it extremely difficult to believe a soldier could have a meaningful life with both legs, one arm, or part of his brain missing.

The physical environment of the wards was kept spartan to help avoid complications in the healing process. Many patients had malaria attacks and high fevers and the metal Quonset huts tended to trap the hot air. Amoebic dysentery would sometimes spread resulting in rampant diarrhea among patients and staff. Americans and allied forces were evacuated as soon as possible, sometimes after receiving several units of whole blood to help stabilize them. The air force would pick them up, often only to bring them back the next day because they were bleeding somewhere. The patient would then be given more blood in the hopes that it would be enough for the flight out of Vietnam. The air pressure experienced during flight could make the red-blood cell value drop, so a good blood level was imperative before flying out. The medical staff tried to keep the civilians as long as possible because the local Vietnamese hospital was woefully understaffed and inadequate. There were portable field suction machines that were used to suction respiratory secretions from tracheotomies and one machine was used for two or more patients. Each patient had their own suction catheter that was kept in a bowl of special solution, and they rinsed the catheter out before and after each suctioning. They taught a young boy how to suction his grandfather, as he was to accompany him to the civilian hospital. Later it was learned that at the civilian hospital there was only one machine for fifty or more people, so all of their training was for naught. Relatives were allowed to come and help give care, and were able to stay in a large tent nearby, although sometimes the parents or other relatives of young patients slept in the child's bed or under their crib. Many Vietnamese helped in cleaning the concrete floors, bathing the children, and other janitorial duties in exchange for food from the mess hall. They also picked up and rocked the crying children and babies. There were many days Wendy held a crying, brain-injured toddler while continuing to perform her other duties. Even some American casualties would manage to pick up and try to comfort a crying child. To this day, Weller cannot tolerate being around crying babies, just remembering back to all those crying infants with their pain, confusion, and missing their parents, many of whom had been killed. Sometimes relatives did come to care for the orphaned children, but many did not; in their culture people with brain damage were often shunned. She felt very helpless with these crying kids, as nothing she could do would really help them, and she did not want to think about where and how they would end up. Trying to care for them seemed so hopeless and futile.

Many casualties with brain injuries had corresponding paralysis or weakness on one side of their body. The nurses themselves had to mix penicillin and chloromycetin solution and add both to the intravenous (IV) bottles—there were no small plastic bags to piggyback into the main lines as there are today—so they would line up the patients and get everyone to shake the small bottles until the meds dissolved, which had the side benefit of providing a bit of crude physical therapy. Sometimes the nurses made modest attempts at more strenuous physical therapy by putting patients in a circle and having them push a large beach ball around, but it was just too hot for the patients to keep up even this modest degree of physical activity for long. Patients in comas might not blink naturally, so their eyelids would be taped shut; a fly landing on an open eye could infect it and the patient could lose eyesight within a day or two. The staff also took small bandages and taped them together to make mosquito and fly nets to put over patient faces. Wendy brought a strong knack for problem solving back from the war zone!

Rocket Attacks

During enemy rocket attacks you first felt the ground shake; then you heard a kind of whooshing, thumping sound; and then you waited to see where the rocket would hit. The 95th Evac grounds sustained damage from time to time and Wendy recalls the motor pool being hit while she was there. Bit by bit she began to accept the dangers of the situation. During attacks there was a combination emotion of misery, but comfort for her amidst her fellow staff members; there was an attitude of "If I am going to get killed, I won't be alone"; and besides, she couldn't be concerned much as to where or whether the hospital would be hit since she was busy covering patients with mattresses or helping them get under their beds during the attacks. There were underground bunkers, but they had their own risks of snakes or more interesting, but embarrassing, trysting couples. She tried a bunker once, but somehow, it didn't seem to offer much protection. Unlike some veterans, Wendy's wartime experiences didn't strengthen her spiritual faith; she remembers thinking that if there were a real God, he/she would not let there be any wars and suffering such as she experienced. One of the most tragic recollections embedded in the dark recesses of her mind is of reports of VC going through a village looking for people who had been treated by the Americans, and then cutting off the limb that had a bandage on it. It is so hard to imagine babies with arms, legs, and heads removed by machetes because they had received hospital treatment under her love and care.

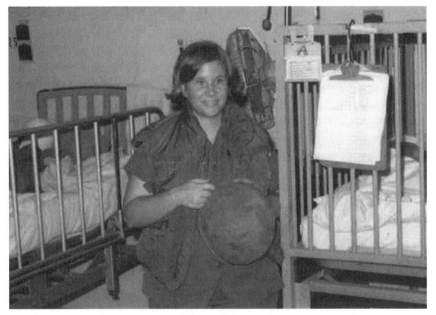

Army nurse Capt. Wendy Weller in Ward 6A of the 95th Evac Hospital, Da Nang, during a nearby rocket attack.

Breaks in the Monotony

When off duty the nurses talked shop such as wounds that had been treated, but also more weighty philosophical subjects such as what a drop in the bucket their work seemed in contrast to the enormity of generally poor health of the people of the underdeveloped country of Vietnam. Their entertainment was rather mundane: chess, cards, and occasional movies that were shown outside.

Some of the highlights of her tour were when she went on humanitarian medical missions such as joining one of their neurosurgeons to visit patients on the German hospital ship where she was able to use her French to speak with the Germans. After the patient rounds they savored freshly baked rolls and sweet butter from the ship's galley. The German nurses wore white cotton scrubs and clogs for shoes, very cool and comfortable compared to Army fatigues and combat boots. Once, Wendy and three other army nurses participated in a medical mission that was sponsored by a missionary group and they found themselves on cast-off U.S. Army helicopters flown by Vietnamese pilots who spoke some English and proudly proclaimed that they had been trained at Ft. Rucker, Alabama. Somehow, the stateside location of their training was not enough to inspire much confidence in the apprehensive nurses. Some of the German staff accompanied the Americans and they flew over the South China Sea to a nearby island. As she practiced her fractured French with the Germans Wendy was suddenly struck by the realization that the four of the 95th Evac nurses were in their uniforms, on an island somewhere, and they were the only Americans.

They landed on one side of the island, were met by Vietnamese men in black pajamas and sandals, carrying AK 47's and carried medical supplies through jungle terrain to the village on the far side. Interestingly, the lettering on the supplies was either in French or German, no English at all. She never knew the name of the island or who exactly were the people they were visiting. The village seemed lost in time, reflecting a way of life that had probably been in existence there for thousands of years. The barefoot villagers' boats resembled the tub Winken, Blinken, and Nod of nursery rhyme fame sailed in. The locals circled their group and just stared at the strange white people; it was as if they were visiting an aboriginal village that had been cut off from the outside world for centuries. One of their patients appeared to have tetanus and another showed symptoms of polio. The Vietnamese pilots contacted someone by radio and made arrangements for them to be taken to the German hospital ship for treatment.

Coming Home

Upon Wendy's return to the *real* world in the United States, she stored all these sights, sounds, and stories away, outwardly attempting to remain detached and organized, but always there was the constant, never-ending screaming and chaos in her head. She tried to keep very busy to avoid remembering and processing what she experienced as an innocent, young army nurse in a combat zone. She poured herself into being as perfect as possible in her nursing, always striving to do everything correctly, becoming as knowledgeable as possible in an after-the-fact effort to compensate for her lack of experience and knowledge while in Vietnam. Whenever she began to work in a new specialty area Wendy learned as much as possible as quickly as possible in order to become certified in that area.

Throughout her thirty-two year civilian nursing career she took her responsibilities very seriously, but there were very difficult times during which she agonized, trying to maintain her self control while caring for patients who had tracheotomies or other serious surgeries. Dressing changes were especially difficult because she could not do them without recalling the hot and horrible times in Da Nang, but she continued to bury those feelings as deeply as possible.

Wendy Weller has never regained a spiritual faith and has a fatalistic philosophy of life, despite how her creative and problem-solving abilities grew during her service at the field hospital. Coupled with the negative of the numbing of her feelings are positives such as an increased sensitivity for the plight of others and her lifelong dedication to serve others, almost as atonement for her inexperience during her tour of duty.

Combat in the Souls

Nurse Weller remained on active duty after Vietnam, but then left the army in 1978 in order to return to San Antonio and finish a master's degree while working fulltime at the Audie Murphy VA Medical Center. While helping to organize a seminar for the critical nursing group, she met a nurse whose husband was a counselor at the local VA Vet Center. In 1987 she attended the dedication of the San Antonio Vietnam Veterans Memorial, which depicts a sculptured scene of a navy corpsman (medic) aiding a wounded marine at Hill 881, a hill surrounding the embattled and encircled base at Khe Sanh. Bob Hope had come to town and performed a radiothon to raise the needed funds.

This ceremony upset her for days afterwards and encouraged by her nurse friend she made an appointment to visit her friend's husband at the Vet Center. He had been a marine at Khe Sanh. Initially Wendy and another nurse joined a group of male combat vets meeting at the Vet Center. The inclusion of two women in the group caused one of the men to quit the group saying, "Women can't be classified as combat vets." A small but troublesome issue related to the men's use of *colorful* language. They were concerned that the addition of the women to the group would inhibit their discussions, but the nurses quickly disposed of that notion remarking that they had heard everything during their service, nothing could shock them. Soon the entire group bonded because they recognized they shared the common emotions of unexpressed anger and even rage.

Eventually there were enough local nurse vets in need of counseling that a new group was formed. Surprisingly, everyone was so busy with work and activities that they never could agree on a meeting time. Wendy and the other nurses coped with the horrors of their Vietnam hospital experiences by staying busy. All these nurses possessed advanced degrees and certifications but the advanced education didn't diminish the need to address the emotional traumas from their war.

Aftermath

Wendy Weller mentioned that, for most of our Americans being assigned to Vietnam, there were varying degrees of orientation as to their combat mission, but has already indicated her own exposure to treating horrendous combat injuries was severely lacking. One glaring inadequacy for most Americans deployed to Vietnam was that they knew nothing about the *people* as opposed to the *enemy* and nothing about the country's rich history, culture, and traditions. Although based adjacent to Da Nang she never knew that it was, "A repository of traditional art objects and architecture from the Cham dynasty, which dates from the second century A.D. . . . an ancient city with a rich cultural history . . . was named Tourane by the French . . . the Cham Museum houses . . . more than 300 artifacts . . . many dating to the fourth century." (Dulles: 399-403) The United States, as magnificent as it is, was a newcomer in world history to the country we fought to save from Communism.

On March 29, 1975 Da Nang became the scene of chaos and confusion as ARVN soldiers and civilians vied and literally fought each other to escape by air or sea. It was a truly pitiful event in the country's history as the South Vietnamese attempted to flee the onrushing Communists: "Some even attached themselves to the wheel wells of one of the aircraft as the planes took off. They met their deaths as they fell hundreds of feet into the South China Sea." (Dulles: 403)

After four years of teaching, in 1978 she returned to work among the veterans at Audie Murphy VA Medical Center in San Antonio where she felt comfortable, satisfied that she was among fellow American patriots, many of whom had also shared the Vietnam experience that had become the period of her life from which she could never escape. Appropriately she was assigned to the mental health unit for fifteen years. Her experiences in this assignment contrasted with her experiences as a green, wet-behind-the-ears nurse when she got to Vietnam. Now she was confident that she could give appropriate, high-quality care to veterans suffering from mental health issues, especially those tormented with post traumatic stress disorder (PTSD). Unfortunately, however, she also witnessed patients who had never been to Vietnam or any other war zone who were intent on embellishing their military service, even creating combat records in order to obtain enhanced benefits that were available to combat vets. These encounters caused her stress, frustration, and anger. She became one of the resident experts at the medical center in uncovering these fakes. (Stories of many "wannabees" are extensively documented by B. G. Burkett and Glenna Whitley in their book, *Stolen Valor: How the Vietnam Generation Was Robbed of Its Heroes and Its History*.)

In 1970, as Wendy Weller was returning from Vietnam to the United States, plans were being drawn up for a surprise visit by Americans deep into North Vietnam.

CHAPTER 12

Mission of Mercy at Son Tay

MAJOR FREDERIC M. "MARTY" DONOHUE, USAF
FIRST LIEUTENANT GEORGE W. PETRIE, USA

Courage . . . is that firmness of spirit, that moral backbone, which, while fully appreciating the danger "involved," nevertheless goes on with the undertaking. Bravery is physical; Courage is mental and moral—Major C. A. Bach, 1917, address to graduating new officers, Ft. Sheridan, Wyoming.

PRISONERS

Given the nature of the war, most Americans taken prisoner by the enemy were U.S. Navy and Air Force pilots shot down over North Vietnam. The longest held spent nearly nine years in captivity. Most were confined in various camps in North Vietnam, including at a place called Son Tay located only about fifteen miles from Hanoi. While a raid intended to free those prisoners came up empty (the prisoners having been moved elsewhere before the operation could be mounted), the North Vietnamese were duly impressed that such an attack could be carried out so deep in their territory. Subsequently most prisoners were concentrated in Hanoi and their treatment noticeably improved, a development they attributed to the raid on Son Tay. When the Paris Accords ended U.S. participation in the Vietnam War, 565 American military prisoners were repatriated. Another number, estimated to be at least 55 and possibly more than twice that number, had died of illness or malnutrition in captivity or were murdered by their captors.

Rescue Pilot

During Colonel Donohue's Air Force career he flew 132 combat missions and conducted over 100 peacetime rescues. His first exposure to counterinsurgency operations was with the Royal Australian Air Force (RAAF) as an exchange pilot where in New Guinea and Malaysia he inserted special operations forces. He commanded the launch site recovery team for Apollo Space Missions 7 through 16. He was the first pilot to complete a hover pickup of an Apollo capsule.

Green Beret on a Personal Mission
Lieutenant George Petrie, U.S. Army special forces, had been one of the Green Berets selected from several hundred volunteers at Ft. Bragg, North Carolina when Col. Arthur D. "Bull" Simons asked for "volunteers" for a "special mission." Petrie's first cousin, U.S. Navy Comdr. Jim Hickerson, was a prisoner of war of the North Vietnamese. George had served in a variety of very hazardous assignments in his previous tours in Vietnam in what were known as Mike Force rapid reaction units and mobile guerilla operations deep in enemy territory.

The Mission
Major Donohue heard the final and complete briefing of their secret mission only the afternoon of the day before the launch to free the American POWs held at Son Tay prison in North Vietnam. He rose to stiff attention with all the other volunteers from the U.S. Air Force, Army and Navy when mission commander Brig. Gen. Larry Manor entered the secure briefing room in the secure compound at the Takhli Royal Thai Air Base in Thailand. They would finally learn the details for the dangerous mission they had been rehearsing for three months. General Manor was a distinguished air force general in command of the USAF special operations forces. He had flown 72 combat mission in World War II and 275 in Vietnam and was highly respected. Manor turned the briefing over to Colonel Simons for the explanation of the mission to the energetic and "pumped" group of military professionals in the room.

A few weeks before the mission kickoff, Major Donohue had been told to report to General Manor for a briefing at Eglin Air Force Base in Florida. At that time he did not believe any of those practicing for the mission knew or had guessed where they were going. Obviously, the concept for the rescue had begun at the Pentagon, but it all only came together under the leadership of General Manor and the team he assembled for the operational planning. Donohue joined General Manor and some members of his planning group in a secure guarded room where he was shown "Barbara," which was a model of Son Tay built by the CIA. Donohue was the first operational member to see the model of their target. General Manor made it clear that Donohue was not to discuss nor tell anyone about what he saw there. Manor began to introduce Donohue to the flight conditions he would encounter and had Donohue put on special goggles that made the mock up look like it was approximately a mile away and then walk toward it as if he were making an aerial approach toward it. He learned that he would have to become accustomed to only the illumination reflected from a quarter moon on the night of the mission. Manor made it clear that this was the target for which they were practicing. At that time Donohue was not entirely sure it was Son Tay; however it was obviously a POW camp. In subsequent practices the words Son Tay were used and it was obviously in North Vietnam.

General Manor retired as a three star general and when asked why Major Donohue had been selected for his part on the raid said, "He was selected due to his extensive experience in HH-53 helicopters, and also he had just completed the first trans-Pacific flight of a HH-53 helicopter." During the war, replacement choppers for the air force were transported in an eight to nine week sea voyage on the flight decks of navy "baby" carriers. Although sealed and covered for the journey, the replacement helicopters always required a week of maintenance at the port of Vung Tau in South Vietnam to repair leaks caused by sea air. A test was needed to fly the choppers all the way to shorten the delivery time. Donohue, piloting one chopper with another beside his, flew all the way from Eglin Air Force Base in Florida to Canada, Alaska, down the Aleutians chain, to Japan and the Philippines to deliver the helicopter to Da Nang. It was a celebrated flight that spanned seven days.

Back to the final briefing where Lieutenant Petrie described legendary Green Beret Col. Arthur D. "Bull" Simons's explanation of the ground plans, "He had stood before us smoking his ever-present cheroot, and with his gruff and to-the-point manner, announced 'We are going to rescue seventy American prisoners of war, maybe more, from a camp called Son Tay. This is something American prisoners have a right to expect from their fellow soldiers. The target camp is twenty-three kilometers northwest of downtown Hanoi!' When he made that announcement, as only he could do, all of us in the room spontaneously stood up, cheered and applauded. I don't know for sure, but I think the colonel's eyes got a little teary when that happened. I know mine did."

The Green Beret volunteers had been personally selected by Colonel Simons and all were subjected to intense mental and physical testing. (Ruhl:

26)

This was one of those incredibly unforgettable times in a warrior's life when the room came together in a demonstration of pride because they now had closure on the months of dedicated and disciplined training for their historic mission. Bold, daring, dangerous were words too weak to define what this group of elite U.S. Army special forces and U.S. Air Force special operations and air rescue and recovery forces would undertake on November 21, 1970.

Early Preparations

In August 1970, the day after Major Donohue returned to Eglin Air Force Base from his trans-Pacific flight, he was ordered to report to Colonel Britton, the helicopter operations officer. Donohue remembers thinking, "What did I do wrong?" when he was asked to close the door behind him. This usually preceded a royal chewing out. Colonel Britton asked him, however, to volunteer for a special, dangerous mission involving much precision night flying. Naturally Donohue volunteered and then he and the other members of this secret mission task force informed their wives they would be on night training for the foreseeable future. The work nights were typically seven at night until seven in the morning.

They began their training to prove out the workability of several helicopters operating at night to conduct a special operation with training for three months at Eglin Air Force Base. The training involved a building block concept, two helicopters flying together, then adding fixed-wing to the exercise, then adding Green Berets as passengers, then aerial refueling, and then landing in unlighted fields. (Donohue: 3) A total of 165 rehearsals were conducted. Donohue's helicopter, a HH-53 gunship *Super Jolly Green Giant* was to lead the force the last few miles and be the first one over the target.

The story of the planning of this operation had begun back in May 1970 when intelligence indicated that American prisoners of war were being held in a small, half-acre installation just twenty-three miles from Hanoi. A joint task force was formed to carry out a rescue mission.

U.S. Air Force rescue personnel had never conducted an assault mission with army soldiers, and every element of the operation had to be coordinated from techniques to equipment to timing. Film was studied from overflights of Son Tay and a replica of the compound was built for rehearsals at Hurlburt Field. (Ruhl: 27) It was dismantled every morning to remove it from the eyes of Russian reconnaissance satellites. (Lamb: 4)

The air force components included Combat Talon C-130Es (four engine cargo aircraft) and A-IEs (propeller-driven, single engine attack aircraft) for providing air-to-ground support for the raid. The plan for the air element was to transport the special forces contingent to the base undetected, provide protection while they assaulted the prison, and rescue the POWs. There was to have been a thirty minute holding period while the ground assault occurred.

Into the Enemy Heartland

On the night of November 20, 1970, the mission was a go and had been moved up one day due to an impending typhoon. Donohue and the other raiders were transported by C-130 the two hundred miles from Takhli to Udorn Royal Thai Air Force Base where Donohue previously had served a tour. He recalled in the past when he had returned there with twenty-nine bullet holes in his chopper, but also the time he had rescued two downed pilots who had ejected from their planes due either to battle damage or mechanical difficulties. He had his own personal history on that base.

At 0130 hours, November 21, 1970, the helicopters launched from Udorn in total radio silence, which was to be maintained until the Green Berets were safely on the ground and inside the camp. The first challenge prior to enter-

Major Marty Donohue (USAF) upon return from a pilot recovery mission in North Vietnam, March 20, 1968.

ing North Vietnam's air space was a thick layer of clouds which kept the helicopters from seeing each other for about ten minutes. Then they broke into the clear in the Red River Valley and saw an unforgettable scene.

Donohue remembered, "Ahead the lights of Hanoi were beautiful . . . and just beyond them the Navy planes had the sky over Haiphong Harbor lit up like the Fourth of July with flares. There was an awful lot of commotion, and there must have been a lot of noise."(Ruhl: 29)

En route Donohue reminded his crew members, Capt. Thomas R. Waldron, SSgt. Aaron P. Hodes, SSgt. James J. Rogers, and Sgt. Angus W. Sowell of their threefold mission. "Number one—to find and identify the camp. Number two—to pass over the wall at twenty knots and twenty feet and neutralize the ground towers and guard barracks. Number three—to land near the Red River and wait until the Army called us in [to carry out POWs]." (Donohue: 6)

The Assault on the Compound

They arrived near the objective, and neither enemy fire nor any force opposed them. The expected quarter moon gave them enough light to descend down and spot the camp. Donohue remembered saying, "Thirty seconds, twenty seconds—there it is, turn left about ten degrees." Initially he didn't see the camp, but then they were there. "Recheck guns and wait till I'm steady, then get those guard towers." Donohue flew the helicopter in and the gunners opened fire, taking out the towers with one totally collapsing. Not a single round went into the compound. Continuing on, they fired on the guard barracks. Then came the word that the other helicopters were arriving. The first part of Donohue and his crew's job was done. (Donohue: 7)

Murphy's Law—If it can go wrong, it will!—kicked in. As he powered up for altitude, an alarm light signaled main transmission trouble. The approved solution for dealing with this alert was to proceed to nearest suitable field and land. Since that would be Hanoi, Donohue landed in a rice paddy one-and-a-half miles away to await the expected call from the assault group to return to pick up the POWs. It turned into a long wait. Donohue kept their engines running and saw many Vietnamese around their helicopter which was on an ox bow bend of the Red River, but the Vietnamese must have been very surprised and quietly watched the three choppers. Sergeant Sowell asked Donohue if he could fire on the peasant audience watching them, but Major Donohue nixed that idea unless they approached or threatened their chopper. To ensure that he did not become trigger happy, Donohue turned off Sowell's gun from the cockpit.

Just prior to leaving the Udorn launch site Capt. Richard Meadows, another legendary Green Beret covert operator and the leader of the assault platoon (code-named Blue Boy), pulled Lieutenant Petrie aside and told him that his cousin, Commander Hickerson, was not supposed to be at Son Tay. As George said, "This hit me pretty hard because I had dreamed about what it would be like to sit next to Jim on the ride back . . ." As they approached Son Tay, Petrie saw a line of perhaps thirty vehicle lights pointed toward Son Tay coming from the direction of Hanoi and only about a mile and a half away. In hindsight they could have been trucks carrying enemy combat troops to Son Tay due to the mission having become compromised. He pointed them out to Captain Meadows who must have thought, if they arrive at Son Tay during the raid, we will deal with them then.

Son Tay raider
1st Lt. George
Petrie, 1970.

Blueboy 3 team of the assault platoon consisted of Lieutenant Petrie, team sergeant MSgt. Tom Kemmer, small and wiry, but tough as nails, and Sfc. Donald "Pete" Wingrove, a ranger and veteran of Vietnam's III Corps Mike Force. Blueboy 3 accompanied eleven other Green Berets who were to be flown right into the middle of the prison compound on a HH-3 air rescue helicopter named Banana 1. The lead pilot was Maj. Herb Kalen, who really had the most daunting flying challenge because the plan called for him literally to fly his chopper into the compound knowing there was a tree as an obstacle, crash land, place his fourteen special forces soldiers on the ground, wait for the POWs to be rescued, then leave his chopper and be extracted with the assault team. On the approach his rotor blades were completely stopped by the branches of the tree before the chopper touched ground. Mattresses spread on the floor modestly cushioned the crash impact and George and the others rushed to their cell block and other assignments. Crew TSgt. Leroy M. Wright's foot was crushed when a fire extinguisher broke loose. Not realizing he was hurt, he proceeded to his preplanned defensive position and only when airborne after the raid did he remove his boot to find a very bloody foot.

George Petrie and the other thirteen members of the compound assault team exited the chopper and Blueboy commander Captain Meadows used a bullhorn to declare to the American prisoners: "We are Americans ... this is a rescue. Keep your heads down. We are here to get you out. We will soon enter your cells. We are Americans." There were no responses from the cells. George moved toward the east gate to take out a guard tower that had been hidden from the aerial photos by tree foliage. It appeared to be empty, but he threw a grenade into it and heard the scream as the enemy soldier hiding there was hit. During his time in the compound Petrie and Kemmer together took out four enemy soldiers and Petrie alone accounted for four more of the enemy. When he entered the maximum-security cell underneath the tower and it was not occupied by any POWs, he knew there was something wrong. The other special forces raiders found no POWs either. (Gargus: 202) One of the men from the Redwine Security Group, Sfc. Freddie Doss, positioned in a camp outer perimeter protective position, had occasion to greet the convoy spotted earlier by Petrie on the flight when they arrived at the camp. He delivered antitank weapons fire on the first two trucks and destroyed them causing the others all to stop, turn around, and disappear out of the field of fire. As was learned later they constituted a convoy from a school for truck drivers. The drivers probably got their first experience of what they would face later if they ever drove down the Ho Chi Minh Trail in Laos.

Banana 1 was stripped of everything but radios and wired for demolition ten minutes after the raiders' departure while everyone else prepared for extraction. While this was happening in the prison compound, the Greenleaf Group (another assault group) had landed erroneously in an area south of the targeted camp where a short firefight put them in a skirmish with "Enemy soldiers, who appeared to be physically larger than typical Vietnamese soldiers... [who] were coming out of the buildings.... They did not appear to be North Vietnamese. All seemed much taller and bulkier than the Vietnamese men our troops had encountered on their prior tours in the country." A hundred to two hundred attacking enemy were all dispatched by the special forces soldiers who then reboarded their choppers and went to the Son Tay prison compound. (Gargus: 195) Supposedly, Colonel Simons later said he believed them to be Chinese or Russians.

It was all over! All the Green Berets moved to their extraction helicopters and departed. Fifty-five guards at the Son Tay prison were killed or wounded.

The Return
Donohue recalled it had been the longest wait of their lives. They heard the radio transmissions indicating no prisoners were there! The NVA finally woke up and they began launching SAMs (surface to air missiles) and antiaircraft fire. Donohue and his crew were observers, so they waited and waited.

Finally the extraction choppers departed the rice paddy and headed toward the prison to pick up the assault force. Donohue had been "first in" and now was to be "last out" as his chopper was scheduled to be the last one at the compound to pick up any stragglers. They were shocked to receive the message, "All the army troops have been picked and you are clear to depart." As they lifted again, the "chip light" was still lit. A SAM headed directly to them, so Marty Donohue headed down so close to the trees as an evasive maneuver that he scraped the tops. That missile missed them as did two more launched toward them. (Donohue: 8–9) Air force fighters had been providing protective cover for the C-130s and dropping flares to support the helicopters. On the return home one of the fighters was hit by enemy fire and the two men bailed out, but were extracted after first light by mission helicopters. On the return trip Donohue and his other crew members began to run through their minds that they had pulled off their mission precisely as planned but there were no prisoners there, a major letdown.

Donohue's four other crew members received Silver Stars for their valor

and Maj. Frederic "Marty" Donohue, the aircraft commander of the helicopter gunship that was the first American element over the camp, received
the Air Force Cross, our nation's second highest decoration for "extraordinary
heroism in military operations against an armed enemy of the United States
. . . without regard for his personal safety, immeasurably contributed to the
complete confusion and disorganization of enemy forces. He successfully
completed a daring return penetration through numerous surface-to-air
missiles, ground fire, and the threat of enemy aircraft." (Donohue's Air Force
Cross citation)

Even after the return to the United States, Marty kept his wife Pat in
the dark too long as to what he had done. The first time she knew for sure
was when they were flying as a group to Ft. Bragg to get medals from
Secretary of Defense Melvin Laird. One of the wives told her that was where
they were going and for what reason. She had been in the back of plane and
came up to where Marty was seated and really gave him some grief. She
wanted to know why the other wives knew and she didn't; Marty simply told
her it was classified. Being a good military spouse it was enough of an explanation for her.

Summing up, Donohue asks:

Was the raid all in vain? In the minds of my crew and the rest of
the force that participated—a resounding NO. The consensus of the
men I talked to cared enough for our prisoners to voluntarily risk
their lives to secure their freedom. Those U.S. Soldiers, Sailors and
Airmen, part and parcel of American society, showed the North
Vietnamese that the American people cared about our prisoners and
were determined to gain their release. The force was large and
vulnerable, but the risk was more than worth it. Hopefully, the word
got to the prisoners and the knowledge that we were that close will
give them the strength to hold on until they can be released. (Donohue: 10)

Aftermath

Before retiring from the air force, Colonel Donohue served with the Thir-
teenth Air Force in the Philippines where he conceived and organized the
use of U.S. Air Force tactical hospitals to treat rural Filipinos. He subsequently received the Philippine Legion of Honor. Sergeant Wright also
received the Air Force Cross. Lieutenant Petrie received a Silver Star for his

valor during the raid and participated in 1975 in the Evacuation of Saigon. (See Chapter 18.)

In November 1970, air force POW Kenneth Cordier, who later retired from active duty as a full colonel, was being held in Camp Hope, approximately ten miles from Son Tay. He remembers:

> I will never forget that night. We thought President Nixon had resumed the bombing. We were moved back to Hanoi three nights later and all 350 of us were put into the main compound at Hoa Lo prison [Hanoi Hilton]. There was a room full of Vietnamese POWs living in a large room adjacent to the corner of the American rooms 4 and 5. Room 5 could pass notes back and forth out the latrine windows to the Vietnamese, who informed us that the Son Tay raid was a U.S. government attempt to rescue POWs. This info was passed via tap and mute code to the other big rooms. Some of the guys were elated, because it showed our government had not forgotten us nor had written us off. It was a morale low point for me and a few others, because I reasoned, that if our government would mount a high risk operation that close to Hanoi, there was no hope for a negotiated release in the foreseeable future. However, the raid made the Vietnamese feel compelled to concentrate the POWs in one location in central Hanoi. This had the benefit to the POWs of living in large groups of 50–55 men rather than in the small cells and isolated conditions experienced up to that time.

It would be twenty-seven months before Cordier and Hickerson (Petrie's cousin), who also was held at Camp Hope, would be released by the Communists.

Son Tay was a propaganda victory for the United States. Another type of propaganda effort was being conducted by civilian Ron Humphrey in the Delta in the battle for hearts and minds.

CHAPTER 13

Winning Hearts and Minds

RON HUMPHREY (CIVILIAN, VIETNAM 1969–1971)

To seduce the enemy's soldiers from their allegiance and encourage them to surrender is of especial service, for an adversary is more hurt by desertion than by slaughter.—Flavius Vegetius Renatus, *The Military Institutions of the Romans*, c. AD 378, tr. Clark, 1776.

RALLIERS

Vietnamese fighting Vietnamese caused much heartache, especially for families with relatives on both sides of the protracted war. A key South Vietnamese program, known as Chieu Hoi *(Open Arms), was an amnesty appeal designed to induce enemy personnel, especially Viet Cong who were of southern origin, to rally to the government side. An important adjunct of the Phoenix program,* Chieu Hoi *became especially successful when the allied approach changed from search and destroy to clear and hold. During 1969 more than forty-seven thousand enemy personnel rallied to the government side, the equivalent of several divisions and more than half again as many as during the previous year.*

Patriot and Public Servant

Ron Humphrey had already served an active duty army assignment in France where the assignment had been relatively uneventful and significantly different from what would face him in later years. He had enlisted in the Army in 1954 and was a cryptologist and chaplain's assistant in a transportation unit based at Rochefort, France. Later, after returning the United States and leaving the army Ron attended the University of Washington in Seattle where he married Marylou, a majorette with the university's "Husky" marching band. Following their graduation in 1959 they both worked in Seattle for the next six years.

Eventually, they decided to pursue an adventurous life together that they thought could be found through employment overseas. Ron passed the written Foreign Service exam in November 1965 and following interviews both by a senior foreign service officer and by the CIA at Langley in early 1966, by June he was offered positions with both United States Information Agency (USIA) and the Central Intelligence Agency (CIA). He decided on USIA, completed the sixteen-week Foreign Officer Basic Course, and was posted to Hamburg, Germany, in November 1966 to oversee *Amerika Haus*, an American cultural center. He had a part-time undercover, assignment, however: as the United States became more and more deeply involved in the Vietnam War Ron was tasked with infiltrating the expanding anti-American movement in Germany.

Ron donned a hippie disguise with requisite beard, successfully infiltrated the left-wing operation in Hamburg and reported on their leaders and plans. His disguise worked well enough that he fit right into the crowds and their antiwar demonstrations. One night he joined a group of five thousand demonstrators who had gathered to vandalize his own center, the *Amerika Haus*. As the group marched down the city street carrying their torches, waving placards, and shouting "Ho, Ho, Ho Chi Minh", he thought that this must have been how it must have been in the 1930s when Hitler and his followers began their rise. It was planned at the last minute that the movement's notorious leader, "Willie the Red," would suddenly appear and administer the *coup de grace,* a sledge hammer directed at the front glass window of the cultural center. Among the crowd only Humphrey knew that the glass had recently been replaced with a shatterproof type. Willie manhandled the hammer, struck the glass and when the glass remained unbroken, he fell back into the street with a bloody nose.

Mission unaccomplished!

Assignment: Vietnam

Presumably Humphrey's superiors believed his experiences with the war protestors was good preparation for actual war so in 1969 he found himself reassigned to Vietnam. His preparation included a short course at Ft. Bragg to train on weapons and obtain a basic orientation to the war zone. His fellow students were destined for assignments in the American embassy, Agency for International Development (USAID), CIA, or his agency, USIA. Ron would be assigned to be a province psyops (psychological operations) advisor (PPA) in the reportedly peaceful province of Go Cong, south of Saigon on the South China Sea. He was packing his bathing suit. His responsibility would be to utilize psychological operations to win over or maintain the loyalty of the local population to the government cause and to thwart the Communist movement in his part of South Vietnam.

Another student Rick was assigned to the much more dangerous province of Vinh Long, which had the ominous reputation as the province recording the deaths of the most American civilians so far in the war. The beaches of the South China Sea were looking better all the time.

Humphrey had truly begun to adopt and believe in America's commitment to upholding freedom and democracy in Vietnam; it was a worthy goal and he was fully committed to his part in ensuring its success.

When he arrived at Tan Son Nhut Air Base in Saigon, it was evident he had arrived in a war zone when he viewed the myriad of military planes on the runways and the two F-4 Phantom jets loaded with bombs departing for a mission. The contrasts in Vietnam were quickly apparent as several beautiful young Vietnamese girls greeted them at the end of the steps just as if they were excited tourists arriving in Hawaii.

Change of Province

Rick must have heard about the civilian deaths in Vinh Long province and chose to resign his new posting resulting in Ron quickly discovering that he was being reassigned there. (Goodbye South China Sea!) Well, he had been seeking adventure and it looked like he would be seeing some action. After being issued a .38 cal. Smith and Wesson revolver and ammunition he was ready for his war. Ron caught a jeep to the Air America terminal at Tan Son Nhut to begin his air-taxi ride sixty-five miles south to Vinh Long City. There he was met by two Joint United States Public Affairs Office (JUSPAO) members whose operations included Humphrey's USIA responsibilities. It was August 1969 and this would be his new home for the next couple years. The Vietnamese office manager/interpreter was a Mr. Quy, who had worked for Americans for fifteen years and was very valuable to their efforts.

On the way to the compound, which was located on the outskirts of town, they passed the Vinh Long Catholic cathedral, which was believed to have been built by the Catholic bishop who was the brother of assassinated Vietnam President Diem. Humphrey was shown to his new quarters and was quickly became convinced that it was very susceptible to an enemy attack.

Next he went to the small provincial JUSPAO building; it was about the size of a two-bedroom home back in the states.

Humphrey was briefed regarding his two culture-drama teams that visited the countryside villages and hamlets of the province to present entertainment shows. He was also introduced to the leaflet operation which entailed dropping leaflets from the air over the countryside. Ron was now in show business, overseeing civic action and troop entertainment for the Vietnamese. With nineteen Vietnamese entertainers and office workers to assist him, his responsibilities included the production of radio and TV programs and publishing a weekly newspaper.

His Vietnamese counterpart in the Vietnamese Information Service (VIS) was Mr. Thom, whose organization consisted of seventy-five people with offices in all seven districts of the province and many of the forty-four villages, which had a combined population of half a million, fifty thousand of whom were in Vinh Long City. Thom and Humphrey were able to communicate with each other in French.

The Military Assistance Command, Vietnam (MACV) compound was next on the tour to acquaint him with the U.S. military advisors to the ARVN forces in the province. Colonel Roland Tausch was the province senior advisor (PSA) in charge of all Americans officially in the province with a State Department civilian as his deputy.

Before the '68 Tet offensive, three years earlier in 1966, Vinh Long City had been relatively secure because ARVN's 9th Division was based there and a U.S. naval facility was based at neighboring Dong Tam. Also, the Vinh Long airbase had been enlarged for a major U.S. helicopter unit to use as a base of operations in that part of the country.

Ron found safer living quarters in a four-apartment building adjacent to the traffic circle in the city. The traffic circle marked the deepest penetration into Vinh Long City made by the Viet Cong during the 1968 Tet offensive, a year and a half earlier. His new living quarters were surrounded by a fence, guard posts, and grenade screen, which helped him sleep much better than he had in his previous abode on the edge of town. Adjacent to his new living quarters Ron observed some shacks that could be accessed from the highway by means of planks thrown across a swampy area. He glanced out his window and whistled at a tall, slender Vietnamese woman wearing an *ao dai*, the traditional Vietnam women's dress. She looked up at him, but made no greeting as she entered one of the shanties. The woman had just returned from her restaurant/ bar-hostess job to tend to her eight children.

PSYOPS Team

His two *Van Tac Tu* culture-drama teams each consisted of seven vibrant, young Vietnamese performers who were basically "wandering minstrels." Their popularity was soon evident to Ron. There were six girls and eight boys, all of whom were dedicated to their outreach, especially for the boys because it won hands down over serving as a soldier in ARVN from which they were deferred. Members of the troop sang songs, played musical instruments, or performed magical tricks. This type of entertainment had been going on in Vietnam for centuries and was an effective method for telling the government story to the country people.

These wandering minstrels were appreciated by the villagers and remarkably enjoyed an incredible degree of safety: the Viet Cong might murder a local village chief or school teacher, but a sure way to turn the villagers against them was to attack the young entertainers who were their only means of diversion in otherwise tough, colorless lives. These teams performed on makeshift stages and always began by leading the audience in singing the national anthem. Government propaganda was subtly woven into the programs.

The young troubadours were immensely popular and typically stayed several days in each village and between shows helped the villagers in various community projects. The villagers provided the troop's living accommodations during their visits and typically entertainers gleaned useful information from the areas they visited. These young people were also the cast members for the taping of the radio and television programs produced by Humphrey.

One evening, when he was back in his room, Ron received a visitor. It was the woman he had whistled at through the window. She was on her way to work and invited him to come have a drink. Ron declined the drink invitation, but agreed to have his laundry done by the woman's daughter. She said her name was Kim and that she would send her daughter for his laundry. Little did he know how his life would be changed in countless ways by Kim entering his world.

Humphrey's next psyops mission was to drop propaganda leaflets over suspected Viet Cong areas. The leaflets kept coming from Saigon in never ending batches so he figured he had better order an air force psyops plane, a "Bird Dog," and begin learning the geography of the province with its 260 hamlets and other small communities. By the end of his time in Vinh Long Ron would become very familiar with the entire province because of all the time he spent on these leaflet drops. On the leaflet missions he also used the plane's speaker system to broadcast messages to the people on the ground.

When Ho Chi Minh died in late 1969, he made speaker announcements to the village about the death and thought defections might increase; they didn't. Apparently Ho Chi Minh in far away Hanoi had little influence on the motivations of the fighters in the Delta.

During his assignment Ron began to be called "Mindbender," so he adopted it as his radio call sign. Ron became very popular among the Americans stationed at the small outposts and compounds in the province because he eventually volunteered to process and distribute American movies as they became available. He also had a movie projector in his own room, so he could have his own private showings. One night his laundry was returned by Kim, but she was not alone. She held an Amerasian (half-Vietnamese half-American) baby in her arms and was followed by six more children who all became captivated by the John Wayne western Ron was playing that night.

Humphrey soon discovered that Kim had lived a very hard and sad life in Vinh Long. Two years earlier she had lost her husband, Captain Nam, an ARVN officer, to whom she had been married for ten years and with whom she had six children. Kim's father had died and her husband took leave from his unit to attend the funeral. On the way home for the funeral Captain Nam was ambushed and killed by the Viet Cong. As a war widow Kim and her six children were forced to live on a very modest ARVN pension. Then, an American working locally for a civilian construction company met her and after a time they fell in love and agreed to marry. Before they could wed, however, Kim had two more children. And, as if this weren't enough to cap off a complicated and challenging life now that she had eight children, friends of her American boyfriend reported that he had been killed in a construction accident. Then Ron came into her life and literally became "the life of the party" for this almost destitute Vietnamese family of nine by showing them a new movie every night in his apartment. Slowly, but surely, Ron and Kim's life became more intertwined. Another daughter began to do his housework and eventually Kim began cooking his meals.

Kim began to teach Ron about Vietnam and its culture. One of the major differences in their two cultures related to how in Vietnam life was believed to repeat itself in cycles whereas in the West life was thought of more as a straight line in which once a day was lived it was over, never to be repeated. She explained their cultural belief that it was best to have both sides "save face" so there would be no embarrassment or loss of status to either party to a transaction. Many of the Vietnamese military officers studied astrological charts to determine propitious times to attack or delay an attack.

❖ ❖ ❖

In late 1969 Humphrey acquired another role related to the Phoenix program as it was being implemented in Vinh Long Province. He began participating in Phoenix by preparing an organization chart of the suspected leaders of the Viet Cong infrastructure (VCI) from his intelligence sources. When evidence was obtained regarding a VCI leader or member a Phoenix team would attempt to arrest the person. In remote areas, however, these Viet Cong leaders were often protected by bodyguards. In these cases it was necessary to use armed local forces known as Provincial Reconnaissance Units (PRUs) to capture or kill the suspects. Targeted individuals included the actual Viet Cong leaders, their tax collectors who extorted money from the villagers, and couriers who carried messages. When a suspect was discovered in a village, PRU operatives would be dropped into the villages from helicopters, often resulting in violent firefights. The violent nature of the PRU teams and their CIA backing resulted in negative publicity for the Phoenix program and it became increasingly controversial.

Ron Humphrey became the psyops support for Phoenix. He would manage an information program about suspects through distribution of leaflets and posters in the villages and broadcasts over the airborne loud speakers. His friendship with Kim took another step when she assisted in writing the texts for the different media the program used. A major part of the effort was to distribute safe-conduct passes to recruit defectors through the government *Chieu Hoi* program. Kim also began to join Ron on the airborne loudspeaker missions, reading scripts in fluent Vietnamese.

One of the most controversial aspects of Ron's duties was to print wanted posters with the names and pictures of the suspects that had been developed through the Phoenix program. If a wrongly-identified person proved their innocence, he would print and distribute new posters. Humphrey admits a major negative of the poster project was that sometimes innocents were killed with their families not understanding why.

One night Ron awoke to explosions at the nearby airfield. Five helicopters were destroyed and twelve more were damaged from Viet Cong mortar fire. Though short the attack was very accurate. Despite the helicopters being moved nightly to a different space in the aircraft parking area, and with many spaces on the runway being left empty, the Viet Cong mortar squads still seemed to know exactly where to place their fire for maximum effect.

❖ ❖ ❖

Eventually, as might be expected, the relationship between Kim and Ron moved toward a deeper level. She professed her love for him and in the same conversation told him that she was thirty-four years old. He told her he also had fallen in love with her.

Nguyen Thi Kim Cuc (later Mrs. Ron Humphrey) when she was a JUSPAO staff employee in Vinh Long, 1970.

By 1970 the Vinh Long pacification program had become so successful that the province became the destination of choice for distinguished visitors and media people to be briefed on this showcase of pacification. Ron was often the escort officer for tours to outlying villages where he would always have a show presented by his entertainment team. One of the disheartening aspects of these visits by press people was the differences in what the visiting press members witnessed on the trips and how their articles appeared in the news-paper clippings that were later sent to him. A major reason for the successes in Vinh Long was due to the exceptionally talented and dedicated province chief, Vietnamese Army Lt. Col. Duong Hieu Nghia, who was different from many in these positions in that he was honest as well as effective.

Province
Chief Duong
Hieu Nghia
presents
awards to Ron
Humphrey at
Vinh Long,
1971. Nghia
committed
suicide in
1975 when the
Communists
overran South
Vietnam.

Halfway through Ron's tour he added a Kit Carson Scout to his staff, a former Viet Cong soldier who had defected, professing loyalty to the government. The Americans tended to trust these converts more than their fellow Vietnamese trusted them. Kim had become very valuable to his efforts due to her linguistic skills and knowledge of the area, so a position as an office clerk was found on his staff to provide her a full-time job.

Death Threat

In November 1970 Humphrey was scheduled to drive his grey-colored jeep on an eighteen-mile road trip to discuss utilizing his psyops techniques. On the way he would cross the Caumoy bridge. In one of those fortuitous and, in this case, life-changing circumstances in life, Kim came to see him that morning and told him he could not make the trip because she had heard from a friend that the VC had targeted him for death in an ambush on the bridge. Ron was puzzled as well as alarmed because the trips taken by Americans were never announced or publicized. He went to the American operations center and said he was postponing the trip and described what Kim had told him. An American army major exclaimed, "You chicken civilians are afraid of your shadow." Ron had nothing to prove to this individual and since he trusted Kim completely he canceled his trip. A group of Vietnamese soldiers were sent to check out the Caumoy bridge over Ron's original route in a gray jeep that matched the color of his jeep. When they reached the bridge, two Vietnamese soldiers were killed when a large mine was detonated under their jeep. Without Kim's warning it would have been his jeep and his life. Needless to say, this further endeared Kim to Ron. At the briefing the incident was announced, but the American who chided Ron remained silent and never apologized. Much more important to Ron however, was *who* on his staff might have tipped off the VC.

One of the extraordinary Vietnamese warriors Ron came to know was a Lieutenant Ngoc, who had begun his military career as a private, but had worked his way up through the ranks and now commanded a Regional Force (RF) company that was a capable and ferocious combat unit. Lieutenant Ngoc's type of leadership was not often found in the ARNV officer corps. His nickname was "Tiger" and he and his militia unit were constantly in action against the local guerrillas.

Many of the outlying small government outposts were vulnerable not only to direct attacks from small VC units, but also to disloyal unit members who on a night when they were serving as guards, would open the gates to the VC to kill the other government soldiers. Most of the military action in the Delta region was limited to small guerrilla attacks and they did not experience major fighting against NVA divisions as occurred in the Central Highlands and other areas north of the Delta.

One of Lieutenant Ngoc's very competent colleagues was an intelligence officer Captain Khong, who was a key player in identifying and targeting the Viet Cong leadership when intelligence indicated they would be in a certain village on a certain day. Humphrey's people would be transported into the village after the military mission was completed. On one occasion Khong planned a heliborne assault by one hundred of his troops into a village to capture a high ranking Viet Cong leader. Following the troop assault and when the village had been secured, Humphrey and his people offered the villagers important social and medical services. Unfortunately, in this instance the VC commissar escaped. Ron's group went about their entertainment and medical work with their doctors and a dentist attending to a long line of sick and lame. They were transported back to Vinh Long while Captain Khong with three men accomplished a "stay behind," where they hid and waited for the Viet Cong leader to return to his village. Upon his return he was killed. Unfortunately Captain Khong was also killed in the firefight. It was a successful operation, but at a high price. Khong left a wife and an unborn child.

There was a *Chieu Hoi* center in the province where Humphrey took his teams to perform as a part of the reeducation program to indoctrinate the defectors. The center was so successful that in 1969 and through much of 1970 his province led South Vietnam in defections. Ron felt good about the part he played in helping to win the hearts and minds of the local population.

The very talented Kim was a fortune-teller in the ancient Vietnamese tradition and she began a rather unusual activity at the *Chieu Hoi* center that proved to be invaluable in gathering intelligence for the province. She would play cards with the former VC and then pull out her fortune-telling kit; it was much like a child's Pick-Up-Sticks game in America. Kim would shake the can and then spill the sticks into a pile. Each stick had a special marking. She would start at the top and carefully remove each stick, explaining the meaning to the defector. Soon, she would reach a solid black Death Stick, which suggested grave difficulties or even death were on the horizon for the man. Then she would note that the stick immediately below the Death Stick would cancel it out, but it required the man to provide worthwhile information to the government in order to be effective. The ploy worked! Defectors who had resisted trained government interrogators were soon telling everything they knew about VC activities in the province, all because of Kim's trick Death Stick.

❖ ❖ ❖

On a trip home to America Ron Humphrey made a momentous decision that would be a major turning point in his life. After Vietnam he chose to accept another overseas posting. He had fallen in love with Kim and her children; in a new overseas assignment he planned to move Kim and her children with him, and divorcing his wife Mary Lou from whom he had become estranged even before he went to Vietnam. He would marry Kim and adopt her children. He thought it was a good plan. Over the years, however, many barriers and other complications would intervene to thwart his plans. While in the states Ron conferred with his USIA personnel officer in Washington and informed him about his desire to be posted again to Germany.

❖ ❖ ❖

By Tet of 1971 Ron's tour in Vietnam was nearing its end. On a final trip, when Kim accompanied him to perform her loudspeaker work, they came under fire and upon their return found a bullet in the leaflet stack where Kim had been sitting.

Prior to his departure in 1971 Ron came to the conclusion that the hard-core VC members were dedicated, would never capitulate, and the war would probably end in their victory. This caused him to raise the importance of his commitment to save Kim and her children by taking them away from South Vietnam. He finally departed for his new assignment to Germany and was driven to the airport in Saigon by Kim's brother Thanh, who was an undercover policeman. As he left and embraced Kim, he told her he loved her and that he would never forget that she had saved his life; he promised to return for her and the children.

Aftermath

Ron Humphrey admits he had entered Vietnam as a "Super Hawk." He originally thought the Asians were inferior and the Americans had to take over the fight because the security of America was threatened by what was happening in that faraway country. He recalled the negative comments about "gooks" made by many of his American associates. During his tour he had come to respect and love the Vietnamese. He concluded:

> But Col. Nghia was a gook; so were Mr. Quy and the members of my beloved *Van Tac Vu*. And now I was in love with a girl who some would call a gook. Yet it was through those almond-shaped eyes of Kim and the others that I saw a different side to the Vietnam War. . . . I had become "un-gooked."
> I learned to see the Vietnamese as real people, just like myself. They were a proud race with a heritage a thousand years older than America's. They already had culture, art, poetry, opera, music, and religion before Columbus stumbled upon America. But now we newcomers on the world scene were coming to Vietnam to teach the Vietnamese all about civilization. (Humphrey: 135)

On the bigger strategic pictured he decided:

It was never our objective in Vietnam to prevent a North Vietnamese takeover of California or other parts of America. It was our goal to fight a war that would stop communism from taking over South Vietnam. At dawn, May 1, 1975, we had failed. So we lost the war we had set out to win. We put that behind us and we go forward, hopefully having learned some valuable lessons. Maybe the next time that we decide we must defend a part of the free world we will do a better job of it.

In a way, we didn't simply lose the Vietnam War, we forfeited victory. We arrived at game time with less than a full team and had to play catch-up the rest of the way. The enemy was not the Viet Cong or the North Vietnamese, it was the calendar. (Humphrey: 136)

By serving as a civilian in a rural province and experiencing such a close relationship with so many Vietnamese, not to mention Kim, Ron was in a unique position to draw some insightful conclusions. Contrasting the attitude of the warriors on both sides:

It was different for the scruffy Viet Cong guerrilla in his spider hole. He didn't have a DEROS, he was in for the duration, until it was all over or until he was dead. There was no Freedom Bird to carry him back to the World. This was his World.

We Americans made our own problems as we went along. We sought to impose our own values and standards on a culture that we didn't understand. We had been raised in a world of black/white, win/lose. The Vietnamese lived comfortably with ambiguity, happily claiming the middle ground, No Man's Land, the gray areas, searching for solutions to problems so that no one would lose face." (Humphrey: 137)

His province was a success story and it did not fall to the Communists until several weeks after the fall of Saigon in April 1975. In the mid-90s a Vietnam tour book described Vinh Long: "The town of Vinh Long itself is rather dreary . . . just a short ride across the Mekong . . . are islands teeming with tropical fruit plantations . . . is not the kind of place you'll really want to spend a lot of time in. . . ." (Dulles: 245–246) Ron Humphrey spent eighteen months in Vinh Long. To a great extent our lives revolve around love and war. In Vinh Long Ron Humphrey found love for Kim, her children and the

Vietnam people, but grew to believe the war would be lost for that "dreary" town.

Over the next four years, until 1975, Ron was assigned to Cologne, Germany. He went back and forth to visit Kim and her family and she visited him in Germany. He began to work diligently and at times feverishly to remove her and her family out of war-ravaged Vietnam. When the final evacuation of Saigon occurred on April 30, 1975, Kim and her family were still in Vietnam and Ron Humphrey was by himself in Cologne, Germany.

Ron Humphrey's exposure to the Phoenix program and its controversial poster program did not impact him as negatively as it did Lieutenant Chris Russell whose tour in the Delta overlapped Ron's. They attended staff meetings together in the Delta.

CHAPTER 14

The Reluctant Warrior

LIEUTENANT CHRIS RUSSELL, USA (1970–1971)

The surest way to become a pacifist is to join the infantry.
—Bill Mauldin, *Up Front*, 1945

DRAFTEES

The Vietnam War officially lasted, at least for American, from 5 August 1964 through 28 March 1973. During that time nearly nine million people served on active duty in the armed forces, and over two and a half million of them served in Vietnam. Nearly three and a half million others served in Southeast Asia, to include flight crews based in Thailand and crews of naval vessels operating in the South China Sea. Contrary to the folklore of the Vietnam War, most of those who served were not drafted. On the contrary, two-thirds were volunteers, a startling contrast to World War II of "greatest generation" fame in which only one-third were volunteers, two-thirds draftees.

Army Brat

One of U.S. Army Captain Clyde A. Russell's V-grams (letters) sent to his mother from Italy on October 29, 1943 read, "If I ever have any kids, they are very definitely going to put in a hitch in some branch of the service." In 1963 Chris Russell's father had been assigned to General Paul D. Harkin's staff in Vietnam, but prior to leaving for his new assignment Colonel Russell placed Chris in Fishburne Military Academy in the Blue Ridge Mountains of Virginia so that Chris could learn to be a dutiful and disciplined young man on the road to fulfilling his father's World War II pledge to himself. In June 1964 upon his elder sister Polly's graduation from Fayetteville Senior High School, Chris's stepmother Helen, his sisters Polly and baby sister Janet, and he boarded a plane en route to Saigon to join his father.

Chris would never forget this period in his life as he enrolled in the local high school in what later in the war became the home of the 3rd Army Field Hospital (AFH) on Cong Le Street. In early 1964 this was the site of a grades 1–12 school for the American dependents living in Saigon. The last senior class at the American dependents' school enrolled twelve students and at that time Chris was in the 10th grade. The school buses were manned with armed guards escorting the students to and from the school's campus. 1964 Saigon was a marvelous place full of military mystery and mayhem. The fun was to prove short-lived however as a half-year after the arrival of Colonel Russell's family in Vietnam all American dependents were evacuated. Nevertheless, those six months became an incredible and indelible memory that would return in a haunting manner later in Chris's life. At the time, though, he simply learned to love and enjoy being around the bold, beautiful, elegant, and graceful people of South Vietnam. There was Ba, their fortyish cook and also beautiful young Co Lynn who looked after Chris's one-year-old little sister Janet; not to mention all the other help like Mr. Arn, his dad's SOG driver responsible for negotiating the back roads of Saigon and ultimately responsible for his father's security traveling to and from work. The list of his Vietnamese friends *lives* in the recesses of his mind and continues to resurface even today as a smorgasbord of memories both pleasant and haunting.

It was in February 1965 that Colonel Russell told his family that all the American dependents were being evacuated from Vietnam as the war continued to ratchet up. Before he knew it Chris and his family were boarding the last dependent flight out of Saigon. Chris's family left with General Westmorland's family and spent a short time in the military housing near Waikiki Beach before heading back to Fayetteville, North Carolina. Needless to say Chris would have preferred to stay in Hawaii, as Mrs. Westmorland did, but his mother was anxious to get him back to the mainland and enrolled in Fayetteville Senior High School.

Colonel Russell returned from Vietnam in 1965 and was assigned as the XVIIIth Airborne Corps G4 (the corps's senior logistics officer) Ft. Bragg and director of industrial operations (DIO) at Ft. Bragg. In 1968 Clyde Russell retired from the army after a distinguished twenty-eight year career and settled in the Fayetteville community. At his retirement he was awarded the Distinguished Service Medal in recognition of his outstanding performance of duty.

At this time the United States was heavily involved in Southeast Asia and the horrors of the war were broadcast onto America's television sets nightly during shows like the CBS Evening News with Walter Cronkite. For the most part Chris's high school years were uneventful and he graduated in 1967, moving on to East Carolina University in Greenville in the fall.

Not Ready to Follow Father's Footsteps
Going to Vietnam as a soldier wasn't too high on his "things to do list" that year; campus life at East Carolina was fine and dandy with him. While he viewed the war on the nightly news he felt secure in knowing that he was classified 2S (student deferment), which pretty much shielded him from the draft. Chris was not as convinced as his father as to the necessity for the war and he couldn't really picture himself being involved in killing others.

As a child he had experienced a rather shocking example of killing, and although it was only an animal it made a searing impression on him. In 1956 his father was at the Army War College in central Pennsylvania and they went deer hunting together. All of a sudden a deer appeared right in front of them, which shocked Chris, but his father, a calm and cool professional soldier, accustomed to killing from his war years, immediately shot the deer. Chris was overtaken with sadness and cried for several days. He couldn't understand why any creature should be killed, much less a human being. Chris's reaction made such an impression on Clyde Russell that he never hunted deer again. In truth, for Chris the thought of killing his Vietnamese *friends* was an anathema and sickened him. As was the case with many of his contemporaries, in his mind the war in Vietnam was not justifiable. Although the war was beginning to bother him, for the time being he was safe and didn't have to worry too much about becoming involved as he continued to attend college, hoping and praying to defer being drafted if not avoiding military service all together.

Surprise! Surprise! Surprise!
All of his smug complacency about the war changed however one night in June 1968 when he opened an official-looking letter from the U.S. government and discovered his 2S draft classification had been inexplicably upgraded to 1A. There was also a notice in the envelope stating that he had been drafted and another one giving him a time and place to report for his induction physical! Surely, Chris thought, there had to be some sort of a mistake; none of his friends had ever heard of anyone receiving all of these

notices in a single envelope. Little did he realize who was really behind all of this change in his draft classification. Chris's mind always goes back to that letter that his father had written home from somewhere in Italy in 1943 saying that if he ever had any kids that he'd make sure that they did some time in the military serving their country. Apparently his father had actually contacted Chris's draft board to force him to enter military service as he had not been impressed with his son's academic performance.

What a tumultuous summer that turned out to be; it was one that very few in the Vietnam generation would ever be able to forget. Famed civil rights leader Dr. Martin Luther King had been assassinated in Memphis and there were race riots in the U.S. heartland and people were killing one another in droves overseas . . . then all of a sudden Chris was called to join in the mêlée. To a nineteen-year-old kid from North Carolina it seemed like the whole world was involved in a struggle for survival and there wasn't anywhere he could go to avoid the onslaught. Everywhere around the globe he looked people were killing each other. It was sheer madness. All he knew was that he didn't have anything against anyone and certainly didn't relish the idea of having to join in on any fight that required him to kill another human being. Chris admits that had his father been anything but a career army officer, he could well have become an antiwar protestor. He was caught between a rock and a hard place, between becoming a warrior like his father and fulfilling his duty to his country in the military, but truly abhorring war unless it was clearly justified as was the case in Chris's mind with World War II.

You're in the Army Now

In September of 1968 he reported to basic training at Ft. Bragg. What a shock! The shock of basic training was followed by another eight-week training session called advanced individual training (AIT) at Ft. Polk, Louisiana. All the trainees at Ft. Polk knew that they were being trained to go to Vietnam. That Christmas they were given leave to go home for the holidays. It was during this holiday period that his father threw one of his famous parties for all of his army friends. One of Clyde's guests was Brig. Gen. John J. Hennessey, who was an assistant division commander of the 82nd Airborne, Colonel Russell's old World War II outfit. (Hennessey retired as a four-star general in 1979). General Hennessey asked Chris about his plans and he told him that he was being trained to go to Vietnam. The general asked him if he would consider going to OCS (officer candidate school) followed by Airborne School and then assignment to the 82nd to be his aide-de-camp. This was an easy decision for Chris and he quickly agreed to the plan because he would rather do anything than go to Vietnam. Hennessey told him not to worry, that he would ensure that everything proceeded as they'd discussed. Therefore, following AIT he entered Infantry Officer Candidate School at Ft. Benning, Georgia, where he'd been born twenty years earlier.

In a demanding twenty-six week OCS course designed to transform young soldiers into officers and leaders of men, only twelve of the original forty-four who had started with Chris actually graduated. The others either dropped out or were recycled, going back and retaking some classes. In June 1969 Chris Russell was commissioned a second lieutenant in the infantry and was assigned to attend Airborne School, which was also at Ft. Benning.

The Airborne School was then commanded by another old World War II soldier and friend of his father's named Colonel Welsh. When jump week, the final week of the three-week course, came around and it was time actually to make the first jumps out of those "perfectly good airplanes," Colonel Welsh picked Lieutenant Russell and Gen. Mel Zais's son, Lt. Mitchell Zais, who was also going through jump school, and personally took the two new lieutenants under his wing and the three of them made all of the five jumps required to qualify for airborne wings on the first day. The other members of the class had to spread out their jumps over a three-day period. Sometimes being an army brat had its advantages. Chris was now airborne qualified and woke up with the realization that he was now not only destined to go to Vietnam but was expected to *lead* others going into battle. He thought, "Lord, what have I gotten myself into?"

Upon graduation Chris received orders sending him to Ft. Bragg to join the famed 505th Parachute Infantry Regiment (PIR). In the interim General Hennessey had departed the 82nd and moved on to Vietnam to command the famed 101st Airborne Division. During the 1969 Christmas holiday season Chris attended the annual Russell Christmas soiree and once again General Hennessey, who was home from Vietnam on leave, was at the party. Chris and the general talked again about Chris's plans. It was at this party that General Hennessey advised Chris that he was going to have him assigned to the 101st in Vietnam as his aide-de-camp. While Chris said that would be an honor, which indeed it would have been, Chris didn't really want to go to the 101st as the general's aide or as a platoon leader or possibly, even eventually as a company commander. He did not tell the general his true feelings or intentions. As far as Vietnam was concerned, a combat assignment was not a role Chris envisioned for himself. While still within the 82nd

Lieutenant Chris Russell during Airborne School before a qualification jump, Ft. Benning, Georgia, August 1969. *U.S. Army photo*

Division and with the intent of doing everything possible to avoid Vietnam, he decided that he would apply to the John F. Kennedy (JFK) Special Warfare School located at Ft. Bragg for the Psychological Operations Course where his schooling would parallel the Special Forces Officer Qualification Course (Q Course) whose graduates earned the right to don the coveted Green Beret. This additional schooling would delay at least for a while Chris going to Vietnam. His father had long served as a Green Beret and possessed the very first Green Beret that was exhibited to members of congress back in 1959 when they asked to see what a Green Beret looked like. His mother Jini made by hand that first beret which was in his father's memorabilia. Chris Russell's admission to the psyops course meant his plan to avoid Vietnam for at least a little while longer was working. The deep military tradition of his upbringing complicated his emotions as he pursued his own personal military service.

Psychological operations were designed to win the hearts and minds of the Vietnamese people; and he somehow rationalized that if he eventually had to go to Vietnam he could convince the Vietnamese fighting for the Viet Cong and North Vietnamese Army regulars simply to *come to their senses* and stop all their foolishness. It was a far better alternative to killing them with a rifle. Boy, was he naïve or what? While he was going through the psyops course he wrote an old family friend, who had been with his father in establishing the Studies and Observations Group (SOG), a retired Lt. Col. Hans Manz and asked him if he could help Chris find a psyops job when he got to Vietnam. Chris had put off Vietnam as long as possible. He was prepared to join the effort in Vietnam, but not the fight.

Chris had first met Hans Manz when he was a youngster at Bad Tolz, Germany, in 1959 when his father had been the executive officer of the 10th Special Forces Group. Networking as an army brat began to really pay dividends for Chris. Hans was a German Jew who had entered the army to fight the evils of Nazi Germany and in 1959 was working with Chris's father when he was stationed in the Bavarian Alps about sixty miles south of Munich. His father had always liked Hans because he thought he was very intelligent. Later in life, when Chris asked his father about his friendship with Hans, Colonel Russell had said he brought Hans into SOG because he needed people he could trust and people who were smart on their feet. Speaking about Hans, Colonel Russell said, "You know, the Jews have been accused of being everything except being stupid," and he always thought of Hans as being one of the best and brightest in the special forces. Hans had retired from the army in the mid-60s and joined the CIA under the cover of United States Aid for International Development (USAID). He returned to Vietnam and took the helm of the fledgling Phoenix Program.

The Phoenix Program, as previously described, was a CIA-sponsored program designed to eliminate the Viet Cong infrastructure (VCI) and Hans was the U.S. government's point man in implementing the Phoenix Program in Vietnam.

While Chris was in the JFK Special Warfare School's psyops course, he received a letter from Hans saying that he'd found him a job within the Joint U.S. Public Affairs Office (JUSPAO) working with psyops out of the American embassy. He added that this was all contingent on Chris being able to process into Vietnam from Saigon and not Cam Ranh Bay in the north, which was where the 101st was located. General Hennessey had seen to it that Chris's orders were to have him assigned to the 101st and therefore his plane was supposed to land in Cam Ranh Bay.

Needless to say it was going to get ticklish. Somehow he had to find a way to get those transportation orders changed so he could fly into Saigon and avoid duty with the Screaming Eagles. So, he went to the transportation office located right there at Smoke Bomb Hill at Ft. Bragg where there was a small trailer with several ladies working behind desks and organizing the transportation manifests for the assignments to Vietnam. Once he had reconnoitered the office he went to a local florist and bought a small bouquet of flowers and two small soft drinks and entered the trailer, sitting down to wait for his turn to speak with one of the transportation clerks. When his time came, the woman looked at Lieutenant Russell with those flowers and soft drinks, smiled and said, "Now what can I do for you, lieutenant?" He said, "You've got me on orders for Cam Ranh Bay and I need to go into Saigon." She said, "Why's that?" and he told her his story. She said, "You know that I'm not supposed to do this . . . but seein' as how you've bought me those flowers and really want to go into Saigon, I guess I'll do it." With that small gesture, his life changed in a flick of a pen. His orders were rewritten to send him to Tan Son Nhut Airbase, Saigon, Vietnam. He was elated to be going "home" to Saigon.

Winning the War One Heart at a Time

All U.S. Army personnel not already assigned to a specific U.S. Army Vietnam combat unit in-processed into South Vietnam through the Army's 90th Repo Depo (replacement depot) at Long Binh, north of Saigon. This holding company was where you received your M16, ammunition, and other equipment necessary for your war while awaiting orders assigning you to a unit. Hans had told him to call as soon as he landed as it would take some last minute maneuvering to get him assigned to JUSPAO. Therefore, upon arriving he called the number Hans had given him and went through the signing-in procedures. Hans told him to stay put and that he'd have someone come to pick him up. Later the next day, a Sunday afternoon, an army sergeant major in civilian clothes picked him up in a staff car and took him downtown to the Continental Hotel, checking Chris into an air-conditioned room. He couldn't believe his seemingly good fortune. Thus far this was definitely a better alternative than a division in combat in the Central Highlands.

Leaving Russell with the room keys, the sergeant major instructed him to report to the American embassy in the morning for his in-processing briefing. The next morning he reported as instructed and began a week-long briefing in which he was schooled on the U.S. efforts in winning the hearts and minds of the local populace, the propaganda effort. As part of his briefing he was given a civilian ID and official papers allowing him to wear civilian clothes, hire locals, perform duties, and go to locations that normally were not permitted or allowed for American military personnel. In short, he became an embassy spook and reported to a full colonel named John Warren.

Colonel Warren told him that he was going to assign him in the Delta, Military Region 4 (MR4, also known as IV Corps), to work on a team headed up by American grade 2 Foreign Service Officer Jerome J. Novick. (Grade 2 ranks just under ambassador.) Further, he was told that Mr. Novick was infamous for being difficult and not to worry if Novick didn't approve the addition of Chris to his staff as Colonel Warren had previously sent two other officers to interview for the same job and both had been rejected.

During the "briefing week" Chris was able to visit his old haunts in Saigon, which had been called the Paris of the Orient. Riding in one of the ubiquitous Saigon cyclos, Chris traveled out Cong Le Street towards Tan Son Nhut airfield and stopped to stand in front of an ornate white French colonial two story building with columns and a porch high up on the second floor. This beautiful building, which had been Chris's school when he lived in Saigon in 1964, now housed the very busy 3rd U.S. Army Field Hospital, the premiere in-country U.S. Army hospital.

As he stood there looking down the same halls he had walked down six years before, he couldn't help but feel a flood of emotions that simply overwhelmed him: the sounds, smells, and very distinct energy that seemed to permeate the atmosphere. Standing there now he couldn't help but think that Saigon was just about the same as it had been five years earlier; only now it was even more alive, exotic, and filled with a very distinct and tumultuous energy. It was time to head back for the important interview. While Colonel Warren suspected the same fate would befall Chris as had the previous two officers, he wanted Russell to do his best to make the grade with Novick. Lieutenant Russell traveled to the heart of the Mekong Delta to the city of Can Tho.

When Jerry Novick interviewed Chris he passed muster and was welcomed to the staff to work with Maj. Tommy Neatherlin. Their task was to liaison with and coordinate psychological operations support to the fifteen provincial headquarters within MR4. Generally, Russell was tasked with planning psychological operations for the Delta Military Assistance Command as well as coordinating all Phoenix operations within the region.

Specifically, he worked with the 4th PSYOPS Group, the area's ARVN political warfare battalion, Delta Company, 5th Special Forces Group, the U.S. Air Force special operations squadron at Can Tho air base and the U.S. Navy river patrol headquarters in Can Tho City. It was quite a diverse group of units. His everyday routine was to brief the MR4 commanding general and his staff on all psychological operations taking place within the region's area of operations, including tabulating all *Hoi Chan* who came over under the MR4 *Chieu Hoi* program. *Chieu Hoi* was a campaign that aimed to convince enemy soldiers, VC and NVA, and VCI to defect to the side of the South Vietnamese. Once an enemy combatant surrendered and came over he would be called a *Hoi Chan*, would be debriefed, and then employed to support RVN activities. (During Russell's one-year tour his *Chieu Hoi* program was officially credited with over five thousand *Hoi Chan* rallying to our side.)

As part of his duties while in MR-4 he participated in a campaign in the U Minh Forest. This was an operation through the U Minh Forest at the far southern tip of South Vietnam on the Ca Mau Peninsula. The aim of the op was to clear the forest of enemy combatants. He remembers one day when he helped gather enemy corpses and weapons and arrange the corpses and equipment in a display. He carried enemy bodies out of the swamps and forests and stacked them beside the captured weapons. The intent was not only to document this victory but also to use the photographs in future psyops campaigns. He remembers how they stacked the bodies as you would stack firewood. The bodies were already stiff and decaying, with swarms of flies and mosquitoes buzzing around them. The stench was overpowering and he was sick to his stomach and threw up. A feeling of somehow being guilty followed, not just for not having the stomach for this grisly work, but also for allowing others, for whom he was the leader, to witness his throwing up. It was a confusing set of experiences to say the least. These experiences would affect his emotional state even long after the war.

About six months into his tour Russell was sent on a psyops reconnaissance mission to film combat operations then taking place in the Seven Mountain area on the Cambodian border. The Seven Mountain campaign was a classified 5th Special Forces/CIA operation targeting the enemy logistic trails entering South Vietnam from Cambodia through the mountainous area.

The 5th Special Forces Group had placed a small team of advisors in a village and armed them with a 155mm howitzer and what was advertised as the "biggest set of night binoculars" in the world with 8-inch diameter lenses. With the binoculars they could spot the enemy at night and then they could use the howitzer to immediately fire on them. This was a secret outpost only manned by a young SF captain and a couple of enlisted men. The captain was without a doubt one of America's best warriors as the night before Lieutenant Russell arrived, the Green Beret captain had taken three gunshots to the abdomen at close range from a would-be assassin, but refused to be immediately medevaced for medical care. He greeted Russell looking like something out of a Boris Karloff movie, wrapped up from his neck down in white bandages looking like an Egyptian mummy. As Russell surveyed the area, he noticed that he was becoming surrounded by a throng of about a hundred local villagers and he was becoming wary of the look in their eyes. Chris decided bribery was the order of the day, so he distributed radios, wrist watches and other bric-a-brac and left as soon as he had won all of the hearts and minds he could on that trip.

A Wartime Love

It was also about halfway through his tour that he fell in love with a young local Vietnamese woman. Just for the record, in Chris's humble opinion Vietnamese women are the most beautiful of the Orient. In any event, the young lady that he had fallen in love with was the most beautiful girl he had ever seen. Her striking beauty literally took his breath away and he fell head over heels in love at first sight. She worked at the bakery down the street from his office and he would meet her surreptitiously every day after work. She didn't speak much English and his Vietnamese wasn't anything to write home about, but the two of them got along just like the two young lovers who they were. They would go out for a cruise in an air boat that he had commandeered from the navy's river squadron or they would simply ride around in his Toyota jeep or simply picnic in the little park in front of the JUSPAO complex. They spent evenings together in his BOQ room, always mindful of getting her home before the nightly curfew. One night they were not paying attention to the time and he could not return her home before the 11:00 PM curfew so she had to spend the night in his room. The next day when he went to pick her up at the bakery, she wasn't there. Although puzzled by her absence, he went back to his quarters, returning the next day to pick her up. Again, she wasn't there. He began to worry that something had happened to her. On the third day when he went back by the bakery and waited for her to appear, a Vietnamese man who he did not recognize approached him and told Chris that the young women would not be coming back to see him anymore and that he was not to come to see or meet her anymore. In no uncertain terms

Russell was advised to stay away from her. He could see in the man's eyes that he meant business and Chris left, mildly alarmed for her wellbeing and safety.

He asked his Vietnamese interpreter, Sergeant Chung, to try to find out about what had happened to her. Two days later Sergeant Chung came to Russell with some photos that showed she had been badly beaten, almost beyond recognition. Chris couldn't tell if she was dead or alive and he was again overcome with grief. He asked his interpreter why someone would do this to her. Chung told him that her brother had beaten her up because he'd found out that she'd spent the night with Chris. When Russell asked if she were still alive, Sergeant Chung said that he didn't know. Could he go speak with her brother? Chung advised him to stay away. Worry beset him all week and finally he asked Chung to get him some pictures of her brother, but the sergeant never did. Chris had begun to think that her brother must be either demonic or perhaps he was Viet Cong as he couldn't understand why he would have done something like this to such a beautiful young women. Russell couldn't help but blame himself for what had happened ... if only he had gotten Lyn home on time, or better yet not been involved with her at all she'd still be alive ... and beautiful. His mind wouldn't allow him to forget and move on.

In his anxiety he started to rationalize that in order for Lyn's brother to do such a thing that the brother must hate him. Russell thought, "How can he hate me when he doesn't even know me?" Out of his romantic fantasy Russell came up with a *solution*: he would ask Sergeant Chung to get a photo of Lyn's brother and Chris would have a Phoenix poster printed up with the photo on it, a kind of "wanted dead or alive" complete with reward. Actually, the posters were not new to the Phoenix program. They were printed all the time when word was received that a person was reported to be a Viet Cong. Admittedly, not all of those shown on the Phoenix posters nor even all those killed as a result of the wanted posters were necessarily actual Viet Cong soldiers, or even sympathizers, but in the press to report results, printing posters and paying rewards for VC became a booming business. Chris had personally turned in names he had received from special forces personnel of locals who were purported to be Viet Cong.

That week he had gone over to the bar in the 4th PSYOPS Battalion area and shared his plan with the battalion executive officer, a young captain who was thought to be the grandson of New York Senator Jacob Javits. Admittedly under the influence of heavy drinking, Russell told the XO how he had made a *Phuong Huong* (Phoenix program) poster with the brother's picture on it. Russell tried to be very convincing and make it sound as if he had actually followed through with his plan, which he hadn't, but the captain became quite alarmed saying that what Chris had done amounted to *murder*. These are the kinds of situations that the stress of war sometimes does to people. In any event, once Russell told him the story and the captain, who must have been drinking heavily, too, accused Russell of murder and could not be convinced that it had not really happened, that it was all a figment of the imagination of a love struck, broken-hearted young man. The captain still believed Russell had printed the poster and threatened Chris with an investigation and court-martial. Since Russell could not convince the captain that he really never had printed the poster, he simply advised him that as the battalion executive officer in charge of the 4th PSYOP printing presses he was just as guilty as the captain would have had to sign off on and approve any such poster. Russell informed him that he had been complicit in many such murders as the entire Phoenix program was nothing but murder. Chris told him that as far as he knew none of the unfortunate people that had been so depicted on Phoenix posters had ever been tried in court and as far as he knew there was absolutely no *proof* that any of the Phoenix victims were actually Viet Cong infrastructure (VCI). This line of argument drove the captain absolutely out of control and he decided to shut down all the presses without any further investigation of the facts. All he would have had to do was to inspect the Phoenix poster archives to see that no such poster of the brother had ever been printed. Apparently the captain had never really considered what the Phoenix operation entailed. Actually the argument could be made that every one of the twenty thousand VCI who had been *eliminated* in the Phoenix program countrywide had in truth been *murdered* for their political persuasions and beliefs. This bar encounter had far-reaching consequences for both men.

Years later Russell examined a book detailing some of the history of the CIA and read that in 1971 the CIA station chief in Vietnam, William Colby, had been called back to testify before a Senate Intelligence Committee and he was asked if there was any way to prove that those who were *sanctioned* by the Phoenix program were in fact VCI and he replied, "No, there wasn't any way to actually know if they were VCI or not." The record went on to note that the subject was dropped upon hearing Colby's answer. Chris vaguely recalls that a Senator Jacob Javits was on the committee conducting the investigation.

Coming Home

When Russell returned home, left the Army, and returned to complete college he was a *changed* individual. He could not fit into society at any juncture or level nor could he trust anyone. He was psychically afraid and began to worry that he was in some kind of hell. He was immersed in a society that didn't seem to care where he had been or what he was experiencing. No one was remotely interested in the fact that he recently participated in the killing of some of the twenty-thousand VCI. When he went to the Veteran Affairs Medical Center and complained of nightmares in which he saw visions of faces of those he had placed on the Phoenix wanted posters and heard them asking him, "Why did you kill me, I never did anything to hurt you?", he was ignored. He was told, "Suck it up, kid, there is nothing we can do for you." Chris was haunted by the ghosts of those whose faces he had arranged to be placed on the posters. He suffered massive doses of guilt and anger that were not identified until later as the key elements of post traumatic stress disorder (PTSD).

Those around him in the college crowd were very quick to point their innocent little fingers at all Vietnam veterans for being nothing but a bunch of baby killers and warmongers while those friends of his father's were of the opposite mindset. There didn't seem to be any middle ground; nowhere to find any peace or solace. You were either damned if you did or damned if you didn't. There was no place to hide except in drugs and alcohol . . . which is where Chris found his solace and escape.

It seemed that the only folks that he could trust and feel comfortable around were other Vietnam vets. They stuck together out of a sense of self-preservation as they were the only ones who could understand what they were experiencing in their own private hells. Times were different back then and it seemed as if the nation's moral compass had been thrown out the window. President Nixon was appearing on television every night trying to convince the country that he was not a crook when everyone knew that he was. On the other hand Russell was being accused of being a murderer for doing what his country asked him to do. It was his generation and would always be his generation that had *lost the war*. It seemed that no one but veterans cared that fifty-eight thousand other brave Americans had died for nothing. Chris had heated arguments with his own father about whether or not Vietnam was worth the expenditure of all those tax dollars and the sacrifice of all those young Americans.

Then there were those such as Russell who hid in a bottle and found their peace in drugs and alcohol only to end up being unceremoniously thrown into our nation's prison system and labeled criminals for life when in many cases their wrongdoings were directly related to their wartime experiences. Many of his fellow Vietnam veterans managed to avoid criminal activities, but were challenged in employment and holding onto jobs because of their demons, past indiscretions, and stupid decision making. The Vietnam War is still very real for thousands of veterans who were thrown into our prisons and forgotten as well as those being treated in the VA medical system. There are many who still want to *come home*, but may die before they are at peace. We see POW stickers proudly plastered on walls and notebooks and paraded about, but never think of those POWs who are still locked away in their own mental prisons, prisoners of the world's systems, still fighting the conflict that continues to rage in their own minds because of some faraway place that today is a tourist trap called Vietnam. In 2011 Chris began to use his experiences in healing by working in a VA Vet Center to help other veterans.

❖ ❖ ❖

He returned from Vietnam in 1971 at a time when U.S. Navy Lt. John O'Neill was confronting in American society some of the very people who thought like Lieutenant Russell about the war without having personally experienced the war.

CHAPTER 15

Coming Home

LIEUTENANT JOHN E. O'NEILL, USN
(VIETNAM 1968–1970)

Anchors Aweigh, my boys, Anchors Aweigh.
Farewell to foreign shores, We sail at break of day-ay-ay.
Through our last night on shore, Drink to the foam,
Until we meet once more, Here's wishing you a happy voyage home.
—*The Navy March* (1906) Lieutenant Charles A. Zimmerman (Music)
and Midshipman Alfred H. Miles (Lyrics)

SWIFT BOATS

Naval service in Vietnam came in several parts. Warships off the coast of South Vietnam provided important naval gunfire support to units engaged in combat operations. Naval aviators flying off carriers in the South China Sea carried out bombing missions over North Vietnam and provided close air support to ground operations in the South. Those were elements of the blue-water navy. But there was another element, often referred to as the brown-water navy, that played a crucial role in South Vietnam, especially in the watery reaches of IV Corps, the region of the Mekong Delta and the country's southernmost provinces. There shallow draft vessels, including armed, high-speed craft known as Swift Boats, supported ground operations and conducted independent raids. Along with other naval craft supporting the U.S. Army's riverine force, these elements made an important contribution to conduct of the war.

The "Family Business" was the Navy

John E. O'Neill came from an old navy family and it was natural for him to join the "family business." His father, uncles, and brothers graduated from Annapolis. Two of his uncles lie on battlefields at Pearl Harbor and in North Korea. His favorite cousin lies in the watery tomb of the USS *Scorpion*. In 1967 John followed in their footsteps when he graduated from the Naval Academy.

Swift Boats

After service on the minesweeper USS *Woodpecker* (MSC-209)offshore Vietnam it was not surprising that Lieutenant O'Neill volunteered for Swift Boat duty in Vietnam. He was placed in command of PCF (patrol craft fast) 94. The PCFs were 45-foot long craft armed with twin and single .50 caliber machine guns. PCF 94 had previously been commanded for a short time by Lt. John Kerry, an naval officer who not only became well known, but also extremely controversial.

The people with whom Lieutenant O'Neill served in the mangrove swamps of the U Minh forest, Ca Mau Peninsula, and the canals of Ha Tien were the best people he ever met in his life. They were fearlessly brave in protecting each other; had the competence and professionalism produced by repeated firefights at short ranges; were givers and not takers. With a singular exception the Swift Boat sailors were not self-promoters, but instead were the citizen sailors trying to do what their country asked in terrible conditions. Among his awards are multiple Bronze Stars for Valor, but O'Neill prefers to remember only the valor of his fellow sailors, navy SEALs and army Green Berets with whom he served, not his own.

John's boats operated in the narrow canals of IV Corps in the Mekong Delta. They were frequently ambushed by concealed enemy soldiers using tripwire claymores, B-40 rockets, and recoilless rifles. These brown-water sailors' victories and defeats were small and little noticed. Their living conditions were grim with their meals typically being canned C rations, some which had been packaged more than twenty years before. Many sailors were lost to malaria, dengue fever, and a variety of other tropical ailments that are unknown in the developed world. He will never forget the swarms of mosquitoes, so numerous it was hard to breathe, and the shock at discovering bloodsucking leeches. When O'Neill looks back now over the long span of years at the pictures from those days of his fellow sailors he is most shocked their emaciated appearance, which reminds him of nothing so much as the prison camp pictures of World War II. He is also struck by the men's eyes, which are incongruously bright and full of spirit.

Navy Lt. John O'Neill, with his back to camera, the officer in charge of PCF 94 (Swift Boat), picking up special forces advisors and Montagnards after an unsuccessful sweep to find and rescue POWs in the U Minh Forest in 1969.

Lieutenant O'Neill experienced tragic death in Vietnam of young sailors dying of terrible wounds, gray from shock, looking into a world beyond this one. He also saw true self-sacrifice and courage: not the phony words of politics, but the act of laying down your life for your shipmate, rescuing and protecting your friends, serving with honor. Two of his crewmen were wounded and another sailor died in his arms.

His friend Lt. Elmo Zumwalt III was the bravest of the brave. On one occasion Zumwalt took his boat out of its assigned ambush position along the Cambodian Border and actually into Cambodian waters without authorization or notice. (Zumwalt: 81) He ended up fighting one of the most successful small unit naval engagements of the war killing more than thirty North Vietnamese soldiers. His father, Admiral Elmo Zumwalt Jr., who was the commander of American naval forces in Vietnam, had a navy captain investigate the incident. The investigating officer's conclusion was that Elmo should clearly be court-martialed for directly disobeying orders, and endangering his boat and crew, but on the other hand should be awarded at least the Navy Cross, if not the Medal of Honor, for his courage in the fierce fighting. Not surprisingly, after the report was submitted, the incident was forgotten. Elmo and his crew had the last word: after his death in 1988—he was only forty-two and the cancer that killed him was probably a result of his exposure to Agent Orange—it was a sculpture of PCF 35, the boat that Zumwalt and his crew had taken into Cambodia, that was placed at the Navy Memorial in Washington to represent Navy participation in Vietnam. Zumwalt had a very positive opinion of O'Neill and after a joint operation he said, "After our firing run [against an NVA camp], John O'Neill said that was the only time in Vietnam that he was sure he was going to be killed." (Zumwalt: 96)

Mike Brown (USNA 1965) was the captain of the Naval Academy track team and one of America's best pole-vaulters. In 1968, as he sat off the Cua Lon River in the Ca Mau Peninsula in charge of a Swift Boat, he saw that the North Vietnamese were using the entire area as a sanctuary. This made no sense to him and so against his orders he entered the river seeking NVA and VC targets. He immediately found enemy flags and troops, which he took under fire receiving scattered return fire from very surprised opponents. After a couple of miles of this Brown realized he had stirred up a hornet's nest behind him and it wouldn't be a good idea to try to go back the way he'd come. So he went forward, down the length of the Cua Lon River to where it met the Song Bo De River and raced another thirty miles, shocking many VC and NVA along the way. Near the end of his run he received minor wounds from a B40 rocket. The Swift Boat exited the Bo De out of ammo, with its machine gun barrels burned out, having inflicted tremendous damage on this enemy sanctuary. As Brown pulled up to an LST (landing ship tank), the ship's captain told him, "You're going to be court-martialed for this. Return to base immediately." As it turned out, he was awarded a Silver Star and Brown's Run became the stuff of navy legend.

Coming Home

Upon O'Neill's return home it was from a world thirteen thousand miles away and full of terrible hardships, in which death waited around every corner; and how could people who slept in safe beds in prosperity and freedom and comfort ever understand? This always has been his predicament even up to the present day: how to describe his long ago times in troubled waters.

It was the summer of 1970 and his father had a Mariachi band giving it their best with *When Johnny Comes Marching Home* when John returned home to San Antonio, a strong military town, supportive of our forces. He was deeply struck by the misreporting of the Vietnam War on television. The actual war where he had watched the North Vietnamese losing in the real world of Vietnam was converted on network news, *presto*, into a war of colonial oppression by Americans. The South Vietnamese, held almost as slaves by the Communists in the areas he had operated in were converted, *voila*, by magic, into a sullen population, hostile towards America, at least as reported nightly on network television. The voyage home was not the happy one wished for in *Anchors Aweigh*.

In the late summer 1970 John O'Neill began his final year in the navy at Holy Cross College, a Catholic school in Worchester, Massachusetts, where he was a Naval Reserve Officer Training Corps (NROTC) instructor. John was deeply shocked by what he saw. The ROTC building had been burned to the ground. Radical groups like the Students for a Democratic Society (SDS) and Black Students Union (BSU) were active on campus. O'Neill was shocked, as a Catholic and an American, at the conduct he observed at Holy Cross ranging from the rude to the violent, all by students in the lap of luxury, whose biggest decision was what to do on a Saturday night.

At the end of the 1970–71 school year the NROTC celebrated the graduation of the seniors with a special Mass to which the students and their parents were invited. He will never forget that day. As they entered the chapel, throughout the sanctuary were North Vietnamese and Viet Cong flags. Over the altar hung a banner that proclaimed, "Long Live the Democratic Revolution of Workers and Farmers of Vietnam," in the national colors of North Vietnam. John remembers, "The sermon consisted of a rant by a Jesuit priest who told us we were each like Romans, driving nails into Jesus, whom he compared to Daniel Berrigan, who was at the time a celebrated antiwar Catholic priest." It certainly was a strange service for the parents much less the young students, at least two of whom later died in Vietnam serving their country. The reaction was stunned silence and in hindsight O'Neill wishes that he or someone else had protested.

That spring of 1971 was an especially emotional time for O'Neill. On March 13, 1971, his friend and Naval Academy classmate Lt. "Bart" Creed, was shot down over Laos. He was alive for at least a short time as the search and rescue (SAR) helicopters tried to recover him, but to no avail due to heavy enemy ground fire. Various reports through the years led his family to hold out hope that he had survived and was being held captive. Lieutenant

Creed is one of nearly six hundred Americans who disappeared in Laos. He had married Susan four days after his 1967 graduation at Annapolis. Creed's two children, Scott, a marine aviator, and Judith, a five-year navy veteran, both graduated from Annapolis ensuring continuity in their heroic father's family business. Service such as Lieutenant Creed's in flying off navy carriers on dangerous missions into heavily defended enemy territory were extraordinary examples of valorous lives dedicated to service.

The combination of his experience at Holy Cross and sacrifices like that of his classmate Creed affected O'Neill in a very special manner when he witnessed efforts to smear the patriotic service of his fellow Vietnam vets.

Around this time he turned on his television where none other than John Kerry, O'Neill's predecessor on PCF 94, was delivering to the Senate Foreign Relations Committee a speech not dissimilar to that of the Jesuit priest's sermon. Theatrically dressed in army green fatigues, Kerry catalogued a series of American war crimes in Vietnam, comparing our forces there to the "army of Genghis Khan." O'Neill was dumbstruck. He knew John Kerry was lying (and that Kerry knew he was lying) about the nature of our efforts in Vietnam. He knew many of O'Neill's friends had died in Vietnam and accepted that as the nature of the war. O'Neill could not believe that, unable to defend themselves, they would now be symbolically killed again by people like Kerry. He wrote to the committee to testify, but received in return a letter turning him down. Then O'Neill became determined to debate Kerry. He discovered a small group overseen by a Marine Corps veteran named Bruce Kessler, which operated from his mother's apartment in a rough neighborhood of Brooklyn. United in a cause to counter Kerry's testimony Kessler and O'Neill joined to pursue Kerry for a debate.

He was shocked by Kerry's comrades in Vietnam Veterans Against the War. Many members of the organization, like its president, Al Hubbard, were simply fakes; they wore fake medals and had never been to Vietnam. (Burkett: 137) Others were radicals, who carried guns and threatened to kill members of O'Neill's group. He often felt in more danger in New York than he had in the U Minh Forest.

John O'Neill ultimately debated John Kerry on the Dick Cavett Show on ABC on June 20, 1971. Many years later the debate was repeatedly shown during the presidential campaign of 2004. The audience was stacked for Kerry, but by the end of the show they booed him, even though they were mostly antiwar. Most importantly to O'Neill was that Kerry, the king of the war crimes story, admitted he had never seen a war crime during his short tour in Vietnam. This was important to O'Neill because he believed that as far as blood and muscle permitted he kept faith with his friends who died in Vietnam and who would have laid down their lives for him. He had fought the good fight.

Lieutenant John O'Neill resigned from the navy the summer of 1971 to attend the University of Texas (UT) Law School where he graduated first in his class in 1974. He was shocked by the radicalism which overwhelmed UT in those years ranging from the SDS chapter on campus to leftwing intolerance and replacement of intellectual curiosity with radical dogmatism. The voyage home had not gotten any happier.

In 1972 John O'Neill was invited to give one of President Nixon's seconding speeches at the Republican National Convention in Miami. Elmo Zumwalt III was invited to attend. As Zumwalt and O'Neill walked toward the convention one night, Zumwalt wrote, "We confronted a group of Vietnam War protestors burning an American flag and waving a Viet Cong flag. This incident outraged me beyond words. . . . The realization that the Viet Cong had been responsible for the death of many people I knew . . . made that protest all the more unbearable." Zumwalt reflected on the essence of what had become the core issue of Vietnam veterans when he expressed our lot this way: "In other wars, the sacrifices of the returning veterans were rightly recognized and applauded. . . . The Vietnam veteran was given no support from his countrymen . . . when we were not shunned, we were reviled as war criminals on baby killers."(Zumwalt: 125–126)

When the Republic of Vietnam fell to the Communists in 1975 O'Neill cried for one of the few times in his adult life. He lost confidence in government and political institutions and has never regained it. It was time to put Vietnam behind him and for the next thirty-five years he did so. Few if any of his friends or even his children knew he had been in Vietnam. He could count on one hand the times he had spoken of it since. He was content to simply leave Vietnam as a place of memories, some very sad and some very inspiring, especially regarding his fellow warriors who served with him in the war.

After the setback of the debate, Kerry faded from political view following a failed campaign for Congress. In the early 1980s he reinvented himself and, irony of ironies, ran as a Vietnam hero surrounded by old *comrades*.

Aftermath

John O' Neill has been an attorney all the years since he "came home." In

2004 he coauthored the book *Unfit for Command* and was a founding member of the 527 Committee Swift Boat Veterans for Truth that questioned Senator Kerry's Vietnam record.

Lieutenant Bart Creed never did come home and when John O'Neill debated the future Senator Kerry, it would be twenty-one more months before army doctor Captain Hal Kushner had his homecoming. When John O'Neill enrolled in law school in the fall of 1971 combat medic Jess Johnson was in the steaming jungles of the A Shau Valley where the shooting war was still very much in progress.

CHAPTER 16

Ghosts in the A Shau Valley

SPECIALIST 4TH CLASS JAMES W. "JESS" JOHNSON, USA (101ST AIRBORNE DIVISION 1970-1971)

God has fixed the time for my death. I do not concern myself about that, but to be always ready, no matter when it may overtake me. That is the way all men should live, and then all would be equally brave.
—General Thomas "Stonewall" Jackson

MEDICS

Every medic was inevitably known to his fellow soldiers or marines as "Doc." During service in Vietnam many, especially those serving with special forces, came close to actually qualifying for that appellation. The widespread availability of medevac helicopters, and the routine courage of the medevac pilots and crews, meant that many badly wounded men, casualties who might have expired on the battlefield in earlier wars, could be plucked from the jungle and rushed to hospitals in time to be saved. The medics who worked over them until the dustoffs arrived, and medics on board those mercy ships saved many, many lives by their skill, compassion, and determination. So skilled did many become that after the war their experience evolved into establishment of the recognized role now known as physician's assistant.

Open the Attic Footlocker

When Captain Clark asked me write to this, he said he wanted a past, present and future story. I thought that this story would be easy, but it wasn't. As a matter of fact I can only write small sections at a

time because the combat is too difficult to write about. It's like going up into the attic of my childhood home, sweeping away the cobwebs, and looking for my old army footlocker under all the old Christmas ornaments. Dust was everywhere and in the corner of the attic, there it was. It's been there for over forty years, untouched and unmoved, a time capsule if you will. What comes to mind is panic, anger, sadness, fear, screaming, the hissing of the PRC-25 [radio], the sounds of medevacs, M16, AK and M60 fire, mortars, RPGs, land mines, navy and air force jets dropping ordinance, incoming . . . all the experiences and emotions I wanted to forget. Now I have to face them, all of them; what would I find when I opened this Pandora's Box? Could I close the lid again or would these demons haunt me again?
—Jess Johnson

When he was fourteen Jess Johnson had a dream. In his dream he remembered rows and rows of bright white grave markers all identically the same, in geometrically perfect lines on a bed of green manicured grass against a cloudless powder blue sky. As he walked through these graves, he stopped to look at one. How strange it had his name on it. There it was: Spec.4 James W. Johnson, KIA, 101st Airborne, Phu Bai, Vietnam. He couldn't relate to the dream, so he put it away. Six years later in 1970 near Phu Bai, Vietnam, when he was a Screaming Eagle of the 101st Airborne Division, he would recall that dream after a day and night he came close to having his name on a monument at a veterans cemetery.

Family Military Heritage
In World War II Johnson's father had been a technical sergeant with the 78th "Lightning" Infantry Division driving a Sherman tank in Belgium. He suffered with great difficulty over the years from the memories of his experiences in the Battle of the Bulge. After his platoon captured *the* bridge at Remagen, Tech Sergeant James Johnson lost his right leg in Germany when his tank hit an antitank mine, killing his crew who had been his friends and military family.

Throughout Jess's early life, his father spoke of his adventures in the old army, but he never spoke of the combat. Jess remembered one time during Christmas his mother, waiting for her husband to return home, was playing records and she put on Bing Crosby's "White Christmas." It was about 5:00 PM when his father returned from work. When he heard that song he walked over to the record player, took the record, and broke it. He was angry and Jess couldn't understand what was going on. His father told him that during the Battle of the Bulge, on Christmas Eve 1944, the Germans played "White Christmas" over and over again, which was terribly depressing to the American soldiers who were freezing in their foxholes, jeeps, halftracks, and tanks. His father said that when he heard the song, he was instantly transported back to that time in the war when he felt the loneliness, the fear, and the cold of that dark forest in the Ardennes where he had endured heavy combat.

Jess Johnson's basic training was near Augusta at Ft. Gordon, Georgia, followed by basic combat medical training at Ft. Sam Houston in San Antonio, Texas and Airborne School at Ft. Benning, Georgia. On leave before going to Vietnam, one of the first things he said to his father was, "Well, Dad, I guess I'm a man now." It's a rite of passage that most men go through, becoming a man in the eyes of their father. Before Airborne School his father had said that graduation from jump school would make him a man, but now his father added new conditions. His father said, "So you think you're a man? Come with me." They went upstairs to the bedroom and his father pulled four blue boxes that Jess had never seen before from the top drawer of the dresser. One by one his father slowly opened them, carefully laying them on the bed. He had earned the Silver Star, the Bronze Star, and two Purple Hearts for his actions in Belgium and Germany. and said, "When you have these," he said, "you'll be a man." Jess left home for the jungle war in far off Vietnam. Upon his return Jess would be a man, for sure, even without all of the decorations awarded his father.

Welcome to Vietnam

His Vietnam experience was truly a once in a lifetime adventure for him. When Jess landed in Vietnam he had no idea what he would be doing or where he would be going. He flew to Phu Bai, the major American combat base that was just south of the ancient imperial capital city of Hue, that was the headquarters of the 101st Airborne Division. Medics were always in short supply as were RTOs (radio operators), FOs (forward observers), and lieutenants due to high casualty rates for those positions.

The medic Johnson was replacing had been in combat for ten months and was very close friends with the men of the platoon. He had demonstrated his bravery and competence under fire; he exemplified what it meant to be a combat medic. Before he left two days later for the "World" he told Jess, "Good luck, you are going to need it." There Jess was in the jungle with nineteen other guys looking at him thinking "who the hell is this guy?" The platoon lost their medic and best friend and now here's an untested new guy with their lives in his hands. One of the old timers, a laid back surfer from LA with beach blond hair and moustache, slid over beside Jess and said, "This isn't personal, but we've talked and we have decided that if we ask you for anything in that aid bag of yours, you had better be able to get it without looking, we don't like you and want our Doc back." Welcome to Vietnam! That was Jess's initiation to the platoon and his new home in the triple canopy jungle of I Corps.

Combat Medic Jess Johnson, 101st Airborne Division, Ashau Valley, April 1970.

Blending into the Jungle

At night, it was so dark you really couldn't see your hand in front of your face. The jungle sounds; birds, lizards, monkeys, insects were part of larger consciousness and it took time for the jungle to accept you as belonging there. Early in his tour during a night patrol Johnson stepped on a branch, breaking it in half. The night sounds of the jungle instantly ceased and, figuratively speaking, you could have heard a pin drop.

Months later, with no showers to wash off the built up sweat, oil and dirt, the jungle had grown on everyone in the platoon. A fortunate side effect of their *gaminess* was that it masked their natural odors, which kept the insects from harassing them. At night you developed the ability to see shades of darkness. The senses of hearing and smell were amplified and intuition helped to preserve life time after time. Later, on another night patrol, he again stepped on a branch breaking it in half, but this time the jungle kept up its sounds and activity without missing a beat; Johnson was now part of the jungle and accepted as one of its own.

Walking through the jungle is like swimming, slowly negotiating the "wait a minute" vines, carefully walking by giant fallen trees, up and down mountains, mile after mile. You learn always to look up and down, side to side, looking for that one thing that doesn't look quite right, that doesn't fit.

A Day in the A Shau Valley

After serving with the Screaming Eagles for several months Jess Johnson had learned a lot about jungle warfare in the. His platoon was back in the A Shau Valley for the umpteenth time. On one patrol, in the middle of the jungle, intuition grabbed him by the throat. He put his right fist in the air, the platoon froze in place, and he told his platoon leader he thought there was an ambush about eighty meters down the trail. The relatively new platoon leader halted his men, everyone listened and then the point man slowly crawled forward. The point man, who always had the authority to investigate and make or break contact depending upon the situation or circumstances, pulled the safety pin from a grenade, threw it as far as he could, and then all hell opened up from the enemy ambush. The explosion of the grenade tripped the ambush and the platoon peeled away at as fast as they could with their eighty-pound rucksacks to get as far away as quickly as possible.

The next day was September 11, 1971, and it would be a day Jess would never forget. He had awakened in the jungle on many patrols, but this time something was different. He had a feeling of dread that something was coming, but he couldn't put his finger on it. The previous night they had established their night defensive position (NDP), on a high speed trail, which was contrary to all standard operating procedures (SOPs). It was about 0700 and dawn was breaking on a beautiful Sunday morning. He noticed that they had actually set up in the middle of six trails coming together in a circle. Then something happened that absolutely freaked him out and continues to disturb him to this day. Johnson saw a vision of a dark, hooded figure, clothed in a long black robe with no arms or face, looking like death personified, which appeared and walked through a thick stand of bamboo, disappearing in the blink of an eye in the direction of one of the six trails. Jess remembers saying in an unusually loud voice to one of the platoon members, "Did you see that?" The other soldier replied, "Doc, you've got to quiet down." Five minutes later the entire platoon moved out. They could have gone in any direction in a 360-degree circle that morning, but the point man started chopping into the same patch of bamboo where Jess's vision had disappeared. It was at that moment, as they all moved into the jungle, that Johnson remembered the dream from his teenage years.

That morning, he began to weave his teenage dream and current events together. When he came to the 1st Battalion, 501st Parachute Infantry Regiment (PIR), 101st Airborne Division, he was a private first class (Pfc.) and he had been promoted to specialist fourth class (Spec. 4), his rank in the dream. Was this his time? Other members of his platoon who had been wounded or died often talked about feelings or premonitions of dread. About 1000 hours the platoon halted and eight men had gone ahead while Jess and the other ten platoon members remained in place. Suddenly he heard an exchange of automatic weapons fire mixed with rocket-propelled grenade (RPG) explosions. The radio came alive, "Send Doc ASAP." Jess had long before completed his combat apprenticeship and been accepted by his platoon as their Doc, the universal title for American combat medics. He ran to their location where he found five of the eight with wounds to their stomachs, arms, or legs. He used almost all of his medical supplies until the arrival of the dustoffs" the medevac helicopters from Phu Bai. Also arriving was a Red Team of two AH-1 Cobra gunships to provide covering fire. The Red Team loomed overhead like killer angels ready to strike at the enemy with a ferocity that was almost indescribable. With one gun run a Cobra can put a round in every square foot of a football field. The deadly accuracy of their miniguns and rockets was truly awesome. The wounded were lifted from the jungle floor by being hooked up to a jungle penetrator, but they sustained even more injuries with this method of extraction from the battlefield.

Bunker Complex

After the wounded were evacuated to the Phu Bai hospital, the rest of the platoon split up their ammo and continued the mission. Jess had requested new medical supplies to replenish his kit, but they had not yet been delivered. He only had one glass saline-solution IV bottle and two morphine syrettes left. About two in the afternoon the platoon leader told Johnson and another platoon member to go a kilometer or two into the valley to the north front of their position. As the two walked along they kept as quiet as they could. Jess didn't know what they were looking for, but all of a sudden they were on some elevated terrain looking down on forty or so perfectly-camouflaged command-sized bunkers. They were made of concrete and steel, then buried in the ground and connected by tunnels or spider holes. It was probably a headquarters and staging area for a later attack on Hue. Panic was not a strong enough word for the emotions of the two soldiers when they radioed their lieutenant. In the conversation Jess remembered only that the USS *New Jersey* was on station off the coast, well within range of the ship's massive 16-inch guns, and incoming naval gunfire from the battleship could be expected soon. If they didn't quickly get out of the impact area for the *New Jersey's* fire mission, they might not get out at all. As best they could they rushed through the jungle running, falling, and running and falling again. As they were running up the hill back to their platoon's location, the first 16-inch rounds started falling. The projectiles were so huge you could actually watch them impact. With so many things happening at one time, he did not realize his right boot was in the middle of a red ant mound. That quickly got his attention as they were now down in his boot, their bites like fire. He bent over brushing them off as fast as he could and pulled the boot off at the same time.

He heard and felt a rush of hot wind or air by the right side of his head after which one of the guys in the platoon found some canvas and picked up a glowing red four pound piece of shrapnel which had traveled over one kilometer from its impact point. For an extended period navy and air force jets dropped tons of bombs, Cobra gunships raked the area, and the *New Jersey* continued to pour naval gunfire on the bunker positions. What had been lush green jungle now looked like a moonscape. At about 1700 hours the severely depleted platoon, now with only fourteen men remaining, moved out to reconnoiter and assess the battle damage. The sun was heavy in the sky so it was going to be a clear night. The first sign of the damage near the bunker complex were six fresh graves, which the FO wanted to dig up for field intelligence. Johnson, a veteran now with several months of experience, said in no uncertain terms, "No Way!" due to possible booby traps. As they continued to patrol another vision appeared to Johnson. This time the hooded figure was about eighteen inches off the ground walking to Johnson's right about ten feet away. Besides being upset—What the hell did this mean? —he was wondering what was next for the platoon. The previous apparition had definitely signaled the direction of the enemy when the morning patrol had moved out. The new NDP was set up near the bunker complex. Sitting on his rucksack he was thinking back on the events of the day when he heard someone say out loud to him, "Don't take any unnecessary chances." He looked around, but nobody was there. The next patrol of eight men, including the platoon leader and forward observer, was getting ready to leave for recon and although he usually accompanied every patrol, he did not this time. For some reason he remained behind. In the next few minutes he would understand why. After the patrol left, someone said in a louder voice, "Get ready!!" Again, no one nearby had spoken. Johnson got ready by putting on his helmet, something he never did in the bush, pulled out what little was left from his rucksack: he still had not received a resupply of medical supplies.

Then Jess heard a powerful explosion followed by the inevitable screaming for the medic. He took off running as fast as he possibly could across an open field when something picked him up and threw him to the ground. When you're running across an open field you're not likely to fall down, and he had not tripped on anything or hit an obstacle or stepped in a hole. The fall was totally unexpected, but, as it developed, very lucky for Specialist Johnson. The moment he hit the ground, a member of the patrol yelled out, "Doc, you're in the middle of a mine field! Stop! Find our tracks and follow them very closely . . . and hurry!" Someone in the patrol had stepped on the pressure detonator of a 105mm howitzer projectile. When Jess finally came up the trail, he saw eight of his men in various positions on the ground; one man was on his hands and knees, bleeding from his eye and searching for his missing eyeball. The forward observer had a concussion from being thrown twenty feet, face first into a tree, causing his skin color to turn gunmetal grey. Most of his uniform had been blown off and his radio had three good size holes torn into it from the shrapnel from the explosion. The radio had saved his life by absorbing the shrapnel which came from behind him.

Everyone was in rough shape, but first Jess had to work fast on the badly-burned machine gunner, who was lying in a five foot crater with his eyes rolled back in his head, his uniform almost gone, and both legs severed above the knees. His remaining upper legs looked like barbecued hot dogs that had been cooked too long. The explosion had seared his legs, so thankfully there was not much bleeding. Jess needed to start an IV, but since the gunner now appeared to be experiencing circulatory shutdown from shock, Jess asked himself, "Should I give him morphine or not?" It seemed like minutes had passed when it really was just seconds. Doc Johnson was losing the gunner. He tried to wash the dirt off one arm to get the IV started, but it did not work, so he tried the other arm and it worked! He noticed small flecks of dust in the ground surrounding him and he realized a sniper was shooting at him. They were receiving heavy small arms fire. He needed to call for the medevacs, but remembered that one of the radios wasn't working because of the dampness of the jungle floor and the other radio had been damaged by the blast. He had one more brainstorm and ran over to take the radio from the FO's back. It sounded like a box of broken china (the PRC-25 was a tube radio), but when he turned it on he heard the hiss: it *worked*! Another miracle to add to those that he had already witnessed. Had the radio not worked, all his wounded would have died, and Jess and the few remaining members of the platoon would have been killed. Jess was shocked, but he could now call for an emergency dustoff.

The medevac choppers brought a Red Team with them and thank God they did! In about twenty minutes the Cobras were on station firing on the enemy. As one of the medevac choppers flew overhead, they threw down the cage litter used to carry up the wounded, but it was a combat loss because it landed among the enemy who were firing on them. The firing was so loud that he could not hear himself talking to the few men left in the platoon whom he was coaching to assist the other wounded. Knowing he was about to die he began to panic. Then he heard another voice say to him, "Son, take a deep breath, everything is going to be okay." All of a sudden, after he heard this voice, the most seriously wounded were being lifted out of the jungle into the dustoff choppers hovering overhead. Burned into his mind was the sun about half set and the double amputee's legs silhouetted black against the center of the yellow orange or golden sunset as the machine gunner was being lifted up to the helicopter. There were now six platoon members left in the middle of a minefield, near a large NVA bunker complex with almost all of their ammunition and supplies gone. Even in the pitch dark of the night, they knew where they were, but so did the enemy, who owned the night. It started to get cold.

Medevaced

Jess found it incredible that the six remaining members of the platoon were left in the jungle all by themselves without being extracted. They couldn't do anything but pray to survive through the night. About midnight or a little later one of the men crawled up to Jess and exclaimed, "Doc! Doc! I was just bitten by a snake! Look at this bite on my hand!" Jess looked at the wound and said, "You just cut yourself, didn't you?" Jess decided to try for a night medevac. Another man in the group called on the radio, "Eagle Dustoff, Eagle Dustoff, over." Amazingly, thirty minutes later the medevac bird arrived. Utter chaos ensued: one soldier was holding a strobe light to signal their position, two or three enemy mortar rounds hit nearby, a jungle penetrator was dropped through a hole in the jungle, and Jess started toward the lift point with the platoon member with the supposedly self-inflicted wound. Jess is carrying him to the penetrator when he trips on someone's rucksack, hits a rock, and passes out. It is now Specialist Johnson's turn to be medevaced. He was taken to the hospital at Phu Bai where he awoke the next day with a swollen and very painful head. On his bed he felt the blood which had seeped down from his head wound.

During Jess's first day in the hospital, a K-9 dog team with a white German shepherd went out to locate the remaining four members of his platoon. The battalion sent out two engineers with minesweeping equipment to help safely remove the last four soldiers, but they hit a mine and both engineers sustained horrific wounds, losing both arms, both legs and half their faces. Remarkably they both survived, but with a horrible future ahead of them. Jess saw them in the Phu Bai hospital; unfortunately, the sight of their wounds was indelibly implanted in his memory. It had been one helluva day, but he lived through it, as did all fourteen members of his platoon.

Finally He Was a Man

About a month later Jess's father sent him a letter which was a surprise because it was his one and only letter from his father while he was in Vietnam. It went something like this:

> Dear Jim,
> I had too much to drink last night since I was trying to drown my sorrows. I miss your mother so much. Anyway, about six this morning, I dreamt you were sitting on the edge of my bed, you had a helmet on, no jacket, a t-shirt, pants, boots, you looked sad and I think you said, "Dad, I am about to die." I said, "Son, take a deep breath, everything is going to be okay." After that you disappeared and I rolled over back to sleep for about ten seconds, then I realized

it wasn't a dream! I lost my balance and fell out of bed. After I put my leg on, I wrote this letter. I hope you are okay.

Love, Dad.

Jess Johnson remembers, "The letter was written the day in the jungle I heard those exact words. Who can say that there is no supernatural? It had to have been my God transmitting a message from my father to help calm me down."

Aftermath

In his prayers several years ago Jess Johnson asked God why he was saved amidst so many opportunities that day to have been killed. God spoke to him that he was spared so that the soldiers he treated and saved would return to perform Christian service for others.

Doc Johnson went to a reunion of his unit several years ago and met some of his fellow platoon members. One of them was involved in a prison ministry, one worked with veterans suffering from PTSD, another was in a ministry to help the homeless. The wife of the double leg amputee he saved came up to him to thank him for saving her husband on that fateful day in the A Shau. Unfortunately, Jess heard after the reunion that several months later the machine gunner committed suicide.

He has often thought about the second apparition that was suspended off the ground and has speculated that it was a warning about the mine field. Jess is quick to know that many will dispute the happenings of the dreams, the words he heard, and the visions, but as far as he is concerned they occurred and no one ever can dissuade him of their existence. People who know Jess find him to be credible.

He received two Purple Hearts in Vietnam and completed his full Vietnam tour. He studied nursing at a community college and graduated with a liberal arts undergraduate degree from Southern Methodist University. Johnson remained in the reserves, receiving training as a weapons specialist, and retired as a master sergeant. He spent three decades of continuing work in U.S. Army special forces and contract employment in national defense activities.

Men who choose to be combat medics obviously have a heart for service to others and this desire to serve and comfort others continues today for Jess Johnson. He is active in a variety of endeavors, but particularly is focused on helping hospitalized veterans. In Dallas, Texas, fifteen years ago with the partnership of Rotary International and many other generous entities, he founded an organization called Vet-to-Vet (www.vettovetusa.com), a ministry to serve the veterans in our Veterans Affairs Department medical centers. Under his leadership, Jess and his loyal volunteers provide meals on special holidays and celebrations at North Texas Veterans Affairs Department medical facilities, and roam as far as Waco, Temple, and San Antonio hospitals to provide gifts for hospitalized veterans. His motivation is so that the vets know, "You are not alone and are appreciated for your service to our nation." There was a reason that he also survived the A Shau Valley engagement that day and other days. He and his wife, Peggy, distributed Bibles to the troops returning to Iraq and Afghanistan when they departed DFW Airport. He helps many others heal, but his own healing from the scars of war on his soul and spirit are an ongoing challenge requiring constant attention. Peggy and his outreach activities to help other veterans are important in keeping at bay the horrid memories of those days in the A Shau.

When Johnson left Vietnam in January 1971, Captain Hal Kushner, captured more than three years previously, was still in a Viet Cong jungle prison camp.

CHAPTER 17

A Will to Survive

Captain Harold Kushner, M.D., USA
(1,931 DAYS A POW)

A man of character in peace is a man of courage in war. —Lord Moran, personal physician to Winston Churchill in World War II

The first requirement of the soldier is not bravery or courage, but the ability to suffer and endure. —Napoleon Bonaparte

ENDURANCE
Those held prisoner either by the North Vietnamese or the Viet Cong suffered almost unimaginable hardship and deprivation, illness, malnutrition and, for many, systematic torture. It would have been easy to just give up and decide to die. Some did. Others were murdered by their captors. But many others persevered, sustaining one another with demonstrations of personal courage and determination to survive. Three POWs subsequently received the Medal of Honor for their leadership and valor during long years in captivity.

Two Wars
F. Harold Kushner, M.D., probably was not aware of it at his then age six months, but he was in his first war when Pearl Harbor was bombed, just next door to his family's home at Hickam Air Field, on December 7, 1941. After receiving his M.D. degree from Medical College of Virginia in Richmond in 1966 and before deploying to Vietnam in August 1967, he received aviation medical training at Ft. Rucker, Alabama and Pensacola, Florida. He spoke the following words at his 9th Cavalry Reunion at Ft. Hood, Texas in

June 1999. No amount of editing or revision can be an improvement on his story in his own words.

Colonel Harold Kushner in his words:

I want you to know that I don't do this often. I was captured 2 December 1967, and returned to American control on 16 March 1973. For those of you good at arithmetic, that is 1,931 days. Thus it has been thirty-two years since capture and twenty-six years since my return. I have given a lot of talks . . . about medicine, about ophthalmology, even about the D-Day invasion . . . as I was privileged to go to Normandy and witness the fiftieth anniversary of the invasion in June 1994. But, not about my captivity. I don't ride in parades; I don't open shopping centers; I don't give interviews and talks about it. I have tried very hard *not* to be a professional PW [prisoner of war]. My philosophy has always been to look forward, not backward, to consider the future rather than the past. That's a helluva thing to say at a reunion, I guess. In twenty-six years, I've given only two interviews and two talks. One to my home town newspaper . . . which my dad made me give . . . one to the *Washington Post* in 1973 . . . which the army PIO [public information office] made me give, and a talk at Ft. Benning in '91 . . . which Col. Ted Chilcotte made me give . . . and to the Military Flight Surgeons in '93 . . . which they made me give. I've refused about a thousand invitations to speak about my experiences.

But you don't say no to the 1st of the 9th, and you don't say no to your commander. Colonel Bob Nevins and Col. Pete Booth asked me to do this, and so I said "yes sir", and prepared the talk. It will probably be my last one.

I was a twenty-six-year-old, a young doctor who had just finished nine years of education, college at the University of North Carolina, med school at Medical College of Virginia, [with] a young wife and three-year-old daughter. I interned at the hospital in which I was born, Tripler Army Medical Center in Honolulu, Hawaii. While there, I was removed from my internship and spent most of my time doing orthopedic operations on wounded soldiers and marines. We were getting hundreds of wounded GI's there, and [they] filled the hospital. After the hospital was filled, we erected tents on the grounds and continued receiving air-evac patients. So I knew what was happening in Vietnam. I decided that I wanted to be a flight surgeon. . . . I had a private pilot's license and was interested in aviation. After my internship at Tripler, I went to Ft. Rucker and to Pensacola and through the army and navy's aviation medicine program and then deployed to Vietnam. While in basic training and my "escape and evasion" course, they told us that as doctors, we didn't have to worry about being captured. Doctors and nurses they said were not PWs, they were "detained personnel" under the Geneva Convention. If they treated us as PWs, we should show our Geneva Convention cards and leave. It was supposed to be a joke ... and it was pretty funny at the time.

I arrived in Vietnam in August '67 and went to An Khe, the HQ of the 1st Cavalry Division. I was told that the division needed two flight surgeons ... one to be the division flight surgeon at An Khe in the rear, and the other to be surgeon for first of the ninth [1st Squadron, 9th Cavalry, or 1/9] a unit actively involved with the enemy. I volunteered for 1/9. The man before me, Capt. Claire Shenep, had been killed and the dispensary was named the Claire Shenep Memorial Dispensary. Like many flight surgeons, I flew on combat missions in helicopters ... enough to earn three air medals ... and one of my medics, SSgt. Jim Zeiler, used to warn me: "Doc, you better be careful: we'll be renaming that dispensary, the K & S Memorial Dispensary."

I was captured on 2 December 1967 and held for five and a half years until 16 March 1973. I have never regretted the decision that I made that August to be the 1/9's flight surgeon. Such is the honor and esteem that I hold the squadron. I am proud of the time I was the squadron's flight surgeon.

On 30 November 1967, I went to Chu Lai with Maj. Steve Porcella, WO1 Mr. Giff Bedworth, and Sgt. McKeckney, the crew chief of our UH-1H [helicopter]. I gave a talk to a troop at Chu Lai on the dangers of night flying. The weather was horrible, rainy and windy, and I asked Major Porcella, the A/C [aircraft] commander, if we could spend the night and wait out the weather. He said, "Our mission is not so important, but we have to get the [helicopter] back." I'll never forget the devotion to duty of this young officer ... it cost him his life.

While flying from Chu Lai to LZ [landing zone] Two Bits, I thought we had flown west of Highway 1, which would be off course. I asked Steve if we had drifted west. He called the ATC [air traffic controller] at Duc Pho and asked them to find him. The operator at Duc Pho said that he had turned his radar off at 2100. He said, "Do you want me to turn it on and find you?" Major Porcella replied, "Roj" and that was the last thing he ever said. The next thing I knew, I was recovering from unconsciousness in a burning helicopter which seemed to be upside down. I tried to unbuckle my seat belt and couldn't use my left arm. I finally managed to get unbuckled and immediately dropped and almost broke my neck. My helmet was plugged into commo [the communications line] and the wire held me as I dropped out of the seat which was inverted. The helicopter was burning. Poor Major Porcella was crushed against the instrument panel and either unconscious or dead. Bedworth was thrown, still strapped in his seat out of the chopper. His right ankle bones were fractured and sticking through the nylon of his boot. Sergeant Mac was unhurt, but thrown clear and unconscious. I tried to free Porcella by cutting his seatbelt and moving him. However, I was unable to. The chopper burned up and I suffered burns on my hands and buttocks and had my pants burned off. While trying to free Porcella, some of the M60 rounds cooked off and I took a round through the left shoulder and neck. My left wrist and left collarbone were broken in the crash, and I lost or broke seven upper teeth.

We assessed the situation: we had no food or water, no flares, no first aid kit or survival gear. We had two thirty-eight pistols and twelve rounds, one seriously wounded WO [warrant officer] copilot, a moderately wounded doctor, and an unhurt crew chief. We thought we were close to Duc Pho and Highway 1 and close to friendlies. Bedworth and I decided to send Mac for help at first light. We never saw him again.

Later ... six long years later, Colonel Nevins told me that Sgt. Mac had been found about ten miles from the crash site, shot and submerged in a rice paddy. So on that night of 30 November 1967, I splinted Bedworth's leg, with tree branches, made a lean-to from the door of the chopper, and we sat in the rain for three days and nights. We just sat there. We drank rain water. On the third morning, he died. We could hear choppers hovering over our crash site and I fired most of the rounds from our .38s [pistols] trying to signal them, but the cloud cover was so heavy and the weather so bad, they never found us.

I took the compass from the burned out helicopter and tried to go down the mountain toward the east and I believed friendlies. My glasses had been broken or lost in the crash and I couldn't see well, the trail was slippery, and I fell on rocks in a creek bed and cracked a couple of ribs. I had my left arm splinted to my body with my army belt. My pants were in tatters and burned, I had broken teeth and a wound in my shoulder. . . . I hadn't eaten or drunk anything but rainwater for three days. . . . I looked and felt like hell.

One of the cruel ironies of my life ... you know how we all play the what if games ... what if I hadn't done this or that. . . . Well, when I finally reached the bottom of the mountain, I estimated four hours after first light, the weather cleared and I saw choppers hovering over the top. I knew I couldn't make it up the mountain, and had to take my chances. But if I had only waited another four hours.

I started walking up the trail and saw a man working in a rice paddy. He came over and said "Dai-wi, Bac-si": Captain Doctor. He took me to a little hooch, sat me down and gave me a can of sweetened condensed milk and a C-ration can opener and spoon. This stuff was like pudding and it billowed out of the can and was the best tasting stuff I had ever had. I felt very safe at that point. One minute later, my host led a squad of fourteen VC with two women and twelve rifles upon me. The squad leader said, "Surrenda no kill." He put his hands in the air and I couldn't because my left arm was tied to my body. He shot at me with an M2 carbine and wounded me, again in the neck. After I was apprehended, I showed my captors my Geneva Convention card: white with a red cross. He tore it up. He took my dog tags and a medallion which had a St. Christopher's on one side and a Star of David on the other, which my dad had given me before leaving. They tied me with commo [communications] wire in a duck wing position, took my boots and marched me mostly at night for about thirty days. The first day they took me to a cave, stripped my fatigue jacket off my back, tied me to a door, and a teenage boy beat me with a bamboo rod. I was told his parents were killed by American bombs. We rested by day, and marched by night. I walked on rice paddy dikes, and couldn't see a thing. They would strike these little homemade lighters and by the sparks they made, see four or five steps. I was always falling off the dikes into the rice paddy water, and had to be pulled back up by my bonds. It was rough. On the way, I saw men, women, and kids in tiger cages, and bamboo jails. I was taken to a camp, which must have been like a medical facility as my wound was festering, and full of maggots and I was sick. A woman heated up a rifle cleaning rod and gave me a bamboo stick to bite on. She cauterized my through and through wound with the cleaning rod and I almost passed out with pain. She then dressed the wound with Mercurochrome and gave me two aspirin. I thought, what else can they do to me? I was to find out.

After walking for about a month through plains, then jungle and mountains, always west, they took me to a camp. I had been expecting a PW camp like a Stalag with "Hogan's Heroes": barbed wire, search lights, nice guards and Red Cross packages . . . and a hospital where I could work as a doctor. They took me to a darkened hut with an oriental prisoner who was not American. I didn't know whether he was Vietnamese, Cambodian, Laotian or

Chinese. He spoke no English and was dying of TB [tuberculosis]. He was emaciated, weak, sick and coughed all day and night. I spent two days there and an English-speaking Vietnamese officer came with a portable tape recorder and asked me to make a statement against the war. I told him that I would rather die than speak against my country. He said words which were unforgettable, and if I ever write a book, will be the title. He said, "You will find that dying is very easy; living, living is the difficult thing."

A few days later, in a driving rain, we started the final trek to camp. I was tied again, with no boots, and we ascended higher and higher in the mountains. I was weak and asked to stop often to rest. We ate a little rice which the guards cooked and actually needed ropes to traverse some of the steep rocks. Finally, we got to PW Camp One. There were four American servicemen there . . . two from the mainland U.S. and two from Puerto Rico. Three were marines, and one in the army. These guys looked horrible . . . they wore black PJs [pajamas], were scrawny with bad skin and teeth and beards and matted hair. The camp also had about fifteen ARVNs [Army of the Republic of Vietnam . . . our allies], who were held separately, across a bamboo fence. The camp was just a row of hootches made of bamboo with elephant grass roofs around a creek, with a hole in the ground for a latrine. This was the first of five camps in which we lived in the South . . . all depressingly similar, although sometimes we had a separate building for a kitchen and sometimes we were able to pipe in water thru bamboo pipes from the nearby stream.

I asked one of the marines, the man captured longest and the leader, if escape was possible. He told me that he and a special forces captain had tried to escape the year before, and the captain had been beaten to death, while he had been put in stocks for ninety days, having to defecate in his hands and throw it away from him or lie in it. The next day I was called before the camp commander and chastised and yelled at for suggesting escape. My fellow PW then told me never to say anything to him that I didn't want revealed, because the Vietnamese controlled his mind. I threatened to kill him for informing on me. He just smiled and said I would learn.

Our captors promised us that if we made progress and understood the evils of the war they would release us. And the next week, they released the two Puerto Ricans and fourteen ARVN PWs. The people released wore red sashes and gave anti-war speeches. I was deeply shocked and shaken by the event. Just before the release, they brought in another seven American PWs from the 196th Light Infantry Brigade who were captured in the Tet offensive of 1968. I managed to write our names, ranks, and serial numbers on a piece of paper—ironically, that was the only time during three and a half years in the jungle that we had paper and pencil—and slip it to one of the Puerto Ricans who was released. They transported the information home, and in March '68 our families learned we had been captured alive. I still have a Xerox of that paper scrap, by which my dad identified my handwriting and confirmed that I was captured alive.

We were held in a series of jungle camps from January 1968 to February 1971. At this time, conditions were so bad, and we were doing so poorly, that they decided to move us to NVN [North Vietnam]. They moved twelve of us. In all, twenty-seven Americans had come through the camp. Five had been released and ten had died. They died of their wounds, disease, malnutrition, and starvation. One was shot while trying to escape. All but one died in my arms after a lingering, terrible illness. Five West German nurses in a neutral nursing organization, called the Knights of Malta, similar to the Red Cross, had been picked up—I always thought by mistake—by the VC in the spring of '69. Three of them died and the other two were taken to NVN in 1969 and held until the end of the war.

The twelve who made it were moved to NVN on foot. The fastest group, of which I was one, made it in 57 days. The slowest group took about 180 days. It was about nine hundred kilometers. We walked thru Laos and Cambodia to the Ho Chi Minh trail and then up the trail across the DMZ [Demilitarized Zone] until Vinh. At Vinh, we took a train 180 miles to Hanoi in about eighteen hours. We traveled on the train with thousands of ARVN PWs who had been captured in Lam Song 719, an ARVN incursion into Laos in 1971.

Once in Hanoi, we stayed in an old French prison called The Citadel or as we said, "The Plantation," until Christmas of '72, when the Christmas bombing destroyed Hanoi. Then we were moved to the Hoa Lo or Hanoi Hilton for about three months. The peace was signed in January '73, and I came home on March 16th with the fourth group.

In the north, we were in a rough jail. There was a bucket in the windowless, cement room used as a latrine. An electric bulb was on twenty-four hours. We got a piece of bread and a cup of pumpkin soup twice each day and three cups of hot water. We slept on pallets of wood and wore PJs and sandals and got three tailor made cigarettes per day. We dry shaved and bathed with a bucket from a well twice per week, and got out of the cell to carry our latrine bucket daily. Towards the end, they let us exercise. There were no letters or packages for us from the south, but I understand some of the pilots who had been there a while got some things. In the summer it was 120° Fahrenheit in the cell and they gave us these little bamboo fans . . . the kind funeral homes in the south used to give out at funerals. During the summer, we all had heat rash, and sweated as if in a steam bath twenty-four hours per day. In the winter, it was cool and damp.

But there were officers and a rank structure and commo done through a tap code on the walls. No one died. It was hard duty, but not the grim struggle for survival which characterized daily life in the camp in the south. In the north, I knew I would survive.

In the south, we often wanted to die. I knew that when they ordered us north, I would make it. In the south, each day saw a struggle for survival. There were between three and twenty-four PWs at all times. We ate three coffee cups of rice per day. In the rainy season, the ration was cut to two cups. I'm not talking about nice, white, Uncle Ben's. I'm talking about rice that was red, rotten, and eaten out by bugs and rats, cached for years, shot through with rat feces and weevils. We arose at four, cooked rice on wood ovens made of mud. We couldn't burn a fire in the daytime or at night unless the flames and smoke were hidden, so we had these ovens constructed of mud that covered the fire, and tunnels that carried the smoke away. We did slave labor during the day, gathering wood, carrying rice, building hootches, or going for manioc, a starchy tuberous plant like a potato. The Vietnamese had chickens and canned food. We never got supplements unless we were close to dying, then maybe some canned sardines or milk. We died from lack of protein and calories. We swelled up with what is called hungry edema and beriberi. We had terrible skin disease, dysentery, malaria. Our compound was littered with piles of human excrement because people were just too sick or weak to make it to the latrine.

We slept on one large pallet of bamboo. So the sick vomited and defecated and urinated on the bed and his neighbor. For the first two years, we had no shoes, clothes, mosquito nets or blankets. Later, in late '69, we got sandals, rice sacks for blankets, and a set of black pajamas. We nursed each other and helped each other, but we also fought and bickered. In a PW situation the best and the worst come out. Any little flaw transforms itself into a glaring lack. The strong can rule the weak. There is no law and no threat of retribution. I can report to you that the majority of the time, the Americans stuck together, helped each other and the strong helped the weak. But there were exceptions . . . and sometimes the stronger took advantage of the weaker ones. There was no organization, no rank structure. The VC forbid the men from calling me "Doc", and made me the latrine orderly to break down rank structure and humiliate me. I was officially forbidden from practicing medicine. But I hoarded medicine, had the men fake malaria attacks and dysentery so we could acquire medicine and keep it until we needed it. Otherwise, it might not come. I tried to advise the men about sanitary conditions, about nutrition and to keep clean, active and eat everything we could ... rats, bugs, leaves, etc. We had some old rusty, razor blades, and I did minor surgery, lancing boils, removing foreign bodies, etc. with them ... but nothing major.

At one time, in the summer of '68, I was offered the chance to work in a VC hospital and receive a higher ration. The NVA political officer who made the offer and was there to indoctrinate us, said it had been done in WW II. I didn't believe him and didn't want to do it anyway, so I refused and took my chances. Later, upon return, I learned that American army doctors in Europe in WW II, particularly those captured in the Battle of the Bulge, had indeed worked in hospitals treating German soldiers. But I'm glad now I did what I did.

We had a first sergeant who had been in Korea and in WW II. He died in the fall of '68, and we were forbidden from calling him "Top." He was experienced and courageous, and a potential leader. The VC broke him fast. He had a terribly wounded hand. He was reduced from a proud and tough noncom to just a little old man. I was not allowed to practice medicine unless a man was thirty minutes away from dying, then they came down with their little bottles of medicine and said "Cure him." At one point we were all dying of dysentery, and I agreed to sign a propaganda statement in return for chloromycetin, a strong antibiotic, to treat our sick. Most of us were seriously ill, although, a few never got sick, maintained their health and their weight. I never figured it out

When a man died, we buried him in a bamboo coffin and I usually eulogized him with some words over his grave and marked it with a pile of rocks. Sometimes we had Mercurochrome to mark the rocks or we built a cross of bamboo. I was forced to sign a death certificate in Vietnamese. I did this thirteen times. The worst period was the fall of '68. We lost five men between September and Christmas. Shortly before the end of November, I thought I was going to lose my mind. All of these fine young strong men were dying. It would have been so easy to live ... just nutrition, fluids, and antibiotics. I knew what to do, but had no means to help them. I was depressed and didn't care whether I lived or died myself. At this time, we were simply starving to death. As an example of how crazy we were, we decided to kill the camp commander's cat. Several of us killed it, and skinned it. We cut off its head and paws and it dressed out to about 3 pounds. We were preparing to boil it when one of the guards came down and asked what was going on. We told him we had killed a weasel by throwing a rock. The guards raised chickens and the chickens were always being attacked by weasels. Well the guard, who was a Montagnard, an aborigine, found the feet, and knew it was the cat. The situation became very serious. The guards and cadre were mustered . . . it was about 3:00AM. The prisoners were lined up and a marine and I were singled out to be beaten. He was almost beaten to death. I was beaten badly, tied up with commo wire very tightly—I thought my hands would fall off, and knew I would never do surgery again—for over a day. I had to bury the cat. . . . And I was disappointed I didn't get to eat it. That's how crazy I was.

About a month later, the marine who had been beaten so badly died. He didn't have to. He simply gave up, like so many. They said, "Doc, I just can't hack it anymore. I don't want to live" . . . and they didn't. Marty Seligman, a professor of psychology at University of Pennsylvania has written a book about these feelings called *Learned Helplessness and Death*. This marine simply lay on his bamboo bed, refused to eat, wash or get up, and died. So many did this. We tried to force them to eat, and be active, but nothing worked. It was just too hard and they were too weary. This marine wavered in and out of coma for about two weeks. It was around Thanksgiving, the end of November. The rains had been monstrous and our compound was a muddy morass littered with piles of feces. Sergeant David Harker of Lynchburg Virginia, and I sat up with him all night. He hadn't spoken coherently for over a week. Suddenly, he opened his eyes and looked right at me. He said, "Mom, Dad, Sis, I love you very much. Box 10, Dubberly, Louisiana." That was in November '68.

We all escaped the camp in the south. Five were released as propaganda gestures, Ten Americans and three Germans died, and twelve Americans and two Germans made it back. I am the only PW who was captured before 1968 to survive that camp. I came back March 16, 1973, and stayed in the hospital in Valley Forge, Pennsylvania, for a month getting fixed up with several operations, and then went on convalescent leave. The first thing I did was go to Dubberly, Louisiana, to see that marine's father. His parents had divorced while he was captured. I went to see five of the families of those that died and called the others on the phone. Every family but one was extremely grateful for the call or visit. One mother didn't want to talk to me.

It was a terrible experience, but there is some good to come from it. I learned much. I learned about the human spirit. I learned about confidence in oneself. I learned about loyalty to your country and its ideals and to your friends and comrades. No task would ever be too hard again. I had renewed respect for what we have and swore to learn my country's history in depth— I have done it—and to try to contribute to my community and set an example for my children and employees.

I stayed on active duty until 1977 when I was honorably discharged and entered the reserve from which I retired as an O6 [full colonel] in 1986. I have had a busy medical practice down in Florida and been remarkably successful. I am active in my community in a number of ways and despite being drenched with Agent Orange a number of times, and having some organs removed, have enjoyed great health. Except for some arthritis and prostate trouble, I'm doing great. So I was lucky . . . very lucky and I'm so thankful for that. I'm thankful for my life and I have no bitterness. I feel so fortunate to have survived and flourished when so many braver, stronger, and better-trained men did not.

Thank you for your attention . . . *Garry Owen*!

Major Harold Kushner is released March 16, 1973, at Gia Lam airport in Hanoi after five years as a POW. *U.S. Air Force photo*

Aftermath

After his Vietnam service he continued the practice of medicine in several overseas medical missions. His military decorations include the Silver Star, Soldier's Medal, three Air Medals, three Purple Hearts, and the Republic of Vietnam Campaign Ribbon with ten battle stars. Since September 1977 he has been engaged in the practice of ophthalmology in Daytona Beach, Florida. He is a healer who was healed himself after the horrors and traumas of his captivity.

❖ ❖ ❖

The final withdrawal of American ground combat forces had occurred in spring 1972. When Dr. Kushner was released from captivity in spring 1973, the Republic of Vietnam would survive only 775 more days before the evacuation of Saigon.

CHAPTER 18

Evacuation of Saigon, 1975

BRIGADIER GENERAL RICHARD E. CAREY, USMC
CAPTAIN GEORGE W. PETRIE, USA

The tumult and the shouting dies;
The captains and the kings depart:
Still stands Thine ancient sacrifice,
An humble and contrite heart.
Lord God of Hosts, be with us yet,
Lest we forget-lest we forget!
—Rudyard Kipling (1865–1936) "Recessional"

FINAL DAYS

The swift collapse of South Vietnam's final defenses, while shocking and dramatic, was also inevitable. Later wrote former South Vietnamese Lt. Gen. Dong Van Khuyen, chief logistician of the Republic of Vietnam Armed Forces (RVNAF), "the survival of South Vietnam depended in a large measure on the viability of the RVNAF. The RVNAF performance, their capabilities to win or lose, in the final analysis depended entirely on the level of U.S. financial and materiel aid." Those somber lines closed his book on the war.

As Communist forces closed in on Saigon, valiant evacuation efforts by American military forces resulted in all the remaining Americans in South Vietnam being taken to safety by aircraft ferrying them to ships standing offshore, along with 130 thousand at-risk South Vietnamese. Many more South Vietnamese fled by whatever possible means, land, sea, and air.

For those who remained in Vietnam the future proved ominous indeed. The Communists arrested many thousands and incarcerated them in primitive "re-

education" camps, where some languished for nearly two decades. Thousands more perished due to sickness, malnutrition, or harsh treatment. A quarter century after the war ended those figures were estimated, at 400 thousand taken prisoner and 50 thousand dead.

Estimating the human costs of the war, let alone those material in nature, was difficult. Douglas Pike calculated that South Vietnam's military forces had lost 200 thousand killed and three times as many wounded. But South Vietnamese civilian casualties, said Pike, were "staggering," amounting to 465 thousand killed and 935 thousand wounded. While some of the civilians were hurt by the spillover of military battles, many more were deliberately targeted by Communist forces, who shelled and rocketed cities and refugee convoys, rounded up and executed civilians, and sent terrorist bombers into pagodas and schoolyards.

While the costs to the United States were modest compared with those suffered by the South Vietnamese, they were substantial nonetheless. There were, to begin with, more than 58 thousand lives lost, over 47 thousand of them due to enemy action. There was the money expended, perhaps not very significant in the long run, but still substantial money: $150 billion by one estimate. Also there was the splintering of the social compact in American society, which was already under great stress for other reasons and could not easily, if at all, be put back together.

North Vietnam, meanwhile, had sacrificed much of a generation to achieve domination of the South. Pike's figures for the North are 960 thousand military deaths (later stated by Hanoi to be 1.1 million) and more than three times that number wounded. Other sources report that, two decades after the war, the North Vietnamese still listed some 300 thousand missing in action, most assuredly dead. The major contrast, though, is in civilian deaths, put by Pike at only 25 thousand in North Vietnam, a mere fraction of the comparable losses in the South.

Not satisfied with their conquests to that point, the Communists then went to war with Cambodia, and then with China, which occasioned yet more death and destruction.

Key American Participants

Brigadier General Richard E. Carey's first war was Korea, where he served as a marine infantry platoon commander during the September 1950 Inchon landing and later was a battalion S-2 (intelligence) officer in a unit that fought its way from the Chosin Reservoir in November and December 1950 when Chinese *volunteers* crossed the Yalu River into North Korea to assist their fellow Communists who had been driven north out of South Korea. In March 1951 Carey was wounded in action and after his recovery he earned his aviator qualification and returned to Korea in a fixed-wing aviation unit.

The first time he visited Vietnam was in 1963 when he conducted an inspection to determine potential aviation activity sites. In the final days before the evacuation of Saigon, which ended on April 30, 1975, he was in Saigon as CO of the 9th Marine Amphibious Brigade: he commanded five thousand marines and one hundred helicopters, fifteen of which were air force Jolly Green Giants.

Brigadier General Richard E. Carey, commander of the 9th Marine Amphibious Brigade, on the bridge of attack aircraft carrier USS *Hancock* enroute to the Republic of Vietnam in 1975. *U.S. Marine Corps photo*

Special forces officer Captain George W. Petrie was in Saigon assigned to the Defense Attaché Office's Special Planning Group (SPG) for the Evacuation of Saigon. In several previous assignments in Vietnam he had been involved in heavy combat, including thirty-day mobile guerilla operations in enemy areas.

Both these men were originally interviewed by the author in a Veterans Forum conducted at the Dallas Veterans Affairs Medical Center on April 30, 2005, the thirtieth anniversary of the evacuation of Saigon.

Evacuation Planning by Petrie

Petrie was assigned to Vietnam in this his fourth tour as a field officer for the Joint Casualty Resolution Center (JCRC). There were special forces officers working in each of the four corps areas, gathering intelligence on Americans missing in action (MIAs), bodies not recovered, and crash sites. The JCRC headquarters was in Thailand with a small liaison team in Saigon. By late March 1975 the countryside had become quite dangerous and the other three captains who had been working in the other corps areas had been sent back to Thailand. Although George was still assigned to III Corps he was also unable to operate in the field anymore so he had returned to Saigon.

At that time Maj. Gen. Homer Smith, the defense attaché, asked for Petrie and marine Captain Tony Woods, also on the JCRC Saigon office staff, to assist in evacuation planning for the Saigon area. At that time the peace treaty only allowed fifty U.S. military personnel to be assigned in all of Vietnam. The two captains detailed to the attaché office along with marine Major Jaime Sabater, from the Four Party Joint Negotiating Team, special forces Sfc. Maurice Brakeman, and two special forces medics from the JCRC, Staff Sergeant Whitener and Sergeant Gallagher, comprised the Special Planning Group for the Evacuation of Saigon.

Initially the group was tasked to conduct a population survey of the Saigon area to determine how many Americans were there to include not only defense attaché civilians and defense attaché Department of Defense (DOD) civilians, but also expatriates. There were many Americans living in the Saigon area: retirees and civilian contractors working for the big American firms. It was necessary to perform a density study to determine where they were living and where to locate them in the event an emergency evacuation became necessary.

About the 1st of April 1975, Da Nang in I Corps had fallen to the North Vietnamese and there had been total chaos on the runways and in the streets. This prompted Major General Smith and the embassy planners to realize that the old American embassy emergency evacuation plan for Saigon wasn't feasible anymore because all the landing zones they had for downtown areas to remove the embassy people were in open areas that could not be controlled. They learned from the Da Nang experience that the Vietnamese population panicked and overran the helicopters and airplanes. A new emergency plan was needed for downtown Saigon. The plan at that time was to utilize buses and Air America helicopters.

Thirteen downtown buildings leased by the United States government as quarters for the Americans were identified and determined to be capable of a rooftop helicopter landing. The Air America (Central Intelligence Agency) choppers were UH-1Bs (Hueys). SPG crews physically cleared the roofs for landings. For each building one of its occupants was trained and equipped by the SPG to control the eventual helicopter landings on their building's roof once the evacuations were ordered. All the building occupants were alerted and prepared. The next step for the SPG was to plan bus movements and volunteer drivers were recruited from the Defense Attaché Office (DAO) and the embassy employees. If an emergency evacuation was triggered, the Americans living downtown would be transported to Tan Son Nhut (TSN) Air Base on busses at night to avoid arousing alarm in the civilian population.

There actually were twenty-six different buildings downtown where the Americans lived. It was desirable to bring as many people as possible out to TSN during the night and then the next day during daylight hours collect those remaining using the Air America helicopters off the rooftops. As often happens, all did not proceed according to plan.

Preliminary Evacuations

When the evacuation began, the members of the SPG had to adjust quickly because Major General Smith independently decided to begin by evacuating his DAO employees, Americans first and then, as the list grew, he included his Vietnamese employees and their families. Initially, an evacuation processing point was established at the Tan Son Nhut air base movie theatre.

The group to be evacuated grew tremendously and they began to use fixed-wing airplanes, C-130s and C-141s from the 13th Air Force that flew from Tan Son Nhut to Guam and the Philippines where the military established refugee processing points. The movie theatre soon began to overflow so they utilized the mall complex in the rear of the DAO compound. The Defense Attaché Office compound at Tan Son Nhut had been the Pentagon East during the war where General Westmoreland's headquarters had been located. Even the gymnasium was used as a processing center. A big two-story building that was later named "Dodge City" was converted into an overnight holding area and stocked with C-rations, other canned foods, and food stuff. A large swimming pool was drained and used as a holding area. Customs people were flown in from the Philippines. The two special forces medics established a dispensary to provide basic medical care for the refugees. Even a nursery was organized with everything needed to care for infants including diapers and formulas. Then the State Department approved what they called laissez fair passes because by that time they were being overwhelmed by Vietnamese trying to escape the inevitable North Vietnamese victory and capture of Saigon.

The handball court was used as a jail because some deserters decided to come out of hiding. One day a pretty scraggly looking character walked by Captain Petrie. Petrie said, "Who are you?" He said, "I work for Sears Roebuck." Petrie said, "Sears Roebuck hasn't been here lately!" The man was handcuffed and marched to the handball court and eventually transported to Guam in handcuffs.

Army special forces Captain George Petrie, during the late April 1975 evacuation of Americans and South Vietnamese from Tan Son Nhut Air Base, Saigon.

The Americans assigned to the embassy wanted to save their Vietnamese employees and naturally each Vietnamese employee wanted to escape with their entire extended families which included not only spouses and children, but grandchildren, grandparents, nephews, nieces, aunts and uncles. These families could eventually encompass as many as sixty members. By April 20th the base processing center was processing five to six thousand refugees per day. The only security forces were the Da Nang consulate marines who had come to Saigon upon the fall of that city. In the final week security became a major problem. Brigadier General Carey, commander of the task force, sent a marine infantry platoon which placed a blanket of needed security on the processing area.

Perhaps it should not have come as a surprise, but Major General Smith had to cut off all PX sales to force the American retiree population to accept evacuation because very unrealistically they were sitting back thinking, "Well, there will be an emergency evacuation one of these days and they'll have to take us then." Major General Smith eventually terminated all their services at the base and most of them relented and accepted evacuation. Between the 20th and 30th of April, eighty thousand people, mostly Vietnamese, were processed without major complications. The next task was to establish the Defense Attaché's compound which Brigadier General Carey's liaison team had told them needed to be prepared for an emergency final evacuation if that became necessary.

The DAO complex began to be called the "Alamo." Once again the SPG members were pressed into action. In an incredibly short time frame the DAO compound was prepared not only as a defensive position, but also as a helicopter emergency evacuation site. Within two days over a hundred concrete bunkers were constructed and placed into defensive positions throughout the compound and surrounded by barbed wire.

The Last Stand at the Alamo

By that time, the NVA were tightening the noose around Saigon. There were at least seventeen enemy divisions around the perimeter which by now was the Saigon city limits. Now it was only a question of when, not if the enemy would take the city. Five landing zones (LZs) capable of landing CH-53s, the Jolly Green Giant helicopters, were constructed by the SPG to be utilized for the final evacuation when the go signal was finally given.

Air Marshal Nguyen Cao Ky described the precarious and dangerous conditions facing everyone: "Nothing was done to stem the onward surge of the enemy. By April 26 the Communists had cut Saigon off from its main source of food, and the only remaining port, Vung Tau, forty-five miles southeast of the capital." (Ky: 222)

The NVA conducted an air strike on Tan Son Nhut using F-5 fighters that had been captured at Phan Rang air base. By the time the enemy had moved close enough to destroy an American C-130 sitting on the ground at

Tan Son Nhut, the final warning bell was ringing. That night, April 28th, Ambassador Graham Martin held a late meeting at the embassy. Throughout all this time the ambassador had been very reluctant to declare that there was going to be an evacuation even up to two days before the final emergency evacuation.

Martin had a message from the International Control Commission (ICC), which was a peace-keeping group who was supposed to maintain peace between the four parties that were negotiating. The ICC reported it was possible that the North Vietnamese might be able to arrange something wherein the Americans could maintain a small diplomatic element in country if the South Vietnamese would capitulate. Actually, it was nothing but a smoke and mirrors attempt, but Martin was grasping at anything that would allow a continuing American presence. He was blinded to reality. Major General Smith and some of the other more realistic people in the room were trying to convince the ambassador to go ahead that night and declare the emergency evacuation so the busses could begin moving downtown. It was obvious there was absolutely no hope left. It was over! The capital city was completely surrounded.

The afternoon of the 28th, two NVA battalions had captured the bridge that led across the river into downtown. The final conquest of Saigon was imminent. The NVA were perched just outside Tan Son Nhut and could be seen right across the fields of the air base, which was surrounded. But Martin was adamant. He gave General Smith what amounted to a direct order: "Tomorrow you will evacuate one hundred thousand key Vietnamese officials on fixed-wing aircraft. I want to shoot for a hundred thousand. How many fixed-wing assets can we get into Tan Son Nhut tomorrow?" The military was exasperated and members of the SPG told marine Colonel Pat Howard that they believed the trigger would be pulled by the enemy at 0500 on April 29th when they would begin their final assault.

After the late night meeting Petrie returned to his room and decided, "We may as well not go to bed because it is three o'clock already; we may as well go sit on the veranda and have a cigarette and a beer." They lived on beer anyway because in the heat they had to keep hydrating themselves all the time. They put on their flak jackets and equipment and went to sit on the veranda. Sure enough at 0500 the first enemy rounds hit: rockets and howitzer and mortar fire that quickly intensified. Two of the marines from the Da Nang squad were killed by a direct hit on their position by a 120mm rocket. Petrie and the other Americans joined the seventy-five hundred remaining refugees, moved them to safety and attempted to keep them calm.

At 1000 hours that morning, when Major General Smith told Ambassador Martin that he should go ahead and order the emergency evacuation, it looked like an aerial circus on the runway. Planes were going sideways down the runway trying to get away. Runways had been cratered by the enemy fire; fixed-wing aircraft could not be brought into Tan Son Nhut to satisfy Martin. Yet Martin, rather than listening to his two-star general, however, was telling Smith, "Do it." Even when the general said there was no usable runway, Martin did not believe him. Ambassador Martin came to TSN mid-morning the 29th, but he still would not order the emergency evacuation. Ultimately it took a direct order from Secretary of State Henry Kissinger and the CINCPAC to force the ambassador to finally give order to Brigadier General Carey.

In the meantime at daylight early the morning of the 29th, the downtown emergency evacuation began with the busses and Air America helicopters. There were complications with refueling so the helicopters would fly off the rooftops in Saigon carrying evacuees to Tan Son Nhut and then continuing on to navy ships to refuel for another cycle. When Petrie left the Alamo compound shortly after midnight the morning of April 30th, there were no refugees remaining at there. The last people leaving the area were the marine command group and their security. Major Sabater and Captains Woods and Petrie were flown out to a helicopter carrier offshore.

George Petrie had been awake for most of the previous 120 perilous and busy hours. When he left Saigon that terrible night, he was sitting in the rear of the helicopter and had a panoramic view of the place he was leaving. He could see hundreds of fires throughout the area and the Long Binh ammo dump exploding. His mind was overwhelmed with a feeling of shame and disgrace for what we were doing. The greatest nation on earth was running with its tail between its legs after sacrificing so many of our young men and women, millions of Vietnamese who had died, and to a lesser degree the billions of dollars of our national wealth that had been spent in a losing cause. He thought of all his dear friends who had died or had been badly wounded, and he cried.

But overall, was it worth it? He thought so.

❖ ❖ ❖

George Petrie had a fixed opinion about the final day when media focused most of the evacuation publicity on the embassy where there was a colossal catastrophe because the embassy was never supposed to be used as an evacuation point. It was only one of many buildings originally planned as evacuation points, and it was only to be utilized by the embassy staffers who were still on the premises. Petrie and his team members had visited the embassy several days earlier and briefed embassy security personnel on how to handle the final evacuation movement and how to set up their road blocks to channel the crowd away from the embassy gates to avoid chaos in the mobs of people who were likely to gather outside the building's walls. Petrie even offered to send work crews to the embassy and make the preparations for them, but they were ignored. International media broadcasted that final sad and tragic rooftop happening when people climbed up a ladder. It was always thought to have been on the roof of the American embassy in Saigon, but actually it was at another building downtown where Petrie's workers had built the ladder. The helicopter in the picture was an Air America aircraft that had been flying one final flight over Saigon. They went down to the roof to pickup a group of Vietnamese they had spotted. The media ignored the final orderly evacuation of almost seventy-five hundred people on the 29th, under fire for a good part of the day, from Tan Son Nhut with no significant difficulties thanks to DAO's Special Planning Group, Brigadier General Carey and his marines, and the proper coordinated planning between the marines and DAO. The press made it look like the evacuation was a complete debacle only because it focused on the embassy on April 30th and ignored the successful evacuation of thousands of people saved from Tan Son Nhut, not only during the emergency evacuation conducted on April 29th, but also over the entire previous month.

The Marines Begin Their Landings

Brigadier General Carey complimented Petrie's efforts at the Alamo. He said they had their operation very, very well planned. Unfortunately the political decisions by the ambassador at the eleventh hour complicated everything. As the commander of the 9th Marine Amphibious Brigade, the one-star General Carey was personally in charge of about five thousand marines and one hundred helicopters with support by four aircraft carriers and forty other ships of VAdm. George P. Steele's Seventh Fleet. There were fifteen amphibious ships and fifteen military sea transport ships (MSTS) which were on standby to transport the refugee evacuees. Carey went to Saigon the first time on April 8th with two members of his staff. One of them was Al Gray, who later became commandant of the Marine Corps. They went to Saigon in civilian clothes to meet with Ambassador Martin because, as Petrie pointed out, there was a limit on the number of American military people who were allowed in the country at any given time and this number was monitored by the Four-Power commission in Vietnam that consisted of Poles, Hungarians, Swedes, and Canadians. There was another commission consisting of representatives of the American government, the South Vietnamese government, the North Vietnamese government, and the Vietnam Cong that was trying to maintain some semblance of order.

Brigadier General Carey's challenge under these circumstances was like "whack a mole." As commands starting in Washington cascaded down through the military chain of command, each link in the chain had to have their input and consequently Carey's orders were constantly changed. He made frequent trips into Saigon for coordination during April from his headquarters on the USS *Blue Ridge*. Brigadier General Carey recognized the importance of the DAO's SPG planning along with the courageous pilots who flew under extraordinarily hazardous conditions to perform the evacuation. One of the threats in the area was an imminent typhoon with thunder storms and lighting that dangerously complicated aerial operations. The pilots were unfamiliar with where their missions would have to be flown, such as, into the embassy or into the DAO compound, especially since most flying was done at night.

Due to all the extensive planning accomplished, the evacuation from the DAO went very smoothly except for a few incidents. There was one instance where the marine control team located on the roof of the DAO was driven off by machine gun fire. They returned fire, but it was puzzling whether it was South Vietnamese who were disenchanted for not being able to be evacuated or whether it was enemy fire. When Carey received word on April 29th, he was cycling his helicopters to the DAO compound. He had never intended to go the embassy as it was not in any of the plans.

When Brigadier General Carey anticipated that, after all, they might end up conducting a last-minute emergency evacuation from the embassy itself, at 1100 hours on the 29th they were able finally to obtain permission to cut down a tamarind tree which was right in the middle of the embassy compound enabling their CH-53's, the heavy helicopters, to land where the tree had been. The giant tamarind tree had been very symbolic because it had been defined by some past ambassador as representing America's strength in Vietnam. (Ky: 53)

The fog of war always demands last minute adjustments to be creatively employed. When Carey received orders from his military chain of command at noon on April 29th, he started his marine helicopters cycling from the ships to the DAO compound to remove embassy staff and embassy-cleared refugees. Already in place on all the MSTS ships were small detachments of fifty marines, each under the command of a lieutenant who had the responsibility for taking care of the refugees who had been evacuated from Tan Son Nhut in the SPG operation. On one ship there were five thousand refugees with fifty young marines and only one navy corpsman to take care of them. Some people came in over the sides and not from our helicopters and since they had not been searched, there were firefights with our marines who needed to disarm the troublemakers.

Final Evacuation

Even at the end, much of the movement to the ships had to be accomplished clandestinely because of the embassy situation; Ambassador Martin remarked to Brigadier General Carey, "Don't stir the ashes too hard. I don't want people to know what's going on." The ambassador was planning to stay until the last minute. To his credit he wanted to remain to help the Vietnamese because he felt very committed to them, so it was difficult both emotionally and professionally for him. Still, this commitment caused difficulty for the military during those final days and hours. The ambassador's foster son, Marine Corps 1st Lt. Glenn D. Mann, who was a helicopter pilot, had been killed in Chu Lai, Vietnam on November 23, 1965 giving Martin a significant personal emotional attachment to South Vietnam; it's likely the ambassador believed a final American departure would reflect negatively on the sacrifice of his foster son.

When the large helicopters landed at Tan Son Nhut, Carey brought ashore a battalion of marines to provide security. That same morning, April 29th, he began to position 180 or so marines in the embassy to help maintain order for the processing of their evacuation. Carey believes there really was limited chaos inside the embassy grounds until the final minutes. Up until that time it had been a fairly orderly transition. The basic problem was in allowing people access through gates, and trying to keep people from coming over the embassy walls to escape on our helicopters. Carey is convinced that some Vietnamese were permitted to come over those walls by his young marines when they saw all those sad faces, crying and begging to leave. They were probably allowed into the embassy grounds by our sympathetic marines. It is also likely that there were people who came in through the back door of the embassy grounds. Every time the evacuation controllers asked for a count of how many people were to come out of the embassy the number was two thousand, even Ambassador Martin said so.

Martin called Carey that afternoon, April 29th, around 1600 hours and he said, "I need some marines." Carey replied, "What do you need marines for?" He said, "People are coming over the walls." Carey said, "When are you coming up to the DAO at the air base?" He said, "I am not going to come down there to the DAO. I'm going to stay here." So, Carey was compelled to begin shuttling his helicopters into the embassy courtyard where the tamarind tree had been removed, especially the large CH-53's. The marines completed the evacuation of all the refugees at the DAO compound on the 29th in eight and a half hours, but Carey was called by Martin at 2030 hours that evening when he still had eight hundred marines to return to their ships. The CH-53s had slowed down coming to the DAO. The ambassador asked Carey, "What's happened to the choppers?" Carey replied, "Why?" Martin responded, "I haven't had a chopper in over half an hour."

Carey tried everywhere to determine what had caused the stoppage of the missions to no avail, so he took matters personally in his hands to get the choppers moving again and boarded the next helicopter that was evacuating marines out of the DAO and landed on the USS *Midway* just in time to witness a South Vietnamese pilot who flew aboard with his family in a small observation aircraft. At 2300 Carey flew to the USS *Blue Ridge*, which was the command and control ship from which Vice Admiral Steele was commanding the fleet operation. It was difficult for Carey not to exhibit anger as he said, "What the . . . happened to my helicopters? Who stopped them?" Commander of the amphibious group RAdm. Donald Whitmire, said, "I did." After being asked an explanation, he said, "Well, they've been in the air for almost twelve hours now and that's way beyond the safety requirement." Carey replied very emphatically, "There's no safety involved here. We've got a job to do." Fortuitously, Rear Admiral Whitmire received a call just then from Adm. Noel Gayler, the four-star Commander-in-Chief Pacific, based in Hawaii. Sitting with Admiral Nayler during the call was Lt. Gen. Louis Wilson, the commanding general of Fleet Marine Forces, Pacific, who said, "My marines don't get tired." (General Wilson, who had received the Medal of Honor in World War II, was appointed the twenty-sixth Commandant of the Marine Corps shortly following the evacuation of Saigon in July 1975.) This high level *encouragement* was enough to convince Whitmire to change his mind.

Immediately, a call from Washington asked, "How many more people are to be evacuated?" The DAO evacuation had been completed by now and an after midnight in the early morning of April 30 call to Ambassador Martin at the embassy gave the answer eight hundred more, which would require nineteen to twenty sorties (trips) of the large CH-53s, and this information was transmitted back up to Washington.

What happened next is a stark example of how Washington often attempted to totally control combat operations in Vietnam in minute detail: Carey was ordered to fly *only* nineteen more sorties. In actuality, at that time there were more than eight hundred people in the embassy, which meant that in the end everyone was not able to be evacuated because Carey had only nineteen sorties left. Former Prime Minister Nguyen Cao Ky related in his memoirs that Ambassador Martin had made a promise to conduct a large-scale evacuation of Vietnamese, but that had now become impossible. Even the firemen who had worked diligently to protect the final helicopter landing at the embassy were left behind. (Ky: 231)

The End at the Embassy
The final exit from the embassy became very tense at the end. The marines there used as much force as possible to restrain Vietnamese who had climbed over the embassy walls to escape. The final group of fifty marines entered the embassy building itself, closed the doors, and climbed to the roof where they were compelled to use tear gas to hold off the last desperate Vietnamese, who recognized their final chance for freedom was quickly disappearing. Up to that time a hundred marines had flown out as the last Americans left by CH-46s from the embassy rooftop.

The final evacuation had now been going on since noon the day before, the 29th, and Ambassador Graham Martin was finally evacuated about 0430 hours on the 30th. It had become very difficult to bring helicopters to the embassy, and the last people, eleven marines who had remained to control the helo landings, left at 0730 that morning.

It literally took a direct order from Washington for the ambassador to leave. This may be the only bit of humor from the horrible final moments of the evacuation. Washington told Carey to remove the ambassador on the next aircraft, but the ambassador, a crusty old guy, maintained he was still not leaving. Unfortunately, at that time he was suffering from pneumonia, could barely talk, and was not in the best of shape emotionally or physically.

The question was asked, "He may not come out—how are we going to get him out?" Vice Admiral Steele turned to Brigadier General Carey who said, "Well, Admiral, why don't we ask Washington? Give me permission to put a marine on either side of him and carry him out if he refuses to come out." Captain Jerry Berry, a CH-46 pilot who had flown for eighteen hours straight, piloted the helicopter that had Ambassador Martin as a passenger. General Carey talked to Captain Berry personally and said, "When you get into the embassy, you personally talk to the ambassador and tell him he is to board on your aircraft by direct order from the president in Washington." Apparently the ambassador had already heard the order to board the aircraft, so he did.

The Operation Completed

Carey's young marines oversaw the evacuees and in some instances accompanied them all the way to Guam. Babies were born on board the ships. The refugees were fed rice that had literally been cooked by the barrel-load. Carey is totally committed to his magnificent air crews whom he recommended for over one hundred Distinguished Flying Crosses (DFCs) along with more than two hundred Air Medals. On each of those operations into the embassy compound there was only a ten-foot clearance on each side of the rudders and only ten to fifteen feet in the courtyard for them to descend. The helicopters were designed to carry thirty five combat marines, but on the evacuation missions they typically carried seventy people. For most of the missions they came under enemy fire in very, very hazardous weather conditions for eighty-mile trips each way. Their fuel limits were stretched.

Amazingly, throughout all this only two aircraft were lost, and *no* passengers were injured. Sometimes they flew with only strobe lights signaling the landing zones. Under extreme and dangerous conditions the final duties and involvement of the United States in Vietnam after more than a decade were performed by our American military personnel in a distinguished and valorous fashion that should make them and all Americans very proud.

South Vietnamese Air Force

Just prior to the beginning of the actual American-led evacuation efforts there were several examples of heroic, desperate, last-ditch efforts by South Vietnamese Air Force members to escape the North Vietnamese. They were flying helicopters and aircraft out to the fleet vessels trying to land on the ships. Carey remembers before the actual evacuation when he was down in the combat control center on the *Blue Ridge* and this horrendous bang was heard in the ship: it was a Vietnamese helicopter that had flown right into the side of the ship. Some aircraft would fly right beside the ship and the pilots would just bail out and our crew members would save them. A further four thousand people came by boats to our ships.

One of the Vietnamese Air Force pilots, Tom Nguyen, who now lives in Dallas, flew with his family, his wife and four children, in a small observation aircraft toward the *Midway*. The aircraft was orbiting, and he called and he said, "I'm going to land." He was told, "You can't land here. You can't get stopped on the deck." The pilot said, "I'm going to land. I've got my family aboard." So the aircraft carrier's commanding officer cranked up the ship getting it underway and up to speed to get the maximum wind over the deck and Nguyen safely landed his aircraft with his family. This was an example of a great humanitarian act that took place.

One of the most well-known personalities in the Vietnam War was flamboyant and courageous Air Vice Marshal Nguyen Cao Ky, who also had served in political positions as prime minister and vice president of Vietnam. After witnessing the ambassador's inspection visit of the damaged runways and the Air America planes all over the Saigon skies on the 29th, he decided it was time to depart to save himself. Several days before he had arranged to save his family by sending them on one of the earlier refugee trips. Along with several other pilots he boarded his own helicopter and flew it to the *Midway* on the 29th. (Ky: 229)

Aftermath

Richard Carey retired with three stars as a lieutenant general. He had been involved in the marine air operations around Khe Sanh, the Hue City battle in 1968, the evacuation of Da Nang just before the one in Saigon, and was serving his third tour in Vietnam. This final departure from a country to which he was very committed and attached was very emotional. He also oversaw the May 1975 incident when the *Mayaguez* merchant ship was attacked by the Khmer Rouge from Cambodia.

He had originally become involved in 1973 when contingency plans were being written for a possible final withdrawal from both South Vietnam and Cambodia. As it turned out, when the trigger was finally pulled, he was the right man at the right place at the right time to command the operation.

General Carey is very complimentary of the loyalty, dedication and valor to the end of many in the South Vietnamese military forces who fought to save their country. He concludes that the peace agreement which allowed the North Vietnamese to maintain their troops in the South and the halting of U.S. military aid to the south combined to bring about the horrible final catastrophe.

George Petrie retired as a major in 1980 having spent three years in Vietnam. He was awarded two Silver Stars, two Bronze Stars for valor, three Army Commendation Medals for valor, and amazingly enough only one Purple Heart. During his Vietnam tours he had extensive exposure to many lower-ranking South Vietnamese officers and men. Several of his assignments involved fighting with Montagnard troops under his direct command.

He believes individual Vietnamese soldiers and most junior officers with whom he associated throughout the course of the war were truly fine soldiers. The military's major shortcoming was the middle and senior officers and the overall political leadership of the country. Too many leaders, both political as well as military, were simply incompetent and corrupt. This major leadership challenge, which, in his opinion, was one of several causes for our defeat, is the responsibility of those in our own leadership who oversaw the war. It was totally solvable, but no attempt was ever made to do so.

Major Petrie holds the Vietnamese people in the highest regard. Most of the people he met in Vietnam, who were later safely resettled in the United States following the end of the war, are hard-working, family-oriented citizens who are great contributors to their adopted homeland.

Petrie's love and respect for the Montagnards could not be any higher. When he was a team sergeant and company commander in the II Corps Mike Force, all of his soldiers were Montagnards; he considers them his Brothers in Arms. Petrie sadly concludes, "When we left Vietnam, we deserted them; it is as simple as that. These brave folks continue to defy the Communists and many are still migrating to the United States." The magnificent old warrior George Petrie left us all behind when, after many years of medical challenges, he died on April 15, 2011.

As we shall see, others were left behind.

CHAPTER 19

Left Behind

KIM AND RON HUMPHREY (1975–1977)

Phoenix: A bird that rises renewed from the ashes

AFTERMATH

Any questions as to the sympathies and loyalties of the South Vietnamese people were resolved conclusively in the wake of the Communist takeover. A million or more fled their own country rather than face life under their new liberators, many becoming boat people as they put to sea in whatever craft could be found. The International Red Cross later estimated that some three hundred thousand boat people perished, the victims of storms, piracy, exposure, or simply starvation.

The Communists had always hoped for, and often predicted, popular uprisings in South Vietnam in support of their efforts at conquest. In fact, though, there was never any popular uprising in support of the enemy in South Vietnam. This was not surprising (except perhaps to the Communists, if they really believed their own propaganda) in view of the their record year after year: assassinations, kidnappings, terror bombings, impressments, and indiscriminate shellings of population centers throughout South Vietnam, actions hardly calculated to win the hearts and minds of the victims or their families. Nevertheless, and dismayingly, some people in America argued that the enemy had the superior moral stance, and indeed before the war was over there were some Americans openly pulling for their own country (and the South Vietnamese) to lose the war and for the deliberate and relentless perpetrators of these war crimes to win it.

Fortunately, for them and for America, large numbers of South Vietnamese refugees found new homes in the United States, where they have enriched our society and culture, embracing the American dream of prosperity through hard work and dedication. Other large groups of South Vietnamese refugees are similarly making new lives for themselves in Australia, Canada, France, and elsewhere.

Saigon: April 1975

Kim was in the line on the embassy grounds April 29, 1975, with her four youngest children patiently waiting with hope that she would escape on one of the American helicopters making trips from the embassy grounds to the U.S. Navy ships out in the South China Sea. The past three weeks had been absolutely harrowing and horrible. In early April she returned from Germany, where she had been visiting her fiancé Ron Humphrey, and attempted to obtain exit visas for herself and her children. Many Vietnamese attempting to leave Vietnam just before its collapse to the NVA troops who were tightening their grip around Saigon were not successful in departing. They were turned back at the Tan Son Nhut base gate unless they had official exit papers or paid bribes.

She had visited the Ministry of Interior to obtain exit visas and was directed to the American embassy where, after a three hour wait on the lawn, she was directed back to the Interior Ministry. It was a colossal bureaucratic circus. She had found her oldest son in a hospital with shrapnel wounds in his head. As a seventeen-year-old he had been called into the army in March and thrust into the fighting with little training. A second trip to the embassy was also unsuccessful in obtaining the necessary papers. Money paid to a man who said he could obtain entry for her family to the base became lost when he deserted them right at the gate. She was in jail overnight with a trumped up charge of bribery to a high official until rescued by her policeman brother.

Saigon: The Final Evacuation

Kim was in a Saigon hotel as April 29th dawned and she ran to the window to view American helicopters flying to the American embassy. She grabbed her children and began walking toward it. People flooded the streets and were saying, "The Americans are leaving." Sounds of gunfire could be heard. They reached the embassy and it was surrounded by literally thousands of people carrying all their earthly possessions in suit cases. The marines guarding the gates allowed people entry very sparingly. She went to a back gate and showed a marine a letter from her dear Ron Humphrey and she was allowed into the embassy grounds where she took her place in the line that seemed to move forward only by inches as each helicopter landed and took off packed with passengers.

All of a sudden she saw some remaining marines and other Americans board a chopper, which whirled into the sky. The anguish of the people in line was palpable as they believed there were no more helicopters coming; they thought they had been left behind. However, Vietnamese firemen employed by the embassy who had been helping to load the aircraft said not to worry. They had been promised by embassy staffers that they and their families would be rescued. Their hopes were dashed. Brigadier General Carey, following his orders from Washington, had concluded the evacuation of the embassy compound.

Finally realizing that there would be no further helicopters coming to take her family away, Kim and her children left the compound and began walking through the streets of Saigon.

NVA in the Streets
Adding to the chaos in Saigon, the North Vietnamese Army began firing rockets indiscriminately into the streets. Dead and wounded people littered the ground. As Kim walked aimlessly rocket rounds continued to fall and she now heard machine-gun fire. As they walked past the nearly empty German embassy, a westerner motioned them inside and the children hid behind the furniture.

She looked outside; it was finally over! North Vietnamese Army tanks were rattling down the streets carrying soldiers wearing pith helmets and waving the North Vietnamese flag. The Republic of Vietnam was no longer.

They checked back into a hotel. Kim heard from her brother that Colonel Nghia, the outstanding Vinh Long province chief, had committed suicide rather than take his chances with the Communists. Kim decided she had better return to her home in Vinh Long, sixty-five miles south of Saigon.

Once back home she learned the fate of Lt. "Tiger" Ngoc, the fearless Regional Force Commander, who would not give up and held off repeated Communist attacks on his position with a few stalwart defenders. Once he and his men expended all their ammunition, they were overwhelmed and killed. The Communists built a public latrine over his gravesite.

April 1975—Germany
Ron pursued every alternative in his attempts to get Kim and her family out of Vietnam before the fall. He learned it was possible that a West German plane could transport them from Saigon in a humanitarian mission, but it did not have a pressurized cabin. With Steve Schmidt of *Time* magazine, he visited the Vietnamese embassy in Bonn and eventually they met with a Colonel

Ninh, who they understood to be a close relative of Nguyen Van Thieu, the president of Vietnam. Colonel Ninh told Steve as they conferred in Vietnamese that Steve's *Time* staff, accompanied by Kim and her family, could have the required clearances to leave from Tan Son Nhut, but the Colonel needed something done for him. No big deal: Ninh said he had a special nine-ton cargo he wanted transported to Europe on one of the West German planes. Steve heard the rumor from a Saigon source that President Thieu was attempting to remove much of the Vietnam central bank's gold supply to Europe for his personal use. After *Time* ran an article on the gold story, no one would touch the nine-ton cargo, and another door was closed to Ron.

On April 30 he heard the fateful news in Cologne. The Americans had abandoned Saigon. Over the next several days Ron heard about the boats leaving the country and refugees being picked up by the U.S. Navy. He wishfully thought that she was on one of those boats.

In Washington, Ron's long-estranged wife Marylou was in contact with him; she had been checking the refugee lists of those who had successfully exited. By now she had found out about Ron and Kim's relationship and was both sympathetic and empathetic to their plight. Several weeks after many refugees had been relocated to Ft. Chaffee, Arkansas, Marylou, who worked for German television, talked to a refugee that she knew who had formerly worked for German television. What he told her was pitiful. Her friend reported what he discovered amongst the refugees at Ft. Chaffee, "You rescued every corrupt Vietnamese official who ever served in Saigon. You were so efficient you didn't miss a single one." (Humphrey: 164) It appears that at least many of the rats had been able to leave the sinking ship!

Retribution

Six weeks after her return to Vinh Long, she was arrested when a NVA officer knocked on her door and said he was aware of her relationship with the CIA-agent, obviously meaning Ron Humphrey. Kim was arrested June 9, 1975, Ron's birthday. She and her brother were taken together to the provincial jail (which had a Catholic chapel) where she found about a hundred others who had worked for the government or the Americans. Since her brother had been only a low-level policeman, his incarceration in a re-education camp only lasted until 1977. Kim was slated for much more harsh treatment. Since she surely could have escaped, the Communists suspected that she must have remained in Vietnam to establish a spy cell; because they believed Ron was in the CIA, Kim must be connected with the CIA.

Each day the prisoners were required to write out their personal biography over and over. They were examined for even the slightest discrepancy which would lead to additional interrogation. They were forced constantly to listen to propaganda and Communist indoctrination. For the first three months, the prisoners were treated reasonably well. Then Kim was placed in a bamboo cage, a "tiger cage", for three days followed by solitary confinement in the jail's chapel. On the floor she saw a shattered crucifix. She put it back together and remembered that the figure represented "Jesu." Her Catholic friends and Ron had told her that he was supposed to be much stronger than the Buddha she had known all her life. She began praying to Jesu for protection.

One day she was brought into a room and was told information about Ron from his time in Vinh Long. The Communists knew everything about Ron and his activities. Their source was Khanh, the Kit Carson Scout who had been hired by Ron. Khanh had been the Viet Cong sympathizer who had set Ron up to be killed at the Caumoy bridge.

As the interrogation began about her relationship with Ron, so too did the torture. Pliers were used to pull out her waist-length hair. She was thrown back in the chapel room. She continually refused to sign confessions that she worked for the American CIA. Then two of her jailers ripped off her clothes and raped her over the next few days. She was then thrown back in with the other women prisoners who were so scared after seeing her physical condition that they all signed their confessions. By signing these confessions, however, the women might as well have been signing their death warrants. Two weeks later the Communists began executing the men and women who signed in the prison yard. Ultimately, Kim was the only woman left alive.

She returned to her room and held the crucifix and praised Jesu for saving her. Her prayers had been answered; she was alive. They were fully answered four days before Tet 1976 when she was freed to return home. In a goodwill gesture Hanoi granted amnesty for a small member of prisoners. Kim was one of them.

The Rest of the Story

After nine months in prison Kim was assigned a probation officer, Mrs. Binh, and made a startling discovery! During the war Mrs. Binh had worked at the American helicopter base as a maid, primarily washing clothes for the Americans. Her husband was a South Vietnamese army lieutenant. They had both been secret agents for the Viet Cong. The accurate pinpoint mortar fire by the Communists on the helicopters that resulted in heavy losses was not due to luck or exceptional firing ability by the Viet Cong. Lieutenant and Mrs. Binh fed the spots where the helicopters were parked to the VC mortar crews on the nights of the barrages. Americans had clean clothes, but at the expense of many damaged and destroyed helicopters.

Aftermath

In mid-1977 a Vietnamese army major knocked on her door again, this time with good news. Through Ron Humphrey's continuous efforts with his diplomatic contacts, he had finally succeeded in achieving his long time goal. His Swedish and West German contacts arranged for Kim finally to depart Vietnam only with her four youngest children; the three oldest children were to remain in Vietnam. Kim's oldest daughter had left Vietnam prior to the April 1975 evacuation with a German high school teacher whom she eventually married. By 1989 Ron and Kim were able to bring her remaining three children into the United States.

The very day that the five of them, Kim and her four youngest children, left Tan Son Nhut in a French plane chartered by the International Red Cross, the now unified Vietnam was admitted to the United Nations. Ron Humphrey has always believed the miracle of Kim's release was related to the diplomatic breakthrough of Hanoi's government being officially recognized as a member of the world community.

Kim and her youngest children joined Ron in the United States and they were finally married. Humphrey had worked diligently to effect Kim's release, pulling out every stop he could imagine. Unfortunately, in his desperate attempts to get Kim out of Vietnam some of Ron's actions and one of his Vietnamese contacts had been indiscrete. He was charged and unfairly convicted of a national security violation. In hindsight Ron believes he was duped and took the fall for someone who should have been indicted instead. He served nine years in the Danbury, Connecticut, federal penitentiary. That, however, is another story, which he relates in a thus far unpublished manuscript *For the Love of Kim*.

❖ ❖ ❖

In love and war Ron and Kim's story had a happy ending in contrast to the lives of many of us who live with the ravages and horrific memories of our time in the war. They live together now in the United States, free and peacefully united in their mutual faith as Christians, a fit ending to the histories in this book about two peoples, Americans and Vietnamese, who sacrificed so much for so long in our quest for freedom and peace for the Vietnamese in the Republic of Vietnam.

Reflections

*U*nderstanding the Vietnam War and why it turned out as it did has been
complicated, even these many years later, by self-justifying mischaracteriza-
tions of it by antiwar groups who, as now–Senator Jim Webb observed several years
ago, "have a large stake in having the war remembered as both unnecessary and
unwinnable."

In fact there had come a point at which the South Vietnamese had won. The
fighting hadn't ended, but the South Vietnamese, with crucial American assistance,
had reached a point at which they could sustain their freedom and independence of
action.

This came about during the latter years of declining American involvement.
Under new leadership in both Washington and Saigon, crucially important
differences included wisdom and stability in the ambassadorial post; better field
generalship; a more adept national leadership, even allowing for the vigorous
internecine warfare waged within the Nixon administration; a wholly different
approach to the conduct of the war within South Vietnam, one in which population
security, not body count, was the measure of merit; different tactics in South Vietnam, with "clear and hold" rather than "search and destroy" the mode; an attitude
of nurturing and improving the South Vietnamese armed forces rather than
shoving them out of the way, as had been done earlier; concentration on "one war"
involving pacification, combat operations, and improvement of South Vietnam's
armed forces rather than fixing on American combat operations; and of course the
radical differences in context and the American domestic scene, resulting in
withdrawal of American forces rather than continually building them up, in
eroding political support for the war, and ultimately in abandonment of the South
Vietnamese.

The fact is that the ill-fated South Vietnamese fought valiantly for their
freedom and, so long as America kept her commitments to them, were holding their
own. It was only when the United States defaulted on all its key promises of

support, while North Vietnam's Communist patrons massively increased the where-withal provided their client state, that the South was overwhelmed.

That unnecessary and tragic outcome need not have been. It was the doing of the United States Congress, then led and controlled by the dissident minority not reflective of the will of the American people at large, nor of course of the millions of American servicemen who had served during the war and who, overwhelmingly, said afterward they were proud to have done so.

Author's Afterword

All of us who served there left behind some part of our bodies, souls, or spirit in Vietnam. Most of us returned with a sense of pride that we were courageous and fit enough to have joined the military. We will always remember those whose names are on the Wall in Washington, D.C., and those fellow warriors who stood, fought, bled, and sacrificed beside us. However, it is my prayer as then-Colonel Dave R. Palmer wrote in his book *Summons of the Trumpet: U.S.—Vietnam in Perspective*, "There must be no more Vietnams." (Palmer: 268)

Acknowledgments

My deep and personal gratitude is expressed to my fellow West Point graduate (1956), Lewis Sorley, for providing the interstitial historical comments.

My utmost appreciation is extended to Lt. Gen. Dave R. Palmer, USA (Ret), West Point graduate (1956) and Superintendent, West Point (1986-1991), who provided very valuable guidance to me throughout the manuscript process.

I also need to acknowledge Lieutenant Colonel Roger Cirillo, USA (Ret.), Book Director, Association of the United States Army, who first believed in the merits of our stories; Colonel Ed Sayre, USA (Ret), was invaluable in adding his historical insights to the MACVSOG chapter. Linda, my patient wife and partner in life, provided constant uplifting inspiration and counsel through all the long years of the writing process. My daughters, Elizabeth Clark and Christi Bieberich, and grandchildren Brooke and Beau Bieberich, each day motivate me to continue contributing to others through service in my lay ministry and my writings and to be an example for a life well-lived.

My wonderful word processors, Brittnay Smith and Janet French, who calmly survived with great and good cheer all the editing and rewriting. Gayle Wurst, my loyal agent, of the Princeton International Agency for the Arts, LLC, who represented me in such a dedicated fashion through some very challenging experiences.

Tara Lichterman and Libby Braden of Casemate Publishers were always pleasant and helpful. Richard Kane, my Casemate Publishers editor, was editor for my autobiography published in 2007. His editing talents have substantially enhanced this final product. Being a fellow West Pointer has bonded us together in trust and understanding.

My lifelong gratefulness is extended to all the subjects of these histories who so selflessly shared their lives, their hearts, and their souls from our war.

Glossary

A Team	12-man special forces detachment
AK-47	Standard NVA assault rifle
Amerasians	Children born of an American and Asian parent
AO	Area of Operations
ARVN	Army of the Republic of Vietnam, the South Vietnamese Army
B-52	Air force bomber
CAS	Close Air Support
CBU	Cluster Bomb Unit
CIA	Central Intelligence Agency
CIB	Combat Infantryman's Badge
C-47	Air Force airplane sent to support units under attack
Chieu Hoi	Government program to accept enemy defectors
Chopper	Helicopter
CIDG	Civilian Irregular Defense Group usually sponsored by special forces
Claymore	Antipersonnel mines that shoot steel balls
C-123	Air Force cargo plane
CP	Command Post
C-130	Air Force cargo plane
CV-2	Caribou aircraft (U.S.)
CV-7	Buffalo aircraft (U.S.)

DAO	Defense Attaché Office
D-Day	June 6, 1944 Assault landings in France
Dai Uy	South Vietnamese military rank equivalent to U.S. captain
DEROS	Date of estimated return from overseas
DMZ	Demilitarized Zone dividing North and South Vietnam
Dustoff	Medical Evacuation Huey Helicopter
FO	Forward Observer
Hoi Chan	Defector who accepts the *Chieu Hoi* program
Hootch	Dwelling place
HU1B	"Huey" helicopter
Jolly Greens	Air Force Search and Rescue Helicopters
JUSPAO	Joint U.S. Public Affairs Offic
KIA	Killed in Action
LRRP/LRP	Long Range Patrol units used extensively in Vietna
LZ	Landing Zone
MACV	Military Assistance Command Vietnam
Medevac	Helicopters evacuating casualties from battlefield
MIA	Missing in Action
NCO	Noncommissioned officer
Nasty	Fast patrol boat from Norway
Net	Radio frequency
Nungs	Ethnic Chinese who fought with American special forces
NVA	North Vietnamese Army
NROTC	Naval Reserve Officer Training Corps
PAVN	Peoples Army of Vietnam which the North Vietnamese termed their army. North Vietnamese Army (NVA) to the U.S.
PCF	Patrol Craft Fast

PIR	Parachute Infantry Regiment
PLAF	Peoples Liberation Armed Forces. The North Vietnam name for the Viet Cong (VC) to the U.S.
PRU	Provisional Reconnaissance Unit (Paramilitary unit in Operation Phoenix)
PTSD	Post Traumatic Stress Disorder
Punji Stakes	Bamboo poles sharpened and placed as booby traps
PW, POW	Prisoner of War
RF/PF	Regional/Popular Forces. Comparable to a U.S. State's National Guard/Militia
RTO	Radio telephone operator
RVN	Republic of Vietnam
RVNAF	Republic of Vietnam Armed Forces
SF	Special forces
SIGINT	Signals Intelligence
Snatch	Capturing a prisoner
SOG	Studies and Observation Group
Strike Force	Local men hired to be soldiers for special forces camps
Trung Ta	South Vietnamese Army equivalent to U.S. Lt. Colonel
VC	Viet Cong. Communists Recruited in South Vietnam
VNSF	Vietnamese special forces
WIA	Wounded in Action

Bibliography

Burkett, B.G. and Glenna Whitley, *Stolen Valor*. Dallas, Texas: Verity Press, Inc., 1998. www.stolenvalor.com.

Carter, Marshall N., "To Kill or Capture", *Marine Corps Gazette*, June 1973.

Charlton, James, editor, *The Military Quotation Book*. New York: Thomas Dunne Books, St. Martin's Press, 2002.

Coffey, Jr., William T., *Patriot Hearts*. Colorado Springs Colorado: Purple Mountain Publishing, 2000.

Conboy, Kenneth and Dale Andrade, *Spies & Commandos: How America Lost the Secret War in North Vietnam*. Lawrence, Kansas: University Press of Kansas, 2000.

Cronkite, Walter. "Gulf of Tonkin's Phantom Attack", National Public Radio *All Things Considered*, August 2, 2004 and "Reviewing the Gulf of Tonkin", August 6, 2004. http://www.npr.org/templates/story/story.php?storyId=3810724.

Accessed March 20, 2009.

Dallek, Robert. "How Not to End Another President's War (L.B.J. Edition)," March 12, 2009. http://100days.blogs.nytimes.com/2009/03/12/how-not-to-end-another-presidents-war-lbj. Accessed March 20, 2009.

Donohue, Frederic M., "Mission of Mercy." Report No. 4560.Presented February 1972 at Air War College, Maxwell Air Force Base, Alabama.

Donlon, Roger H.C., *Beyond Nam Dong*. Leavenworth, Kansas: Rand N Publishers, 1998.

du Berrier, Hilaire, *Background to Betrayal*. Boston: Western Islands, 1965.

Dulles, Wink, *Fielding's Vietnam Including Cambodia & Laos*. Redondo Beach, California: Fielding Worldwide, Inc., 1997.

Efros, William G., *Quotations Vietnam: 1945-1970*. New York: Random House, Inc., 1970.

Gargus, John, *The Son Tay Raid.* College Station, Texas: Texas A&M University Press, 2007.

Goldstein, Gordon M., *Lessons in Disaster.* New York: Time Books, Henry Holt and Company, 2008.

Gwin, Larry, *Baptism.* New York: Presidio Press, Random House, 1999.

Jennings, Jack H. and Tran Do Cam, "NASTY!: The inside story of operation 34A and the Nasty–class PT boats–and the crews that manned them during the Vietnam War." *Military Magazine.* Sept. 2004, Vol. XXI, No. 4.

Johnson, Lady Bird, "Selection from Lady Bird's Diary on Johnson not running for reelection." March 31, 1968. http://www.pbs.org/ladybird/shattereddreams/shattereddreams_doc_diary.html. Accessed June 12, 2010.

Karnow, Stanley, *Vietnam.* New York: The Viking Press, 1983.

Ky, Nguyen Cao, *How We Lost the Vietnam War.* New York: Stein and Day Publishers, 1984.

Lamb, Arnie, "TSgt Leroy M. Wright, Air Force Cross Recipient and Son Tay Raid," Air Force Enlisted Heritage Research Institute. Student Paper, 3 Dec. 1996.

Langdon, Al, *Ready.* Fayetteville, NC: 82nd Airborne Division Association Educational Fund, Inc., 1986.

Marshall, S.L.A., *Battles in the Monsoon.* New York: William Morrow and Company, Inc., 1967.

Moise, Edwin E., *Tonkin Gulf and the Escalation of the Vietnam War.* Chapel Hill, North Carolina: The University of North Carolina Press, 1996.

Moore, Lt. Gen. Harold G., (USA-Ret.) and Joseph L. Galloway, *We Were Soldiers Once...and Young.* Norwalk, CT: The Easton Press, 1992.

—*We Are Soldiers Still.* New York: HarperCollins Publishers, 2008.

Murphy, Edward F., *Dak To America's Sky Soldiers in South Vietnam's Central Highlands.* New York: Pocket Books, 1993.

Palmer, Dave, *Summons of the Trumpet U.S.-Vietnam in Perspective* San Rafael, California: Presidio Press, 1978.

Pentagon Papers, New York: The New York Times Company, Bantam Books, 1971.

Plaster, John L., *SOG A Photo History of the Secret Wars.* Boulder, Colorado: Paladin Press, 2000.

—*SOG the Secret Wars of America's Commandos in Vietnam.* New York, NY: ONYX, New American Library, Penguin Group, 1998.

Randal, Jonathan, "Marines Kill 61 Vietcong After a Defector's Tip," *New York Times.* New York, January 16, 1967.

Reimann, James, editor, L.B. Cowan's *Streams in the Desert*. Grand Rapids, Michigan: Zondervan, 1997.

Ruhl, Robert K., "Raid at Son Tay", *Airman Magazine*. August 1975.

Schuster, Carl Otis, "Case Closed: The Gulf of Tonkin Incident", *Vietnam Magazine*. June 2008.

Shanahan, Bill and John P. Brackin, *Stealth Patrol*. Cambridge, Massachusetts: Da Capo Press, 2003.

Sharp, Admiral U.S.G., *Strategy For Defeat*. San Rafael, California: Presidio Press, 1978.

Sheehan, Neil, *A Bright Shining Lie*. New York: Random House, 1988.

Shultz, Jr. Richard H., *The Secret War Against Hanoi*. New York: Perennial, 2000.

Simpson, Charles M., *Inside the Green Berets*. Novato, California: Presidio Press, 1983.

Sorley, Lewis, *A Better War*. New York: Harcourt Brace & Company, 1999.

Stanton, Shelby, *Green Berets at War*. New York: Dell Publishing Co. Inc., 1985.

Stockdale, Jim and Sybil, *In Love and War*. New York: Bantam Books, 1985.

Tsouras, Peter G., editor. *The Greenhill Dictionary of Military Quotations*. London: Greenhill Books, 2004.

Underwood, Lamar, editor, *The Quotable Soldier*. New York: The Lyons Press, 2000.

Westmoreland, William C., *A Soldier Reports*. Garden City: Doubleday & Company, Inc. 1976.

Zumwalt, Elmo, Jr. and Lt. Elmo Zumwalt, III with John Pekkanen, *My Father, My Son*. New York: Macmillan Publishing Company, 1986.

Index